# NONLINEAR AND MULTISECTORAL MACRODYNAMICS

Richard Goodwin
*Photograph by Dorothy Hahn*

# Nonlinear and Multisectoral Macrodynamics

## Essays in Honour of Richard Goodwin

Edited by
Kumaraswamy Velupillai
*Professor of Economics*
*University of Aalborg, Denmark*

NEW YORK UNIVERSITY PRESS
Washington Square, New York

Manufactured in Great Britain

First published in the U.S.A. in 1990 by
NEW YORK UNIVERSITY PRESS
Washington Square
New York, NY 10003

**Library of Congress Cataloging-in-Publication Data**

Nonlinear and multisectoral macrodynamics : essays in honour of
Richard Goodwin / edited by Kumaraswamy Velupillai.
p. cm.
ISBN 0–8147–8762–2
1. Business cycles. 2. Economics, Mathematical. 3. Goodwin, Richard M. (Richard Murphey), 1913– . I. Goodwin, Richard, M. (Richard Murphey), 1913– . II. Velupillai, Kumaraswamy, 1947–
HB3711. N654 1990 89–36886
338.5′42—dc20 CIP

# Contents

## PART III: MULTISECTORAL MACRODYNAMICS



## PART IV: EXOTICA

# Notes on the contributors

**Professor Amiya Kumar Bagchi**
Centre for Studies in Social Sciences
Calcutta

**Professor Andrew Brody**
Institute of Economics
Hungarian Academy of Sciences
Budapest

**Professor Terenzio Cozzi**
President of the Scientific Committee
Luigi Einaudi Foundation
and
University of Turin
Turin

**Professor John Kenneth Galbraith**
Harvard University
Cambridge MA

**Professor Siro Lombardini**
University of Turin
Turin

**Professor Luigi L. Pasinetti**
Universita Cattolica del Sacro Cuore
Milan

**Professor Lionello F. Punzo**
University of Pisa
Pisa

**Professor Paul A. Samuelson**
Nobel Laureate
Institute Professor
M.I.T.
Cambridge MA

**Professor Robert M. Solow**
Nobel Laureate
Institute Professor
M.I.T.
Cambridge MA

**Professor Sir Richard Stone**
Nobel Laureate
Cambridge University
Cambridge

**Professor Björn Thalberg**
University of Lund
Lund

**Professor Jan Tinbergen**
Nobel Laureate
The Hague

**Professor Kumaraswamy Velupillai**
Aalborg University
Aalborg

**Professor Alessandro Vercelli**
University of Siena
Siena

# PART I
# Biographical Notes

# 1 Introduction

Kumaraswamy Velupillai

I first met Richard Goodwin 15 years ago: I was 25 and he was 60 years old. The years rolled along. He left Cambridge and took up a Professorship in the University of Siena. A little later I joined him by accepting an appointment in Fiesole. We celebrated his 70th birthday in February 1983 in our house – minus our respective wives – which was set amongst the gentle hills beyond Fiesole. The ratio of our ages reached 1/2, having been less than that in the previous years! Now, this year, he has reached the venerable age of 75 and I am 15 years older than in 1973 and the ratio of our ages is greater than 1/2. In fact it is about 0.5333 and then any number of 3s as you like. He has, in the intervening years, been growing at the rate of 1.25 and I at 1.6. At this rate, it is easy to see, I could even become older than Richard Goodwin. This is the sort of *linear* nonsense Richard Goodwin has been trying to expose for over 40 years.

The idea of a Festschrift for Richard Goodwin came up during a splendid dinner in Björn Thalberg's house in Lund when Professor Amartya Sen was visiting the University – now more than ten years ago. That is a measure of the length of time this book has been maturing. The hope is that the vintages have aged with splendour and grace, almost as Goodwin has.

There is a particular sadness to report. The late Professor Leif Johansen had enthusiastically agreed to contribute for this volume. Had this book been published as early as it was conceived his prospective contribution would have enriched its contents.

Another apology, and this time to Professor Amartya Sen. He it was who first encouraged and supported me to go ahead with the idea. The various complications and difficulties in his own personal life, at a crucial juncture, made it impossible for him to contribute to this particular collection of essays.

To Professors Brody, Stone, Thalberg and Tinbergen I have a different kind of apology. Their enthusiastic participation was manifested in almost immediate response to my initial requests. They and almost all the others have had to wait several years to see this volume in print. I hope, nevertheless, the final form compensates for the delay.

The contributions are grouped in four parts. Parts II and III are directly and intimately related to two aspects of Richard Goodwin's contributions to analytical economics. These aspects of his work I have tried to summarise in my semi-biographical essay in Part I. The other note in Part I, by Professor Galbraith, is a little gem which, in the terse style that has been characteristic of Goodwin's own writings, gives us a glimpse of how things were not very long ago – but yet 50 years have elapsed, almost.

Frisch, nonlinearities, chaotic dynamics, dynamics of development and the art of using deceptively simple models to illustrate crucial social issues have occupied Goodwin's macrodynamical work for almost as long as macroeconomics has been interestingly dynamic. All of these issues, and more, are discussed by Solow, Samuelson, Stone, Brody, Thalberg and Bagchi. Curious that Goodwin did not exploit the implicit nonlinearities in Frisch's Cassel Festschrift contribution. There is a bare – almost invisible – hint in Thalberg's elegant reflections on Frisch and Goodwin's methodology.

The phenomenological dynamics of aggregate economics is deceptively elegant; the structural dynamics of capital and distribution theories are elegantly deceptive. For as long as he has been occupied with the former, he has also been concerned with the latter. His method, powerful and useful, has been to try to decouple interdependence so as to focus on dynamics – but not, at the same time, to assume away general interdependence. On this path he produced some remarkable results. Some I have documented in the 'Nonlinear Life'. Others, and their analytical implications and possibilities, are broached by Pasinetti, Cozzi and Punzo in three seminal contributions in Part III.

The issues discussed in Part IV are not tightly connected to Goodwin's direct contributions – except that Vercelli takes up part of the difficult question of causality which was once implicit in Goodwin's formalisation of the dynamics of coupled markets. That idea was imaginatively extended by Herbert Simon. Vercelli returns to that theme, albeit partially. However, even although the subject matter of Part IV is not directly connected to Goodwin's many and varied contributions, they are in fact, issues which have interested him all along. That they are here taken up by Tinbergen, Lombardini and Vercelli must give him particular pleasure.

There is left the pleasant task of thanking those who have helped and advised me over the many and long years this project has been going on. Early advice, encouragement and help from Professors Pasinetti, Sen and Thalberg were invaluable. Their patience, generosity and gentleness are impossible to document. I have myself moved from Lund to Louvain-La-Neuve to Cambridge to Florence to Copenhagen and, finally, to Aalborg. So many in these various places have helped and encouraged me that it is quite impossible to name them all. It would, however, be absurd not to mention the efficient help over many, many years that Jessica Spataro and, later, Annete Nicolaisen gave me. They had not only to type and retype my versions but, sometimes, retype (several times) 'others' versions'. They shall not be forgotten. Berc Rustem, Andrea Brandolini, Giorgio Gobbi and Stefano Zambelli belong to that exotic and rare set of critical friends – a set into which I dipped more often than I should have and came out with valuable advice each time. They probably do not realise the extent to which they have helped in the successful completion of this volume.

During the many asymmetric swings of fortune the preparation of this book has undergone, particularly in the long downward phases, I have had the strong and unfailing support of my wife, Aina and our three children: Viveka, Sumithra and Carmina. The children have known Richard and Jacqui Goodwin all their little lives; and Aina has known them as long as I have. They know that he deserves all the warmth, admiration and respect expressed in this volume.

# 2 Richard Goodwin Retrospective

## J. K. Galbraith

Many years ago – now approaching a half century – one of the most interesting of my contemporaries at Harvard was Richard Goodwin. He was a greatly competent economist, who passed easily through the most intricately technical aspects of the subject without, however, surrendering the power of his larger judgement or his larger policy and political concerns. He had the respect, perhaps even slightly the envy, of us all.

In addition, Dick Goodwin and his wife were known for their intensely civilised mood. They were deeply interested in art, especially or more so in music. They stood in contrast to those of us who thought any departure from economics a dangerous neglect of duty. I've told in the past, half seriously, that perhaps Goodwin's interest in the arts cost him promotion to tenure at Harvard. Economists are not meant to have such interests. At our professional best we are naturally committed, sombre, perhaps we should face it, even dull.

In any case, Goodwin left the one Cambridge for the other. It was my pleasure to see him there from time to time. I wish it had been more often. Richard Goodwin stands as one of the most accomplished scholars and teachers of economics in our time. No one did more to rescue the subject from its historically dismal reputation. I join with pleasure in this tribute to him.

# 3 The (Nonlinear) Life and (Economic) Times of Richard M. Goodwin

Kumaraswamy Velupillai

> I first came on a Rockefeller fellowship to Harvard University. The only Professors there with whom I could talk were Haberler and a young man by the name of Richard Goodwin. He later left for England, I believe. They were the only ones encouraging some interaction . . .[1]

## 3.1 INTRODUCTION

> Dick was not only a teacher of mine, but my first teacher of economics. When I studied economics for the first time as a freshman at Harvard, I was quite unhappy in the elementary course until I drifted by chance into Dick's class. That made all the difference; otherwise I might not have gone on.
>
> Letter from R. M. Solow to the author, 29 September 1976

1913 was an auspicious year to be born if one was hoping to become a painter (cf. Harcourt, 1985, p. 412), an applied mathematician (cf. Goodwin, 1985, p. 7) and a Keynesian economist (Goodwin, 1985, p. 9). Richard Goodwin was born in 1913 – he paints, is an applied mathematician in the classic 'Courant-Hilbert' tradition and is one of the leading Keynesian macroeconomists.

The year was apposite in every one of the three senses. Indeed when Ozenfant, one of the founders of the Purist school, came to write his celebrated book on the *Foundations of Modern Art* (Ozenfant, 1952) he divided the 'ages' of painting into a period from before the Flood to the end of 1913 and then to the Modern schools from 1914 onwards. Goodwin, in his paintings, is, if anything a modernist in the truest sense of the word.

And then the budding applied mathematician, the pioneer of linear multisectoral economic dynamics and nonlinear macrodynamics, the perceptive scholar and interpreter of the use of the Auctioneer as a constructive principle of proof of existence rather than an actual device of the real world (cf. Goodwin, 1949, 1950, 1951a, 1951b, 1953) could not have been born at a more opportune time. Frobenius had just published his famous results on the theory of nonnegative square matrices (Frobenius, 1912). In 1913, George Birkhoff proved Poincaré's 'last theorem' (Birkhoff, 1913) – a theorem which began with his efforts to solve the n-body problem and which gave rise to modern topology, qualitative dynamics and the theory of dynamical systems. And, finally, Luitzen Brouwer's famous inaugural lecture initiating his sustained attack on formalism was published in 1913 (Brouwer, 1913) – thus commencing a profound reinterpretation of mathematical logic which has resulted in prominence being given to constructive methods in proof theory. The implications of these important mathematical and methodological innovations and results for the analysis of linear and nonlinear economic systems was first most elegantly shown by Richard Goodwin in a series of fundamental essays (cf. Goodwin, op. cit.).

These essays have, of course, turned out to be fundamental in many other respects. However, it is indisputable that Frobenius's results, the forced van der Pol equation – ultimately the crucial equation in the development of the modern theory of dynamical systems – and an interpretation of Walras's device of the auctioneer to prove existence of equilibrium as a constructive method of proof and not necessarily an actual device, were first introduced in the mathematical economics literature in the above cited and other related essays of the same period by Richard Goodwin.

Above all, for someone who was to become one of the most outstanding and consistent Keynesian macrodynamic economists it was the perfect year to be born; for Keynes himself arrived on the scene as an economist that very same year with the publication of *Indian Currency and Finance* (Keynes, 1913).

In Economics, however, it was a transition period – unlike in art and mathematics where the transition to modernism which took place in these years just before the Great War had been in gestation, so to speak, for over 50 years. The third and final volume of *Principia Mathematica* had, in fact, been published in 1913 bringing to completion the work begun by Boole in 1847 – and, indeed, *Der Blaue Reiter Almanach* edited by Kandinsky and Marc had also been published in 1912.

It was a transition period in economics in that macroeconomics (a word coined, to the best of our knowledge, by Lindahl (1939, p. 52)) as an independent subdiscipline had not yet attained any status. The groundwork, however, had been laid by Wicksell but he was to retire just then. The great architects of the 'marginalist' method were soon to retire – like Wicksell – or had just retired – like Marshall; and others were nearing the end of their great lives: Walras died in 1910; Böhm-Bawerk in 1914; Menger in 1920; and Pareto in 1923. The macroeconomic and the macrodynamic paradigms had to wait for Hayek, Keynes and the Swedes. Schumpeter straddled both paradigms. Thus it was that Goodwin, the brilliant pupil of Schumpeter, carried on that great eclectic tradition which originated in Wicksell – mathematical macrodynamics and disaggregated sectoral analysis – without succumbing to the arid mathematical vices of general equilibrium theory nor to the monetary macroeconomics of the latter-day Austrians (von Mises and Hayek).

Of the three equally feasible paths open to him, art, applied mathematics and economics, it was natural that he concentrated on the last; for, as he reached his own youthful maturity in the mid- and late-thirties, macroeconomics in general and macrodynamics in particular was the obvious canvas for a politically active and socially conscious enlightened intellectual. The subsequent 50 years and more have amply vindicated this choice.

There have been other attempts to provide a sketch of Richard Goodwin's contributions (Harcourt, 1985, Palazzi, 1982; Goodwin 1985). We attempt, in this short note, to complement these other, earlier, essays. In the next section an outline of Goodwin's outstanding contributions to nonlinear macrodynamics is presented. In the third section we try to summarise aspects of the rest of his work in economics. The nature of the task makes it obvious that it cannot be anything but a *sketch*. The concluding section is a statement of hope and nostalgia.

## 3.2 THE (NONLINEAR) LIFE

> Cycles are not, like tonsils, separable things that might be treated by themselves, but are, like the beat of the heart, of the essence of the organism that displays them.
>
> (Schumpeter, 1939, p. 5)

The heart of Richard Goodwin's analytical contributions have been about the contradictions of a capitalist economy that are manifested in growth and cycles of key variables. His first full-length fully published article concerning 'economic cycles' was an attempt to push forward the frontiers of the Wicksell–Schumpeter–Frisch 'shock' theory of cycles (cf. Goodwin, 1946). Wicksell, in a review of Karl Petander's book: *Goda och Dåliga Tider* (Wicksell, 1918) had observed:

> If one strikes a rocking-horse with a hammer, the motion [movement] of the rocking-horse will be different from that of the hammer. The impact is the *cause* of the motion, but its own equilibrium properties will be the *basis* for the *form* of the motion.[2]

'Propagation' and 'impulse' derive from these simple but elegant obervations by Wicksell. Frisch did not try to formalise the stochastic shock theory by explicitly introducing Schumpeterian assumptions on innovation.[3] That was left to Goodwin who was perhaps the first to formalise Schumpeter's theory – at least a version of it – in terms of the method suggested by Wicksell. Now that the economic world and its dynamic phenomena have been reduced to linear difference and differential equations by the new classical macroeconomists the pioneering quality of this long-lost paper by Goodwin may become more evident.

But this discussion is out of place in this section – or is it? The model is linear and we were supposed to wonder about his *nonlinear life*! Not quite out of place – it is about cycles and his later lifelong interest in nonlinearities in economics was essentially because of their power in modelling, with a minimum of assumptions, fluctuations.

He was to make two more linear attempts – both absolutely original ones – before he shifted gear, so to speak, and moved on to the 'higher' and 'nonlinear' standpoint. The next two attempts have become justifiably famous, for having introduced the idea of unilateral coupling and causality (Goodwin, 1947) and the 'flexible accelerator' (Goodwin, 1948). At this point we wish to point out an observation he made in the 'Dynamical Coupling' (Goodwin, 1947) paper which has gone completely unnoticed although he himself has returned to it in his recent Paris paper (Goodwin, 1983) and later papers, in particular Goodwin (1986).

In the 'Dynamical Coupling' paper Goodwin had to – or tried to – analyse the problem of 'coupled markets with production lags' (Goodwin, 1947, pp. 197–203). He was able to show that the periods of the cycles in the two markets do not repeat themselves:

> *even with no outside disturbance or natural damping*. Except by accident the various periods will not dovetail, because they are not integral multiples of one another, and hence in each cycle they will join in a new way, resulting in an ever-changing wave shape.
>
> (Goodwin, 1947, pp. 201–2; italics in the original)

In these days, when the pages of prestigious journals are replete with fashionable models of chaos, much is to be gained by reflection and a perusal of long-lost classics. What Goodwin showed in that article of almost 40 years ago was that the *irregularity* of capitalist fluctuations can be modelled by linear assumptions without the need for postulating *ad hoc* exogenous shocks.

An illuminating geometric way to visualise the power of Goodwin's observation would be to decompose the two complex conjugate cases into a *direct sum* of two systems in the plane – which is natural. Next, take the *direct product* of the two closed curves in each of the planes. The original linear system has now been transformed to dynamics on a generalised torus. Then, Goodwin's above observation is equivalent to the statement that the coupled markets, when rationally independent, give rise to phase curves everywhere dense on a generalised torus.

Ultimately the result depends on the fact that rational numbers are denumerable and the irrational ones are not. Recent results on strange attractors depend ultimately on such exotic properties of the real line. Economists have not caught up, as yet, with John Conway's 'surreal numbers' – but many would consider that to be a blessing given the surreal nature of much of mathematical economics. The simple elegance of the modern classics, exemplified by the type of analysis in Goodwin's 'Dynamical Coupling' paper, is a lost art. However, mercifully, Goodwin himself has returned to these themes and his very latest work, beginning with the Paris paper (Goodwin, 1984) and leading up to Goodwin (1986, cf. especially pp. 7–8) seem to indicate that he has re-evaluated the power of the methods developed in Goodwin (1947).

The three papers mentioned in the beginning of this section were his initial forays into formal, mathematical, trade cycle theory – the initial conditions, if one may say so, for his next, sustained, attempts at formalising the essentials of a fluctuating capitalist economy.

Goodwin has himself given us an almost exhaustive version of the story of his 'nonlinear' life – in the sense of his work on cycle theory (cf. Palazzi, 1982, pp. 18 ff.; also Goodwin, 1985). Victor Zarnowitz was not far off the mark when, in his recent survey article, he noted that: 'The substantive uses of nonlinearities in the theory of business cycles are yet to be systematically explored . . . The early models by Kaldor, Hicks and Goodwin remain influential in this literature' (Zarnowitz, 1985, p. 540).

There is no intention, in this paper, to attempt a comparative study of nonlinear models of the trade cycle (although that has been the subject of an earlier paper, see Velupillai (1986)). It is, mainly, Goodwin's nonlinearities that are of concern; and the story of the nonlinear theories of Richard Goodwin's cycles begins with Tinbergen's (1937) review of Harrod's book on the *Trade Cycle* (Harrod, 1936). This too is a story that has been documented (cf. Palazzi, 1982; and Goodwin, 1985). Simply stated the story has been as follows: Harrod's intuition about the basic upward dynamic instability, once excited, of capitalism is correct; the system encounters the limits of primary factors – mainly full employment of labour: *that* is a sufficient nonlinearity for endogenous oscillations. However, there are other economic complications: the asymmetry between 'prosperity' and 'depression'; the role of functional distribution as an adjustment mechanism; and the nature of the accelerator. This small but potent set of issues and their compact formalisations have been the focus of the various nonlinear models of the trade cycle that Goodwin has produced in the past 40 years.

The main contours of these nonlinearities range from the 'nonlinear accelerator' (Goodwin, 1951) to the 'growth cycle' of 1967. He has, of course, continued to produce the gems we have come to expect from him since then as well – i.e., since 1967. However, the basic structure can be found in the papers between 1950 and 1967 although variations on the themes continue to this day to occupy his fertile mind.

The above collection of key macroeconomic issues – the nature of the full employment constraint; variations in the functional distribution of income as an adjustment mechanism; the asymmetry in the accelerator; the role of innovations – have their counterpart in a series of absolutely fundamental mathematical formalisations that cannot be matched for their sheer brilliance, originality and comprehensiveness by anything else in the field of macrodynamics. In a recent masterly survey of the dynamical systems approach to differential equations the eminent mathematican Morris Hirsch observed that: 'only nonlinear differential equations have interesting dynamics' (Hirsch, 1984, p. 23).[4] If a confirmation, in an applied science, is necessary Hirsch will find it in the nonlinear models of the trade cycle Goodwin has produced over these past 40 years. It is almost as if

Goodwin had Hirsch's dictum in mind as he journeyed his nonlinear way from 1950 to 1967. But even more importantly, when it is remembered that the canonical equations that have been instrumental in the development of the modern theory of dynamical systems are the forced van der Pol, Duffing and Lotka–Volterra equations in addition to the conceptual apparatus provided by the Hopf bifurcation theorem, then the significance of Goodwin's contributions becomes even clearer. To the best of our knowledge the Duffing equation has not been exploited in economics. However, only Goodwin has seen the need to consider the forced van der Pol oscillator in the modelling of macrodynamic fluctuations.

Not only that. In addition to the ease with which the Hopf bifurcation theorem can be introduced in an economically meaningful way using the 'nonlinear accelerator' and the 'growth cycle' it is also possible to discuss the relevance of 'Turing bifurcations' by simple generalisations of the above two papers. (Cf. Prigogine, 1980 for a definition of 'Turing bifurcations' (1967).)

Goodwin's 'Growth Cycle' (1967) is, by now, so well known that there is no need to spell out, explicity, the elegant way he exploited the structure of the Lotka–Volterra system. On the other hand, the combination of a Schumpeterian background with Keynesian sympathies resulted in the highly original model of 1951 where, possibly, the only known example, in economics, of a forced van der Pol oscillator occurs (cf. equation 5(e) in Goodwin, 1951). The use of van der Pol-type equations had been advocated (even by van der Pol himself) even before Le Corbeiller's (1933) article in the first volume of the *Econometrica* – to which Goodwin and others have referred over the years (e.g., Samuelson, 1947, p. 340). It is, however, significant that one may still agree with Zarnovitz's (1985) evaluation – in spite of Hamburger (1934) before and a few sporadic attempts later.[5]

The forcing term in the equation to which we have referred from Goodwin (1951a) is the *innovations* term; the rest of the structure is the results of a Keynesian multiplier-accelerator mechanism. The remaining issues, from the small set to which we alluded earlier, to be formalised macrodynamically were the limits due to primary factors and the role of the variation in the functional distribution of income.

In a concise review article of Hicks's celebrated book on the trade cycle (Hicks, 1950) the problem of the upper limit of full employment was elegantly discussed by Goodwin (1950). It is significant that both Goodwin and Dusenberry (1950) in their respective review articles on Hicks's book were able to point out that it was sufficient, for endogenous oscillations, to assume *either* the ceiling *or* the floor (Goodwin, 1950, p. 318; Dusenberry, 1950, p. 468). The fact that only one of these constraints was sufficient led Goodwin to a fundamental result in the theory of oscillators (cf. Le Corbeiller, 1960 in Goodwin, 1982). We append to this paper the fascinating letter from Le Corbeiller to Goodwin outlining the origins of the 'Goodwin Characteristic'. A rigorous mathematical demonstration proving Goodwin's intuition can be found in de Figueiredo (1958). There was still the problem of the 'limits to growth' due to the full employment of nonlabour primary resources. To that he returned after the illumination – if it may be put that way – that the power of the structure of the Lotka–Volterra system (and its generalisation by Kolmogorov (1936)) seemed to have given him. He had, by this time, become interested in catastrophe theory (cf. Goodwin, 1980a) which coupled to the accidental reading of Fred Hoyle's 'Hull Lecture' (cf. Goodwin, 1978) at a timely moment – the so-called energy crisis was in full swing – provided the ideal setting for an attack on the problem of the limits due to nonlabour resources. At a conference to honour the economist he seems to have respected most – Knut Wicksell, whose own nonlinear path to economics was by way of Malthusian preoccupations – Goodwin, in his mature years, reflected upon a world that may have to face up to the limits of nonlabour primary factors (Goodwin, 1978).

Finally, the role of the variations in the distribution of income in fluctuating growth was encapsulated in the classic 'Growth Cycle' published, most appropriately, in the Festschrift to Maurice Dobb (Goodwin, 1967). At last he seemed to have begun the final synthesis of bringing all these essential macroeconomic elements with which various partial structures had been built, into one model of growth *and* cycles. It was a journey to synthesis that began a very long time ago. Perceptive readers, even without mathematical training, discerned the vital importance of the attempted synthesis right at the outset:

> Goodwin's model is limited, but it is an important step in the right direction, because there is first a recognition of the interdependence of trend and cycle, and secondly an emphasis on the importance of technology. Goodwin assumes continuous improvement in technology, but economic history shows both continuous improvement and also major discrete changes.
>
> (Gordon, 1955, p. 337 on Goodwin, 1955)

History, long waves and discrete changes play an increasingly important role in the analytical synthesis Goodwin has been attempting in his various emeritus years – an emeritus from two ancient institutions: Peterhouse and Siena, places that have seen so much history and borne the brunt of many a long wave in technology.

## 3.3 THE (ECONOMIC) TIMES

> I have picked the most familiar topic of all: elementary supply and demand analysis. I am not the pedagogical innovator here: what I am trying to do is to revive a soon 20-year old paper of Goodwin's that has not seen use that I think it deserves.
>
> (Leijonhufvud, 1970, p. 1)

That paper by Goodwin, which is referred to by Leijonhufvud, is now a 'soon 40-year-old paper' (Goodwin, 1951b) and it has still 'not seen the use ... it deserves' in spite of Axel Leijonhufvud's efforts. It belongs to a strand of thought in Goodwin's eclecticism: the study of structure and dynamics must not be separate. Goodwin's thoughts on growth and cycles, and structure and dynamics, form two sides of the same coin: on one side his insistence on studying *growth* and *cycles* together; on the other, his entreaty to cast light on the crucial interdependence between *structure* and *dynamics*. Hence his insistence that an understanding of the structure of an economic system is best approached by trying to see it in motion.

In his 'nonlinear life' he has concentrated on dynamics following, *ex post facto*, Hirsch's dictum that 'only nonlinear differential equations have interesting dynamics'. For the 'economic times', or *supply* and *demand* (the study of structure), he has pursued a consistent strategy which began with his lucid article on 'The Multiplier as Matrix' (Goodwin, 1949). The strategy has been to be explicit about the diverse disaggregated activities of an economic system by modelling them as interdependent sectors – an attempt, in fact, which goes back and beyond 'The Multiplier as Matrix' to 'Dynamical Coupling' (Goodwin, 1947).

However, he did not get bogged down in the analysis of the equilibrium of the interdependent structure – that he left, wisely, to the general equilibrium theorists. It is almost as if he had the 'wave–particle' duality in mind when he proceeded to study the dynamics of a multisectoral interdependent structure. Those familiar with the standard characteristic equation will recall that the proposition stating equivalence between Heisenberg's matrix mechanics and Schrödinger's wave mechanics is shown by transforming, in the former case, a certain (infinite) matrix into *diagonal* form and, in the latter case, by finding vectors (in an infinite-dimensional space) which when acted upon by a certain linear transformation are just multiplied by a numerical factor – i.e. scalar multiples.

Although we have tried to avoid explicit mathematical formalism, a simple demonstration of the above remark may be of some use in illuminating Goodwin's methodology (to analyse the dynamics of an interdependent structure). The problem is the following: given a Matrix A, can we find a similarity matrix H such that the similar matrix $H^{-1}AH$ is a diagonal matrix? i.e. determine numbers $z_1, z_2, \ldots, z_n$ and the elements of H such that:

$$[H^{-1}AH = z_1, z_2, \ldots, z_n]$$

Put another way, the question is whether we can find a new coordinate system – a new frame of reference – such that the (linear) transformation characterised by the matrix A in the original coordinate system becomes a transformation of the form:

$$y_k = z_k x_k \ (k = 1, 2, \ldots, n)$$

in the new coordinate system. It is, of course, easy to show that the answer is in the affirmative and when the first of the above equations is written (but see ch. 10 for details) as:

$$Ah^{(k)} = z_k h^{(k)}$$

where the $h^{(k)}$ are vectors ($k = 1, 2, \ldots, n$), and finding the similarity matrix H which transforms the matrix A to diagonal form reduces to finding vectors $h^{(k)}$, which when acted upon by A, are multiplied by a scalar. In this form it is the algebraic analogue of the above proposition giving the equivalence between the formalisms of Heisenberg and Schrödinger. Couple to this Niels Bohr's complementarity principle and you have a fruitful research strategy to analyse the dynamics of multidimensional systems.

In an outstanding lecture on the occasion of his retirement, Professor Johan Åkerman proposed exactly such a strategy and interpretation to 'reconcile dynamics and general equilibrium theory' (Åkerman, 1967).

It is, in fact, a parallel of the above technique of transforming coordinates that has been effectively utilised by Goodwin in studying the dynamics of multisectoral interdependent structures. He first exploited the technique, in a specialised form, in 'The Multiplier as Matrix' (Goodwin, 1949 cf. equations (20)ff.). Once again, within the economics profession, he seems to have been unique in systematically employing the device of changing the frame of reference to suit the problem – a 'bread-and-butter' technique for the physicist and applied mathematician. And Goodwin, after his 'war years' as a physicist, probably found it natural to approach analytical economics in such a fashion.

The analytical device of decoupling interdependencies has been used by Goodwin to cast light on deep and controversial issues in economics: from propositions about the standard commodity and the wage–profit curve to issues in international trade (cf. Goodwin, 1974 and 1980b, for example); from the problems faced by the Walrasian auctioneer (Goodwin 1953) to those of trying to 'swing along the turnpike' (Goodwin, 1986) – again a sustained contribution spreading over 40 years of 'nonlinear lives and economic times.'

The 'economic times' have swung him along other turnpikes. Some time spent in India gave rise to reflections of the problems of developing countries. On that turnpike he swung another tool to cast light on the pressing problem facing developing countries – how much to save now and accumulate. Just before the famous results of Pontryagin and Bellman became the much (mis-) used tool of economists as they went about adding Hamilton to Lagrange in the vocabulary of the textbooks, Goodwin reformulated the problem of accumulation in an underdeveloped economy as a classic problem in the calculus of variations. He seems now to have arrived, along some nonlinear turnpike, to the years of reflection.

## 3.4 THE VINTAGE YEARS

> I have very much enjoyed all except the misprints in your book, *Elementary Economics from the Higher Standpoint*.
>
> (Letter from E. J. Nell to Goodwin, 13 February 1973)

There were others, like the reviewer in EJ, who enjoyed 'all' including the misprints. No doubt there were some who enjoyed only the misprints! *Elementary Economics from the Higher Standpoint* (1970) is, in style and content, highly original. Written in the classic Cambridge tradition of being self-contained in every sense of the word – there are no references, footnotes, etc. – it is an *ideal* textbook: the teacher must *work* at least as hard as the taught at least with respect to thought. Felix Klein in the preface to the third edition of his book (Klein, 1945) – the title of which was not uninfluential in the choice Goodwin made for his own book – remarked that he had: 'long ago expressed the belief that, beyond a certain age, one ought not to publish independently' (Klein, 1945, p. iv). Goodwin seems to have followed this advice – at least with respect to books. His recently published Siena lectures are a joint product with his younger colleague, friend and protégé – Lionello Punzo. It seems to be the grand synthesis we have alluded to earlier: a synthesis of multisectoral interdependent structure, dynamics and history; or Walras, Keynes–Marx and Schumpeter with the benevolent Wicksell as the halo.

Goodwin is a modest man. He claims to have become a 'Sunday mathematician', one who 'pursues the black art in his spare time' (1985). Those of us who have understood or made valiant efforts to understand his original, penetrating and honest analysis would find it difficult to agree with the view that he is a 'Sunday mathematician'. His explanation for that judgement upon himself is, partly, elaborated in the 'Personal Perspectives': 'I have always suffered from an inability to understand and deploy pure mathematics. My initial effort, under the guidance of an eminent mathematician, Marston Morse, came to grief' (Goodwin, 1985, p. 7). That explanation may justify our view that he is not just a 'Sunday mathematician'. Another mathematician, quite as eminent as Marston Morse, in a delightful lecture on 'Mathematicians and Their Times' reminded us that: 'In Princeton, it used to be said that if something was obvious for Hermann Weyl, then von Neumann could prove it. If it was obvious for Marston Morse, it was most certainly false' (Young, 1981, p. 328).

Perhaps the sharp Goodwin couldn't absorb all those 'obvious' lectures by Marston Morse – not because of intrinsic deficiencies in the young Goodwin but because they were 'most certainly false' and his intuitions rebelled against putting any effort into trying to comprehend mistakes!

Now the vintage years – the gentle years – are being spent in the heart of the Tuscan hills. It is no longer an uncommon sight to see

Pininfarina's elegant creation – the poor man's Ferrari: the Fiat Dino – being driven by a stately white-haired gentleman, along the winding roads straddling the undulating Tuscan hills. With a mind as fertile as ever, Richard Goodwin continues to spend the vintage years being as active as ever. He continues to paint, to work at the necessary mathematics and to produce the little gems that push the frontiers of macrodynamic analysis a little further each time.

Many years separate the origins in Indiana and the present in Siena – and there have been many lives in between as well. The path, from the middle of one continent to the heart of another, has been quite nonlinear. The years to come, the noble years, may well see the Nobel year as well.

## APPENDIX

21 Gibson Street — Cambridge 38, Massachusetts

March 29, 1958.

Dear Dr. Goodwin:

I have such good memories of our conversations of quite a few years ago. I have enjoyed (and enjoy meeting from time to time in my books) your kind messages from various climes and am sorry, when it comes to a few people like yourself, to be ~~[illegible]~~ such a bad correspondent.

This will make you think that I am writing you about something specific. Here it is. You surely will remember that you came one day in my office in great elation (you may even be able to give me an approximate date) [my earliest homework is of Dec 19, 19 and told me that you had found economic justification for a characteristic F(x) which gave rise

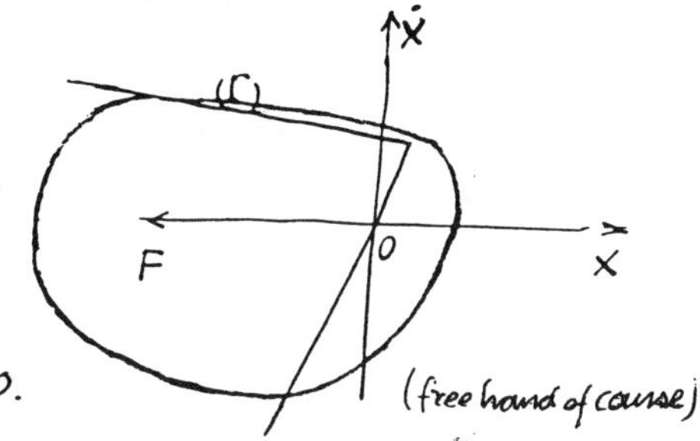


to a limit cycle and hence a periodic solution for Lord Rayleigh's equation

$$\ddot{x} + F(\dot{x}) + x = 0.$$

And you drew on my blackboard (I am still in that same corner office, opposite the Law School) the above characteristic (Γ). I said: But this cannot oscillate. <u>You</u>: Why not? <u>I</u>: Because a characteristic must have an S shape, an inflexion point somewhere, for the system to oscillate. <u>You</u>: But this one does oscillate! <u>I</u>: Impossible! — Whereupon you showed me that by making the first half-line of Γ horizontal, one got a limit cycle very simply, which totally convinced me. I went home and played with a few shapes which did give limit cycles and realized that you had found what no one had been able to find since 1927, an example of a stable oscillator differing <u>essentially</u> from that of Lord Rayleigh and van der Pol.

21 GIBSON STREET — CAMBRIDGE 38, MASSACHUSETTS

Now since that time I have played with the idea off and on and various things always prevented me from pushing it to a conclusion. Now (I) my own ideas are ripe and I plan to write a paper and (II) a graduate student of mine has built up a proof of the existence and unicity of the limit cycle for equations of your type which has been found by a colleague from the Math Department to be a real advance. You may be interested if I tell you that in my own work (which turned out to be conveniently distinct from that of my young man) I believe I have succeeded in finding what I think is a canonical, 1-parameter equation to be put at the side of Lord Rayleigh, viz:

Lord Rayleigh: $\ddot{x} + \rho\left(-\dot{x} + \frac{\dot{x}^3}{3}\right) + x = 0 \quad 0 < \rho < \infty$

Goodwin - ALC : $\ddot{x} + \rho\left(e^{-\dot{x}} - 2\right)\dot{x} + x = 0. \quad 0 < \rho < 1$

Try it out!

I have looked through various papers and manuscript notes which you have been so kind as to give me — and I may have looked badly, but — I have not come across any reference to that characteristic of yours with the two half-lines. If you have published it somewhere, would you kindly give me the reference, so I can quote it? Otherwise I shall say: Dr. R. Goodwin, in an oral communication not later than Dec. 1950, etc.

Well, that is the story. I have given it at two colloquia so far, one of a few graduate students at Harvard last October, and one of the Elect. Eng. Dept. of Rensselaer at Troy, N.Y., two days ago. I don't expect to have time to write up a paper until this summer, so don't feel you have to answer me by return mail. But I'll be happy to hear from you, and I shall keep you informed of the progress of the question.

Please give my regards to Mrs Goodwin and believe me, dear Dr. Goodwin,

Very cordially yours

P. le Corbeiller

**Notes**

1. Karl Brunner in Klamer, 1984.
2. It is my translation from the Swedish original: 'Om man slår på en gunghäst med en klubba så bli gunghästens rörelse mycket olika klubbans. Stöten är orsaken till rörelsen, men föremålets egna jämviktbetingelser äro förutsättningar för rörelsens form' (Wicksell, 1918, p. 71, fn. 1).

   It is generally believed that Wicksell's famous rocking-horse (gunghäst) example can be found in his well-known paper: 'Krisernas Gåta' ('The Enigma of the Business Cycle' Wicksell, 1907). This incorrect impression, due to a mistaken reference by Frisch, has been passed on, from generation to generation. It is time that it was corrected, especially in view of the extreme importance given by Lucasians to the so-called Frisch–Wicksell approach.
3. However, Frisch did have an interesting concluding section on 'The Innovation as a Factor in Maintaining Oscillations' in Frisch, 1933, pp. 203–5, where some discussion along the lines of Schumpeter's theory of innovation is present. But, this last section is independent of the previous mathematical analysis. This intelligent and eminently fair remark should be juxtaposed with Grandmont's remark: 'economic theorists should perhaps look more closely at the sort of mechanisms that may be responsible for significant nonlinearities in the economic system if they wish to have a proper foundation upon which to build a sound business cycle theory' (Grandmont, 1985, p. 1039). Grandmont then goes on to conclude with a plea for taking into consideration 'multiplier or accelerator' effects (without sacrificing the optimisation altar) in an article which is 50 printed pages in length and includes 60 references – but not one single reference to Kaldor, Hicks or Goodwin! Henry Ford's dictum on history has many followers in economics – but then Giovanbattista Vico's cyclical theory of history drops out as a corollary!
4. L. Hamburger seems to have been the first economist to point out the significance of relaxation oscillations for modelling fluctuations in economic variables. Indeed Hamburger had been present when van der Pol presented one of his celebrated papers on relaxation oscillations at the 7 May 1928 meeting of the Batavian Society of Logic and Empirical Philosophy: 'The present writer would like to point out that the applicability of the principle of relaxation oscillations to economic cycles was first emphasized by him in 1928 in a discussion following a paper read by Messers van der Pol and J. van der Mark' (Hamburger, 1934, p. 112).

   Even in the teaching of Keynesian economics Goodwin trekked off the beaten track. In fact Harcourt does point out that: 'Goodwin used a four quadrant, rather than the Hicks–Hansen two quadrant, diagram which he never published though one of his students – he forgets who – did' (Harcourt, 1985, p. 410).

   As a matter of fact Goodwin's four-quadrant diagram has entered the literature by a roundabout method – and hence very productively. One of Erik Lindahl's fundamental 'Keynesian' papers used this very four-quadrant system in Lindahl, 1954. Lindahl acknowledges indebtedness to a paper by Ira Scott (1951–2) where, in turn, we find: 'After preparing the first draft of this paper, the author benefitted greatly from reading an unpublished manuscript in which Professor Goodwin presents a slightly different version of the Keynesian system in diagrammatic form' (Scott, 1951–2, p. 13, fn. 3).

**References**

ÅKERMAN, J. (1967) 'Fyra Metodologiska Moment', *Ekonomisk Tidskrift*, vol. LXI.

BIRKHOFF, G. D. (1913) 'Proof of Poincaré's Geometric Theorem', *Transactions of the American Mathematical Society*, vol. 14, pp. 14–22.

BROUWER, LUITZEN E. J. (1913) 'Intuitionism and Formalism', *Bulletin of the American Mathematical Society*, vol. 20, pp. 81–96.

DUSENBERRY, JAMES S. (1950) 'Hicks on the Trade Cycle', *Quarterly Journal of Economics*, vol. 64, pp. 464–76.

FIGUEIREDO, R. J. P. DE (1958) 'Existence and Uniqueness of Periodic Solutions in Autonomous Oscillators', unpublished PhD thesis, University of Harvard, Cambridge, Mass.

FRISCH, RAGNAR A. K. (1933) 'Propagation Problems and Impulse Problems in Dynamic Economics', in *Economic Essays In honour of Gustav Cassel* (London: George Allen & Unwin).

FROBENIUS, G. (1912) 'Über Matrizen aus nicht Negativen Elementen', Sitzung, B. Deutsch. Akad. Wiss., Berlin Mathematische Nat. K1., pp. 456–77.

GOODWIN, R. M. (1946) 'Innovations and the Irregularity of Economic Cycles', *Review of Economic Statistics*, vol. XXVIII, no. 2, pp. 95–104.

GOODWIN, R. M. (1947) 'Dynamical Coupling with Especial Reference to Markets Having Production Lags', *Econometrica*, vol. XV, no. 3 (July), pp. 181–204.

GOODWIN, R. M. (1948) 'Secular and Cyclical Aspects of the Multiplier and the Accelerator', in L. H. Metzler (ed.), *Income, Employment and Public Policy, Essays in Honour of A. H. Hansen* (New York: W. W. Norton & Co.), pp. 108–32.

GOODWIN, R. M. (1949) 'The Multiplier as Matrix', *Economic Journal*, vol. LIX, no. 236, pp. 537–55.

GOODWIN, R. M. (1950) 'A Non-Linear Theory of the Cycle', *Review of Economics and Statistics*, vol. XXXII, no. 4, pp. 316–20.

GOODWIN, R. M. (1951a) 'The Nonlinear Accelerator and the Persistence of Business Cycles', *Econometrica*, vol. XIX, no. 1, pp. 1–17.

GOODWIN, R. M. (1951b) 'Iteration, Automatic Computers and Economic Dynamics', *Metroeconomica*, vol. III, no. 1 (April), pp. 1–7.

GOODWIN, R. M. (1953) 'Static and Dynamic Linear General Equilibrium Models', in Netherlands Economic Institute (ed.), *Input–Output Relations*, Proceedings of the Conference on Inter-Industrial Relations, Driebergen, Holland (Leiden: H. Stenfert Kroese), pp. 54–98.

GOODWIN, R. M. (1955) 'A Model of Cyclical Growth', in E. Lundberg (ed.), *The Business Cycle in the Post-War World*, Proceedings of the Conference held by the International Economic Association, Oxford, September, 1952 (London: Macmillan), pp. 203–21.

GOODWIN, R. M. (1967) 'A Growth Cycle', in C. H. Feinstein (ed.), *Socialism, Capitalism and Economic Growth, Essays Presented to Maurice Dobb* (Cambridge: Cambridge University Press) pp. 54–8.

GOODWIN, R. M. (1970) *Elementary Economics from the Higher Standpoint* (Cambridge: Cambridge University Press).

GOODWIN, R. M. (1974) 'The Use of Normalized General Coordinates in Economic Analysis', in A. Mitra (ed.), *Economic Theory and Planning: Essays in Honour of A. K. Das Gupta* (Calcutta: Oxford University Press) pp. 26–38.

GOODWIN, R. M. (1978) 'Wicksell and the Malthusian Catastrophe', *Scandinavian Journal of Economics*, vol. 80, no. 2, pp. 190–8.

GOODWIN, R. M. (1980a) 'Catastrophe Theory, Structural Stability, Qualitative Dynamics', *Greek Economic Review*, vol. 2, no. 1, pp. 1–11.

GOODWIN, R. M. (1980b) 'World Trade Multipliers', *Journal of Post Keynesian Economics*, vol. 2, no. 3, pp. 319–44.

GOODWIN, R. M. (1982) *Essays in Economic Dynamics*, (London: Macmillan).

GOODWIN, R. M. (1983) 'The Use of Gradient Dynamics in Linear General Disequilibrium Theory', paper presented at the Conference on economic dynamics, (Observatoire Français des Conjonctures Economiques), Paris, September, 1983.

GOODWIN, R. M. (1985) 'A Personal Perspective on Mathematical Economics', *Banca Nazionale del Lavoro Quarterly Review*, no. 152, pp. 3–13.

GOODWIN, R. M. (1986) 'Swinging Along the Turnpike with von Neumann and Sraffa', Mimeo (February) Siena.

GORDON, R. A. (1955) 'Discussion' of Goodwin (1953) in E. Lundberg (ed.), *The Business Cycle in the Post-War World*, Proceedings of the Conference held by the International Economic Association, Oxford, September 1952 (London: Macmillan) pp. 336–7.

GRANDMONT, J.-M. (1985) 'On Endogenous Competitive Business Cycles', *Econometrica*, vol. 53, no. 5, pp. 995–1046.

HAMBURGER, L. (1934) 'Note on Economic Cycles and Relaxation Oscillations', *Econometrica*, vol. 2, no. 1, p. 112.

HARCOURT, G. C. (1985) 'A Twentieth-century Eclectic: Richard Goodwin', *Journal of Post Keynesian Economics*, vol. 7, no. 3, pp. 410–21.

HARROD (1936) *The Trade Cycle* (Oxford: Oxford University Press).

HICKS, J. R. (1950) *A Contribution to the Theory of the Trade Cycle* (Oxford: Oxford University Press).

HIRSCH, M. W. (1984) 'The Dynamical Systems Approach to Differential Equations', *Bulletin (New Series) of the American Mathematical Society*, vol. 11, no. 1, pp. 1–64.

KEYNES, J. M. (1913) *Indian Currency and Finance* (London: Macmillan and Co., Ltd).

KLAMER, ARJO (1984) *The New Classical Macroeconomics: Conversations with New Classical Economists and Their Opponents* (Sussex: Wheatsheaf).

KLEIN, FELIX (1945) *Elementary Mathematics From An Advanced Standpoint* (New York: Dover Publications).

KOLMOGOROV, A. (1936 'Sulla teoria di Volterra della lotta per l'esistenza', *Giornale Italiano degli Attuari*, vol. I, no. 2, pp. 74–80.

LE CORBEILLER, Ph. (1933) 'Les Systemes Autoentretenus et les Oscillations de Relaxation, *Econometrica*, vol. 1, pp. 328–38.

LE CORBEILLER, Ph. (1960) Letter to Goodwin (cf. Appendix, above).

LEIJONHUFVUD, A. (1970) 'Notes on the Theory of Markets', *Intermountain Economic Review*, vol. 1, no. 1, pp. 1–13.

LINDAHL, E. (1939) *Studies in the Theory of Money and Capital* (London: George Allen & Unwin).

LINDAHL, E. (1954) 'On Keynes' Economic System', *Economic Record*, vol. 30 (May and Nov.).

OZENFANT (1952) *Foundations of Modern Art* (New York: Dover Publications, Inc.).

PALAZZI, M. (ed.) (1982) *Intervista a un economista. Richard M. Goodwin (con la bibliografia deglia scritti* (Bologna: Cooperativa Libraria Universitaria, Editrice Bologna (CLUEB)).

PRIGOGINE, ILYA (1980) *From Being to Becoming: Time and Complexity in the Physical Sciences* (San Francisco: W. H. Freeman & Co.).

SAMUELSON, P. A. (1947) *Foundations of Economic Analysis* (Cambridge, Mass.: Harvard University Press).

SCHUMPETER, J. A. (1939) *Business Cycles: A Theoretical, Historical, and Statistical Analysis of the Capitalist Process* (Vol. 1) (New York: McGraw-Hill Book Co., Inc.).

SCOTT, IRA A. (1951–2) 'An Exposition of the Keynesian System', *Review of Economic Studies*, vol. XIX, pp. 12–20.

TINBERGEN, J. (1937) Review of Harrod *The Trade Cycle, Weltwirtschaftliches Archiv*, May.

VELUPILLAI, K. (1989) 'Nonlinear Macrodynamics', Mimeo, Aalborg; forthcoming in History of Economics Society *Bulletin*.

WICKSELL, K. (1907) 'Krisernas Gåta', *Statsøkonomisk Tidskrift*, pp. 255–85.

WICKSELL, K. (1918) 'Review of K. Petander, *'Goda och Dåliga Tider'* , *Ekonomisk Tidskrift*, vol. 19, pp. 66–75.

YOUNG, L. (1981) *Mathematicians and Their Times* (Amsterdam: North-Holland).

ZARNOWITZ, V. (1985) 'Recent Work on Business Cycles in Historical Perspective: A Review of Theories and Evidence', *Journal of Economic Literature*, vol. XXIII, no. 2, pp. 523–80.

# PART II
# Nonlinear Macrodynamics

# 4 Goodwin's Growth Cycle: Reminiscence and Rumination

Robert M. Solow

## REMINISCENCE

I came to Harvard College as a 16-year-old freshman in September 1940. So far as I had any coherent plan at all, it was to study plant genetics. I can no longer remember where that idea came from; my best guess is that I had heard there were jobs to be had in the US Forest Service. Today's students cannot imagine how large a factor that was in our minds as the decade of the thirties came to a close.

My four freshman courses were Introductory Biology, a first course in the German language, an Introduction to Psychology (the first semester on perception and psychophysics with Professor E. G. Boring as lecturer, and the second on personality, with Professor G. W. Allport as lecturer), and Introductory Economics ('Ec A' in the jargon). I have no difficulty reconstructing why I enrolled in the economics course. The Depression had just ended and the war in Europe had already begun. It did not take a lot of imagination to see that society was in trouble, and to realise that understanding the functioning of the economy was an urgent matter. Any 'scientific' approach to the study of social problems attracted me. My interest in psychology was really directed at social psychology; in my sophomore year I signed up for courses in sociology and social anthropology as well. But in my freshman year, as luck would have it, I began to study economics.

Ec A was taught in 'sections' of about 25 students who met for an hour three times a week with an instructor, called a 'section man'. (I am using the masculine pronoun as a matter of descriptive fact. What is more, all the students were males as well; at that time Radcliffe students in Ec A were taught separately in their own sections.) There was a uniform set of textbooks for all the sections, but each section man was an independent teacher and handled his section in his own style. They were mostly advanced graduate students. Since those were, by common consent, golden years at Harvard, it should come as no surprise that they were on the whole very good graduate students.

Nevertheless, I was unhappy in Ec A. I did not seem to be learning answers to the questions that had brought me to a course in the Principles of Economics. I kept asking 'dissident' questions and I kept getting put down. Readers today will be surprised to learn that my dissidence owed nothing at all to Marxian economics. I had been reading Veblen! It was *The Theory of the Leisure Class*, *The Theory of Business Enterprise*, *The Instinct of Workmanship* and *The Engineers and the Price System* that filled my mind with impious questions and unorthodox thoughts.

On the whole, I had better teachers than I deserved; some of them are now famous economists. But I kept annoying them – I must have been an ignorant pain in the neck – and they kept disappointing me. I say 'they' because I tried drifting from one section to another in search of satisfaction; it was perfectly legal. Then one day – it was probably my fourth or fifth try – I happened into Dick Goodwin's section. I wish I remembered details, or had the courage to fake them. I don't. But I do remember that I knew at once that I had found a home.

No instant enlightenment descended. God knows what he replied to my Veblenian – and worse – questions. Maybe nothing much, though I doubt that. But I liked his style. He was laid back – how did one say that in 1940? – and I do remember that a 16-year-old from Brooklyn was absolutely spellbound by what must have been the only Indiana-Oxford drawl in captivity. There was something more important, however. It is clear in my mind that when I asked what I must have thought were devilishly clever or profound questions, Mr Goodwin did not take a high and mighty – and defensive – line. His answers made it plain that he had plenty of sceptical doubts of his own. I may be inventing this, but I seem to recall that he sometimes suggested that, well, one could not actually believe this or that, but it was an ingenious line of thought, perhaps worth following just to see where it came out. One could always reject it later, and then one would have a better idea of what one was rejecting. If that actually happened, then I was getting my introduction to the theorist's frame of mind. It was probably wasted on me then.

Of course I stayed in that section for the rest of my freshman year. And I continued to study economics. In the next year my teachers were John Dunlop and Paul Sweezy. Only later did I study with Goodwin again. It is a fair guess, however, that if I had not wandered into Dick Goodwin's section of Ec A in the fall of 1940 I would have abandoned economics then and there. It is an awesome responsibility that he must shoulder.

Toward the end of 1942 I decided that being a student of the social sciences – economics and the others – was too boring and, since I had turned 18, I volunteered to join the army. When I came back to Harvard College in the fall of 1945, still an undergraduate, I had to decide what to study, and I chose economics. I will not explain how that decision was made, because it would only enhance my unfortunate reputation as a person who sees the faintly ridiculous side of serious matters. So it goes.

More or less by chance, I was assigned to Wassily Leontief as my 'tutor' or supervisor. For the next few years he was my main teacher and intellectual influence. The Leontiefs and the Goodwins were friends, and so I got to know Dick Goodwin in a less institutional way. Of course I continued to learn from him, both in the substance of economic theory – especially dynamics – and in a more subtle way that I do not know how to describe except as a matter of intellectual style. The unspoken message was that if a thing is worth doing it is worth doing playfully. Do not misunderstand me: 'playful' does not mean 'frivolous' or 'unserious'. It means, rather, that one should follow a trail the way a puppy does, sniffing the ground, wagging one's tail, and barking a lot, because it smells interesting and it would be fun to see where it goes.

There is always a temptation on occasions like this, to focus on personal details and remembered local colour. There is nothing wrong with yielding to that temptation – and I have done so – but there is a limit, and I shall observe it. In the rest of this paper I want to talk about Goodwin's work, and about one piece of work in particular. The example I have chosen is the paper on 'A Growth Cycle' that appeared in 1967 in the Festschrift for Maurice Dobb (Goodwin, 1967). I chose it for several reasons.

(a) It represents, as Professor Velupillai has pointed out in Chapter 3, the approximate culmination of Goodwin's important and insistent search for an integrated nonlinear model of economic growth and fluctuations.
(b) It has the additional advantage of exemplifying what for me has always been one of the most attractive characteristics of

Goodwin's approach to economic dynamics. That is his willingness to analyse a series of small, sharply specified, bare-bones models, none of them intended to describe all or many aspects of the economic system, but each intended to dramatise one or two aspects of economic life. The function of such models is not so much description as it is basic training for the intuition. This way of doing dynamics goes all the way back to his papers of the early 1950s, during my days as a graduate student. That was when I came to the belief that the analysis of small concrete models was the way forward in dynamics. The profession has come to favour generality over specificity. Like Goodwin I have worked both sides of this particular street. I know I am always happier on the small-is-beautiful side; but I am not sure he would agree with me now.

(c) Finally, the 1967 paper is five pages long. It does its business clearly and forcefully and stops. It contains no empty calories. Most economists – belying their own basic principles – write as if they were being paid by the word, though they are not.

Connoisseurs of Goodwin's work will know the model well. It has inspired a literature of its own. (See, for instance, most of the papers in the symposium volume edited by Goodwin, Krüger and Vercelli, 1984.) For others I can give a very terse outline.

There is a single produced commodity; in the usual way it can be directly consumed or accumulated as nondepreciating capital. It is produced by capital and labour in fixed proportions; the constant capital–output ratio is b. Let u be the share of wages in output, the rest being profits. All wages are consumed; all profits are instantly invested and *all capital is operated.* Investment is thus $(1-u)$ times output and the proportional rate of growth and capital and output is $(1-u)b^{-1}$. Suppose that the productivity of labour grows exogenously at the constant relative rate of $\alpha$; then employment grows like $(1-u)b^{-1}-\alpha$. Let v be the employment rate, the ratio of employment to working population; if the latter grows geometrically at rate $\beta$ then

$$v'/v=(1-u)b^{-1}-(\alpha+\beta) \qquad (1)$$

where $v'$ means $dv/dt$.

The second equation of the model comes from a real-wage Phillips curve. The real-wage rate grows faster the higher the employment rate, say $w'/w=-\gamma+\rho v$. Since the wage share u is, by definition, the real wage divided by the productivity of labour, it follows that

$$u'/u = -(\alpha+\gamma)+\rho v \tag{2}$$

So (1) and (2) are the equations of the model. Dividing one by the other, one finds

$$[-(\alpha+\gamma)+\rho v]dv/v = [-(\alpha+\beta)+(1-u)b^{-1}]du/u$$

which can be integrated to yield

$$u^{\eta_1}e^{-\theta_1 u} = Hv^{-\eta_2}e^{\theta_2 v} \tag{3}$$

where, in Goodwin's original notation, $\theta_1 = b^{-1}$, $\theta_2 = \rho$, $\eta_1 = b^{-1}-(\alpha+\beta)$, and H is a (necessarily positive but otherwise freely available) constant of integration. I did not learn to do this sort of thing from Goodwin: I learned it from reading N. Minorsky's *Introduction To Non-linear Mechanics* (Minorsky, 1947/62). But I learned that I wanted to learn it from Goodwin.

Equation (3) describes the trajectories of the model, i.e. the paths traced out in the (u,v) plane by the solution of (1) and (2). It is easily seen from the form of (3) that the trajectory is a closed curve whose general location depends only on the structural parameters but whose amplitude depends only on H. The limiting closed curve is the stationary point at $u = 1-b(\alpha+\beta)$, $v = \rho^{-1}(\alpha+\gamma)$. The other closed trajectories, obtained for different initial conditions (values of H), all surround this point. Thus, given initial conditions, u and v trace out repetitive oscillations. Remember that v is the employment rate; since it oscillates around a fixed average level, employment grows in the long run at the same rate as the working population, and therefore output grows in the long run at its 'natural rate', the sum of population growth and productivity gowth. Remember also that u is the wage share; its trendlessness implies that the real wage fluctuates around a trend that rises at the same rate as the productivity of labour. It really is an integrated trend-cycle model; and it is this neat construction that I want to discuss.

## RUMINATION

1. Goodwin observed, and others have noticed, that (1) and (2) amount formally to the famous predator–prey model of Volterra. The *trouvaille* of predator–prey interaction as a metaphor for the business cycle is often found to be attractive. It is not so often pointed out,

however, perhaps because it is disconcerting, that in this model it is the workers who are the predators and the capitalists who are the prey. I should be more clear about what that means. In the original Volterra model of the interaction of two species, the predator and the prey are distinguished in the following way. The predator population grows faster the larger the prey population, because there are more of them to eat. The prey population grows faster the smaller the predator population, because there are fewer of them to be eaten by. In applying this notion metaphorically to the growth cycle, one cannot just observe that the shares of wages and profits add up to one: that is true of *any* model. Given Goodwin's variables, it seems necessary and natural to identify the employment rate v with 'the workers' and the profit share $(1-u)$ with 'the capitalists'. Then it is seen from (1) that the employment rate increases more rapidly the larger the profit share, and from (2) that the profit share increases more rapidly the smaller the employment rate. The workers thus correspond to the predators. The economics underlying this identification is straightforward. High profits mean high investment and, since all investment is manned, high investment means rapidly growing employment. On the other side, low employment means falling wages and a rising share of profits.

An altogether different interpretation would be to regard the capitalists as passive non-players. The real conflict is between employed workers (identified with u) and unemployed workers (who are favoured by increasing v). Then it is the employed workers who are cast as predators in the model and the unemployed who are their prey. There is an uncomfortable ring of truth in this view. Perhaps the moral to be drawn is just that God made many more stories than differential equations, so one should not pass too easily from formal similarity to story-telling.

2. Here is a related point. Goodwin remarks, at the end of his beautiful paper, that the real wage rises with productivity in the long run, i.e. averaged over the cycle, whereas the profit share, the capital–output ratio, and therefore the rate of profit itself all stay constant. Therefore labour 'is the sole ultimate beneficiary from technical progress'. It seems to me that this conclusion runs into dimensional trouble. Is it really so bad being a capitalist in this model? The literal assumption is that capitalists do not consume at all, but that could be modified in the usual way to allow capitalists to consume a certain fraction of their income. Now imagine a capitalist who starts with

some capital and with a certain standard of living. Suppose she goes on consuming and investing her profits in the common proportion. Her private stock of capital will grow in the long run at the natural rate: the sum of population growth and technical progress. With a constant average rate of profit, so will her aggregate income. With a constant saving rate, so will her consumption. It is perhaps not so great being a unit of capital in this economy, but it is not so bad being a capitalist. Goodwin himself attributes the outcome to the 'tendency of capital, though not capitalists, to breed excessively' (1967, p. 58). That is exactly the point.

3. The model adopts Say's Law. Real consumption is always equal to real earnings and real investment is always equal to real profits. Thus aggregate demand is *identical* to aggregate output. (In the language of elementary textbook macroeconomics, the 'C+I function' coincides with the 45-degree line.) This is what permits the model to trace out fluctuations in output and employment as dictated primarily by the course of wage costs. Students used to pick up the vague notion that Say's Law had something to do with full employment, but that was a confusion. Say's Law permits *any* level of output to be an equilibrium; it takes an additional assumption about the clearing of the labour market to guarantee full employment, and that assumption Goodwin very sensibly does not make.

4. This utter passivity of the demand side in the Goodwin model leaves me uncomfortable. One might be willing to proceed tentatively on that basis so far as trend growth is concerned. That is what I did in the 1950s after all; but I was even then quite explicit that the problem of matching demand with productive capacity was left hanging. That aspect of the integration of growth and cycle theory is still unsettled and almost unexplored. In a model that has a characteristic maintained cycle around trend it seems even more risky to treat demand as adapting passively to fluctuations in production. But the gap is not easy to fill, at least not simply. Any abandonment of Say's Law has to begin with the provision of an unproduced object of desire as a vehicle for saving other than real capital. Fiat money is the traditional choice, but it may not be the best. Within that framework it may be possible to find special formulations that leave the qualitative behaviour of the model more or less unchanged. (See, for instance, the paper by M. diMatteo in the symposium volume already cited.) But that is a very un-robust course, in the sense that apparently trivial variations in the formulation may cause the results to change qualitatively. My

experiments seem to show that a more 'Keynesian' treatment of aggregate demand will replace or supplement (1) with a Saving = Investment equation and will change the model a lot.

Even straightforward modification of the original Goodwin model seems to lead to the same sort of problem. Suppose, for example, we preserve Say's Law by assuming that capitalists consume whatever they do not invest and then let investment depend on extrapolated profit so that (1) becomes

$$v'/v = i_0 + \mu b^{-1}(1 - u - ku') - (\alpha + \beta) \tag{1'}$$

which reduces to (1) for $i_0 = 0$, $\mu = 1$, $k = 0$. One can substitute from (2) for $u'$, but it is immediately clear that the nice conservative property of the Goodwin model is gone. I do not go on to analyse the model consisting of (1′) and (2) because it has nothing in particular to recommend it.

5. It appears that the absorption of effective demand considerations into the Goodwin model is difficult. If it can be done at all it will generally entail drastic changes in the characteristic Goodwinesque result. These considerations suggest a fairly radical conclusion. Perhaps the Goodwin growth cycle is not a model of the business cycle at all, at least not a model of the short-run fluctuations in economic activity that the National Bureau of Economic Research dates and the financial press talks about. Those fluctuations really do seem to be dominated, usually, by exogenous and endogenous movements in aggregate demand. This notion is reinforced by the observation that their period should be approximately $2\pi/(b^{-1}\rho u^* v^*)^{1/2}$ years, which I make to be about 8 to 10 years even with $\rho$ taken as large as 2. Goodwin cycles are then something else. What could that something be? Here I presume we must take seriously the story that the model tells: (a) that there are periods or episodes in which employment is rising because real wages are relatively low and the resulting high profits move avidly into investment and production; (b) these alternate with periods of episodes in which real wages are relatively high compared with productivity, and the profit-driven impetus to faster-than-average capitalist growth is blunted; and (c) the alternation is endogenous, induced by the real-wage Phillips curve. If that rings true to you, then you think there is something in it. My feeling is that the model does capture something real. At least I can think of episodes that seem to conform to that pattern. I think that is all that can be said and all that need be said about a small model. It is no contradiction to

say that the everyday business cycle marches to a different drumbeat. Goodwin can provide – has provided – models for that too. That is why, methodologically speaking, small is beautiful.

6. Does the Goodwin growth-cycle model fit the facts? I must admit that I ask the question mainly to create an opportunity to discuss what it means for a deliberately simple model to 'fit the facts'. I do not think that a flourish of multiple correlation coefficients is really to the point. The current fashion for deadpan 'econometric testing', magnified into an epidemic by the personal computer, is in my view a perversion that does harm both to economic theory and to econometrics. The philosopher John Austin once said – I am quoting from memory – that one might be tempted to describe oversimplification as the occupational disease of philosophers were it not their occupation. Much the same is true of economic theorists, and that must be taken into account in judging their constructions.

The true test of a simple model is whether it helps us to make sense of the world. (Marx was, of course, dead wrong about this. We have changed the world in all sorts of ways, with mixed results; the point is to interpret it.) A reasonable correspondence with the facts is no doubt a necessary condition for a model to be useful in interpreting the world. But the usual sort of over-fitted equation system or vector autoregression, accompanied by inappropriate mechanical tests of significance, does not seem to offer any guidance. I shall go to the opposite extreme and offer the crudest sort of comparison with data. I do not approve of that either. But my intention is not to offer a test of the model; it is rather to begin to see if it belongs in any obvious niche.

In Figure 4.1 I have used annual data, 1947 to 1986, for the US nonfarm business economy to plot the phase diagram of the growth-cycle model, its track in the (u,v)-plane. If the model were an exact description for that place and that period, the successive data points would parade clockwise around a closed orbit. They do not do so, nor is the discrepancy fairly described as noise. What then?

To begin with, there *is* a suggestion of predominantly clockwise motion, but in three separate episodes: the first eight observations, followed by a displacement and then the next twenty or so observations, and then an even larger and longer-duration displacement followed by the last half-dozen or so observations. The displacements are quite large and they suggest that the Goodwin model cannot be the only mechanism governing the relation between the wage share and the employment rate. I do not want to guess what the other mechanism(s) might be; that is a job for younger Goodwinians and it

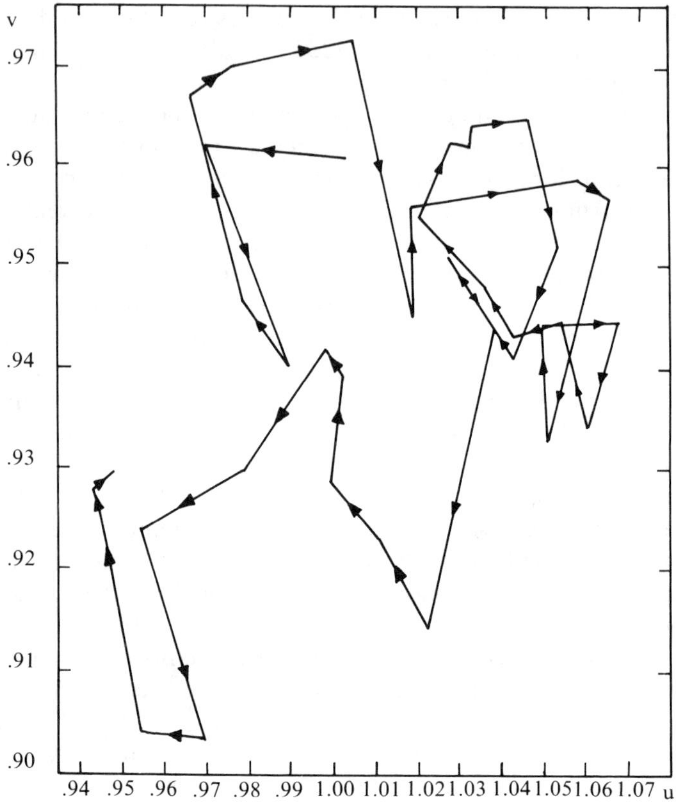


FIGURE 4.1

will clearly involve some econometrics, some intelligently-controlled econometrics I hope. Without that kind of accounting it will be very hard to apply the Goodwin model to concrete events.

It is also worth noting that the phase diagram contains a bare hint of a single large long-period clockwise sweep. It is only a hint, at best a hint. One cycle is not a periodic motion. There may be work for Goodwinians here too, theoretical as well as applied. It would make more sense to me if the Goodwin mechanism were to apply on a time scale considerably longer than the ordinary business cycle. Since the model determines its own period, there is room for some interplay between the facts and the theoretical structure.

Third and last, I should point out that the US may not be an appropriate trial horse for this model. Part of the folklore is that the

US has a nominal-wage Phillips curve, whereas the main European countries do indeed have a real-wage Phillips curve. The difference is very important for the interpretation of the model. In an economy with a nominal-wage Phillips curve, the wage share will be significantly affected by such forces as the speed and strength with which nominal prices respond to the facts of supply and demand (as expressed especially in the behaviour of the mark-up of prices over costs) and the cyclical behaviour of productivity itself (simply ignored in the formal model). It would be enlightening to try the model out on similar data for some European countries. I have seen one or two such exercises, but they do not ask the question in the stark way I have done here.

All this from a five-page paper! If brevity is the soul of wit, as Polonius claimed, then surely this is one of the wittiest papers in our discipline. I hope that my old teacher's more recent students will do him the honour of carrying his model further, *using* it to interpret the world, perhaps in some of the ways I have suggested here.

**References**

GOODWIN, R. M. (1967) 'A Growth Cycle', in C. H. Feinstein (ed.), *Socialism, Capitalism and Economic Growth, Essays Presented to Maurice Dobb* (Cambridge: Cambridge University Press) pp. 54–8.

MINORSKY, N. (1947/62) *Introduction to Non-linear Mechanics*, published 1962 as *Nonlinear Oscillations* (New York: Van Nostrand).

# 5 Deterministic Chaos in Economics: An Occurrence in Axiomatic Utility Theory[1]

Paul A. Samuelson

Edward N. Lorenz, MIT meteorologist, made a pivotal analytical breakthrough when he discovered in 1963 *deterministic chaos* (Lorenz, 1963). Previously scholars tended to regard *stochastic* and *deterministic* models as distinct categories, mutually exclusive. Now we know better.

The present paper pays homage to Richard Goodwin, an aristocrat in the tribe of science, whose aristocratic nose early smelled significance for economics in nonlinear *autorelaxation* dynamics *à la* Rayleigh and van der Pol; in Hopf *bifurcation* theory and Thom *catastrophe* theory; and in Lorenz–Poincaré–Feigenbaum *deterministic chaos*, which can itself be shown to involve the self-similarity phenomena of Mandelbrot *fractals*.

Macroeconomic business cycles, as in Richard H. Day (1982), would be a natural place to expect chaos to appear. My present focus, however, is on the unexpected appearance of *deterministic chaos* in connection with some axiomatic foundations of Bernoulli–von Neumann utility theory.

First, I describe some general features of deterministic chaos, a paradigm that rationalises why the warm El Nino current brings or withholds the crop of anchovy protein; that times the drops from a leaky faucet and paces the heart; that takes the measure of turbulence and gives us this day our daily random numbers; that apes the showers of dinosaur-extinguishing asteroids and kneads for us this day our daily bread.

## 5.1 GENERALITIES

Most important innovations have earlier forerunners. Henri Poincaré's nineteenth-century study of topological dynamics recognised that motions determined by Laplacian deterministic systems could generate probabilistic regularities. We use a roulette wheel or a tossed coin to generate games of chance, Poincaré realised, because the smallest imprecision in control of the system's initial conditions will result in the largest differences in recorded outcomes, even though an *exact* knowledge of the object's initial state would have enabled an omniscient Laplace to know its ultimate state *exactly* even after many turns of the wheel or coin.

The following juxtaposition of quotations from Laplace and Poincaré is therefore illuminating:

> Laplace, 1776
> "The present state of the system of nature is evidently a consequence of what it was in the preceding moment, and if we conceive of an intelligence which at a given instant comprehends all the relations of the entities of this universe, it could state the respective positions, motions, and general effects of all these entities at any time in the past or future.
>
> "Physical astronomy, the branch of knowledge which does the greatest honor to the human mind, gives us an idea, albeit imperfect, of what such an intelligence would be. The simplicity of the law by which the celestial bodies move, and the relations of their masses and distances, permit analysis to follow their motions up to a certain point; and in order to determine the state of the system of these great bodies in past or future centuries, it suffices for the mathematician that their position and their velocity be given by observation for any moment in time. Man owes that advantage to the power of the instrument he employs, and to the small number of relations that it embraces in its calculations. But ignorance of the different causes involved in the production of events, as well as their complexity, taken together with the imperfection of analysis, prevents our reaching the same certainty about the vast majority of phenomena. Thus there are things that are uncertain for us, things more or less probable, and we seek to compensate for the impossibility of knowing them by determining their different degrees of likelihood. So it is that we owe to the weakness of the human mind

one of the most delicate and ingenious of mathematical theories, the science of chance or probability."

Poincaré, 1903
"A very small cause which escapes our notice determines a considerable effect that we cannot fail to see, and then we say that the effect is due to chance. If we knew exactly the laws of nature and the situation of the universe at the initial moment, we could predict exactly the situation of that same universe at a succeeding moment. But even if it were the case that the natural laws had no longer any secret for us, we could still only know the initial situation *approximately*. If that enabled us to predict the succeeding situation with the *same approximation*, that is all we require, and we should say that the phenomenon had been predicted, that it is governed by laws. But it is not always so; it may happen that small differences in the initial conditions produce very great ones in the final phenomena. A small error in the former will produce an enormous error in the latter. Prediction becomes impossible, and we have the fortuitous phenomenon."

## 5.2 HISTORY WITHOUT HYSTERESIS

A simple damped pendulum has an equilibrium state that is a simple *attractor* for all motions. Any past historical event that perturbs the pendulum's initial state, thus, is ultimately forgotten as two nearby motions converge asymptotically toward equilibrium and each other. Chaotic motions, Lorenz discovered, have *strange attractors*, quite different from the globally stable damped pendulum.

Similarly, in Lotka–Leslie standard population dynamics, the one-time perturbation by war of the age distribution is ultimately forgotten by the stable system. Ansley Coale, and his pupil A. Lopez (1961), discovered that past perturbations of age distribution are ultimately forgotten *even if age-specific mortalities and fertilities change in time*. Their beautiful quasi-ergodic theorem would smell sweet to the Goodwin nose, alerted already to the beauties of Frobenius matrixes.

*Theorem*: Let $[a_{ij}] = a$ be a positive square matrix of order n. Then $a^T$, as $T \to \infty$, comes to have columns (and rows) that are almost proportional to each other (so that past age-perturbations asymptotically fade).

Now consider the double sequence of positive matrixes:

$$^{1}a=[^{1}a_{ij}],\ ^{2}a=[^{2}a_{ij}],\ \ldots;\ [^{T}\bar{a}_{ij}]=[^{1}\bar{a}_{ij}]\,[^{T-1}\bar{a}_{ij}] \tag{1}$$

where for all $T=1,2,\ldots$

$$\mathrm{Min}[^{T}a_{ij}/\sum_{k=1}^{\infty}{}^{T}a_{ik}]>\delta>0 \tag{2}$$

Then

$$\lim_{t\to\infty}[^{T}\bar{a}_{ij}/\sum_{1}^{n}\sum_{1}^{n}{}^{T}\bar{a}_{rs}]=[b_{i}c_{j}]>0 \tag{3}$$

Deterministic chaos is not like this. It does generate ergodic-probability distributions. But its strange attractors preclude stable equilibrium points, stable limit cycles, and stable surfaces of a torus. (The concept of an 'attractor', as the sub-locus to which all motions in the space ultimately go, will be taken up after equation (13) below.)

## 5.3 THE LOGISTIC COBWEB

When we add limitation of land to Malthusian population models, the law of diminishing returns negates an exponential rate of growth, as in the simplest Verhulst-Pearl model of *logistic* growth:

$$\dot{x}=rx(1-K^{-1}x);\ K>0,\ r>0 \tag{4}$$

$$=x(1-x),\ \text{under units with}\ (K,r)=(1,1)$$

where $dx/dt$ is written as $\dot{x}$.

The solution, for initial $x(0)$ a fraction, is

$$x(t)=1/1+[X(0)^{-1}-1]e^{-t} \tag{5}$$

$$\lim_{t\to\infty}x(t)=1,\ \lim_{t\to-\infty}[\dot{x}(t)/x(t)]=1 \tag{6}$$

Some economists, such as Roy Harrod, like *differential* equations.

Others, like Goodwin when young, lean toward *difference* equations; they would be tempted to replace (4) by

$$[X(t+h)-X(t)]h^{-1}=r_h X(t)[1-X(t)];\ r_h>0,\ h>0 \tag{7}$$

Biologists, such as Robert M. May (1976), have discovered that (7) can develop chaotic motions for certain innocent choices of the parameters $(h, r_h)$. (Fortunately for our intuition, when these positive parameters are sufficiently near to (0, 1), the solution is qualitatively like that of (4)'s solution.)

I suppose it can be argued, as in Potts (1982), that these chaotic solutions represent *phantom chaos*, which are artefacts avoidable if we replace (7) as our approximation to (4) by the equally satisfactory first-order approximation

$$X(t+1)-X(t)=X(t)[1-X(t+1)](e^h-1),\ 0<h \tag{8}$$

with no chaotic properties in its exact solution

$$X(t)=1/1+[X(0)^{-1}-1]e^{-ht},\ t=0, \pm 1, \pm 2, \ldots \tag{9}$$

## 5.4 CHAOTIC FLOWS AND TRANSFORMATIONS

However the ecology savants decide on this matter, the following difference equation could easily arise in economics:

$$X_{t+1}=f[X_t]=f[f[X_{t-1}]]\equiv f_2[X_{t-1}],\ f[\,]\equiv f_1[\,] \tag{10}$$

$$X_{t+\tau}=f_T[X_T]=f_1[f_{T-1}[X_t]],\ T=2,3, \ldots \tag{11}$$

$$X_{t+1}=bX_t(1-X_t),\ 0<b\leqq 4 \tag{12}$$

This iteration maps nonnegative fractions into nonnegative fractions. The origin $X_0=0$, maps into itself and thus provides a stationary equilibrium point. For low values of b, the origin is globally stable, being approached asymptotically no matter what the initial perturbation of $X_0$ on the interval [0, 1]. When b comes to exceed unity, the origin becomes unstable; and a second equilibrium point is defined at $(b-1)/b$. This is stable for b in the interval [1, 3]. For b greater than 3, no equilibrium point is locally stable and chaos with its strange attractors arises.

Lorenz (1963) himself studied third-order nonlinear differential equations of the following form, which sufficed to define chaos for appropriate choices of the parameter r (and with bifurcation phenomena at critical r points):

$$\dot{x}_1 = -10x_1 + 10x_2 + 0x_3 \tag{13}$$

$$\dot{x}_2 = rx_1 - 0_2x - x_1x_3$$

$$\dot{x}_3 = x_1x_2 + 0x^2 - (8/3)x_3$$

These motions take place in the 3-dimensional space $[x_1, x_2, x_3]$, and, for $t > 0$ and assigned initial $[x_j(0)]$, can be seen to remain bounded inside some specifiable cube. Lorenz wishes to explore where all motions go asymptotically: to what 2-dimensional surface do they all gravitate? He realised that, for certain choices of the parameter r, they could not run into a stable point; by numerical simulation he could verify that they approached no stable limit cycle of the van der Pol–Rayleigh type, and could not wind stably around a doughnut-type torus. So no normal 'attractors' were present.

Lorenz correctly sensed that the (13) flow has the property that two nearby initial points have trajectories that start out diverging exponentially from each other ('instability'). But, since all motions are bounded, such divergence could not persist indefinitely; inevitably the first-spreading-out motions must secondarily fold back on themselves. This qualitative alternation is quite like the kneading of bread: first the baker spreads out the dough; then he folds it over; as the process is repeated endless times, a new blob of yellow egg in the dough gets spread indefinitely evenly through the original white mass. Exactly this occurs with the Lorenz (1963) process and with similar processes of O. Rössler (1986).

The 'strange attractor' that Lorenz inferred as the rendezvous set for the motions has the *fractal* property that, as we examine its points under ever greater scale magnification, we keep seeing essentially the same structure. Dean Swift put this Mandelbrot property presciently: 'a flea/Hath smaller fleas that on him prey;/And these have smaller still to 'bite em;/and so proceed *ad infinitum*'.

Stanislaus Ulam and John von Neumann early studied the (12) iteration by numerical simulations. It is a standard case of *unimodal* iteration with well-behaved so-called Schwartzian derivatives. As shown by A. N. Sarkovskii, D. Singer, M. Feigenbaum, and others, the features of this special instance have amazing universality for all such smooth unimodal cases. See Collet and Eckmann (1980) and Grandmont (1983) for details.

The following cornered cobweb case, although it lacks smoothness and some standard entailments, lends itself nicely to economists' graphical experimentations. It also prepares the reader for this paper's baker's transformation of [6.2] to come.

## 5.5 THE CHURCH-STEEPLE COBWEB

Figure 5.1 plots the following scenario:

$$X_{t+1} = f[X_t] = 1 - 2|X_T - 1/2| \tag{14}$$

To discern the motion generated by any initial point on the unit segment of the horizontal axis, we first go up or down to intersect the ABZ locus depicting (14)'s cornered f[X] function. Then, second, we

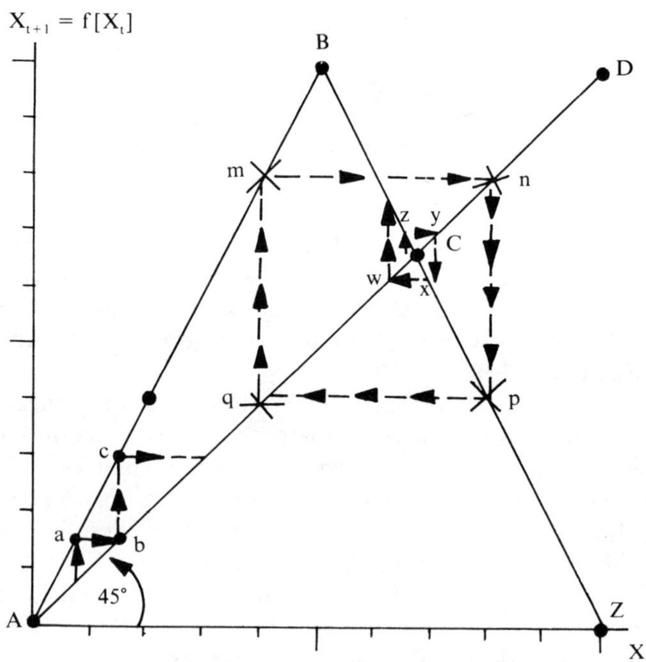


FIGURE 5.1 *Chaos transformation*

go left or right to the 45-degree line AD (thereby proceeding to use $X_{t+1}$ as the new springboard succeeding the previous $X_t$ springboard).

Simply repeat indefinitely these successive up-or-down and then right-or-left processes to generate the solution for the iteration to any desired number of terms. Example: The a b c . . . steps illustrate how perturbed motions run away monotically from the unstable equilibrium point of A. The w x y z . . . steps demonstrate anti-damped oscillations running away from the unstable equilibrium point at C, defined by intersection of AD with the BZ branch of ABZ at the point (2/3, 2/3).

Since the 45-degree line intersects the cornered function ABZ in the points 0 and 2/3, we observe two equilibria. Both equilibrium points are unstable because the slopes of AB and of BZ exceed unity in absolute value. Nearby motions at first diverge exponentially, proportionally to $|2|^t$!

Do periodic motions exist? Yes: 4/5, 2/5, 4/5, . . . is seen to be a motion of period 2; it is traced out clockwise by the closed box m n p q m . . . It can be seen to be locally unstable under the slightest perturbations (because the product of the relevant slopes in a cycle is $|2|^2$, which exceeds unity). Actually, this is the only motion of period 2 (except, of course, for the degenerate equilibria; 0, 0, 0, . . ., and 2/3, 2/3, 2/3, . . .).

There are other periodic motions, of period exceeding 2. The telltale sign of chaos is that all periodic motions are unstable (as the absolute derivatives of $f_t(x)$ are of the form $|2|^t > 1$). By playing with paths in Figure 5.1, the reader can plot the motion of period 3: 6/7, 2/7, 4/7, 6/7, . . . She can also verify the existence of another unstable motion of period 3: 8/9, 2/9, 4/9, 8/9, . . ., which differs from the periodic motions as yet mentioned, in that it does not alternate each time between the AB and the BZ branch.

Almost all choices of initial conditions generate trajectories that go on forever, never becoming strictly periodic. Each such trajectory moves very close to each periodic motion, mimicking it for long intervals of time but ultimately quite ignoring it (most of the time!). If a motion picked at random had its likelihood recorded of visiting each sub-interval of the unit interval [0, 1], a determinate (ergodic) probability distribution would be generated. Chaos, so to speak, lacks *deterministic* good behaviour; but, working the other side of the street, we can discern in chaos very orderly and good behaviour *on the average*!

All this is quite what observers of turbulence in fluid flow have learned to expect.

## 5.6 BAKER'S TRANSFORMATION

Recall how a baker flattens his dough, then laps it over. Recall how an introduced blob of egg at first appears concentrated near one spot; gradually it spreads in fingers through the whole mass until, after many kneadings the yellow appears homogenously through the whole loaf. Prigogine (1980) discusses extensively the following baker's transformation:

$$(x_t, y_t) \rightarrow (x_{t+1}, y_{t+1}) \tag{15a}$$

where

$$[x_{t+1}, y_{t+1}] = [2x_t, y_t/2],\ 0 \leqq x_t < 1/2 \tag{15b}$$

$$= [(2x_t - 1, (1/2)(1 + y_t)],\ 1/2 \leqq x_t < 1 \tag{15c}$$

For my present purpose, (15)'s transformation for $x_t \rightarrow x_{t+1}$ which is quite autonomous in the sense of being independent of $y_t$, is to be modified at $x_t = 1/2$ and $x_t = 1$ from Prigogine's convention.

I need to write

$$x_{t+1} = f[x_t] = 2x_t,\ \text{if } 0 \leqq x_t < 1/2 \tag{16a}$$

$$= 2x_t - 1,\ \text{if } 1/2 < x_t \leqq 1 \tag{16b}$$

$$= 1/2,\ \text{if } x_t = 1/2 \tag{16c}$$

Figure 5.2, which is not unimodal, but is discontinuous, graphs the transformation. It is seen to have three fixed points $\bar{x} = 0, 1, 1/2$, all unstable. $f[x_t]$ exists as a single-valued function, even though no unique $f^{-1}\ [x_{t+1}]$ inverse function exists: for $x_{t+1}$ not at one of the equilibria, 2 different $x_t$'s could have generated it: $x_{t+1}/2$ or $(x_{t+1} + 1)/2$. For $x_{T+1}$ either 0 or 1, a unique $x_t$ can be inferred – namely 0 in the first case and 1 in the second. But for an observed $x_{t+1} = 1/2$, any of three predecessors could be admissible: namely, $x_t = 1/2$, 1/4 or 3/4.

Numerical and graphical exploration reveals the existence of a countable infinity of periodic motions for (16), all unstable. An

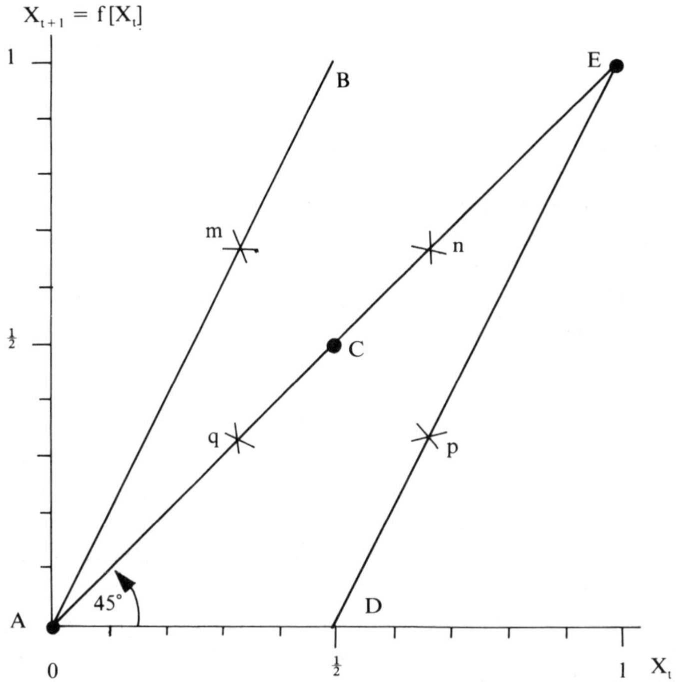


FIGURE 5.2 *Baker's transformation*

example, of period 2, is the motion: 2/3, 1/3, 2/3, . . . Another, of period 4, involves: 3/5, 1/5, 2/5, 4/5, 3/5, . . .

Now, however, we have a phenomenon not possible in Figure 5.1 or (10). Motions that begin out of equilibrium may, in a *finite* number of steps, run into the equilibrium point of 1/2, and then forever afterward remain there. Here are some examples, which the reader can check:

$x_t$: 1/2, 1/2, . . . (17)

: 3/4, 1/2, 1/2, . . . ; 1/4, 1/2, 1/2, . . .

: 7/8, 6/8, 1/2, . . . ; 1/8, 2/8, 1/2, 1/2, . . . ; 5/8, 2/8, 1/2, 1/4, . . . ; 3/8, 6/8, 1/2, . . .

. . . . . . . . . . . . . . . . . . . . . . . . . . . . . . . . . . . . . . . . . . . . . . . . . . . .

: $1/2^k$, $1/2^{k-1}$, . . . , $1/2^{k-k+1}$, 1/2, . . . , after k + 1 steps;

etc.

Let us employ the binary number system, so that any real number on the [0, 1] interval can be written as an infinite sequence of 0-or-1 digits:

$$.d_1 d_2 d_3 \ldots \text{ or } d_1 2^{-1} + d_2 2^{-2} + d_3 2^{-3} + \ldots \tag{18}$$

Then any irrational number requires a sequence with more than a finite number of non-zeros. Almost all rational fractions will involve an infinity of non-zeros, but necessarily in the form of repeating cycles. Any positive number involving only a finite number of non-zero's must be of the finite form

$$d_1 2^{-1} + \ldots + d_n 2^{-n} + 0 + \ldots, \text{ where } n < \infty \text{ and } \sum_1^n d_k > 0 \tag{19}$$

It is those items that satisfy (19) which do reach the equilibrium point of 1/2 after only a finite number of steps.

The beauty of (16)'s baker's transformation is that, as in Prigogine (1980), the solution for any iteration from a specified initial $X_0$, consists of writing $X_0$ as a binary decimal; and then each iteration involves only a Bernoulli shift, in which the left-most digit is omitted while the decimal point is shifted one place to the right.

Then

$$\sum_{i=1}^{\infty} d_i(t) 2^{-i} = X_t \to X_{t+1} = \sum_{i=1}^{\infty} d_i(t+1) 2^{-i}, \; n \leqq \infty \tag{20}$$

where

$$d_1(t+1) = d_2(t),\ d_2(t+1) = d_3(t),\ \ldots,\ d_i(t+1) = d_{i+1}(t),\ i = 1, 2, \ldots \tag{21}$$

For all irrationals the process never ends; for rational $X_0$s the process cycles or does terminate in a finite number of steps.

## 5.7 'WEIGHTED' INTERMEDIATE TEMPERATURES

Consider two equal masses of some identical substance: let them first be isolated from each other, and let each fluid be contained within its own *insulating*, *rigid* walls. Whatever way we choose to measure temperature, there is no reason to require that the two systems have the same temperature; they may, therefore, also have different specific volumes.

Now bring the equal masses into contact with each other through a common externally-conducting wall. Gradually, the two fluids will come into temperature equality or equilibrium: the part with initial higher temperature, say $T^2$, will cool down; the other part, with initial $T^1 < T^2$, will have its temperature increase. It is a recordable law of nature that the final temperature $T^*$, is a determinate *mean* of the two initial temperatures:

$$T^* = M[T^1,T^2] \tag{22a}$$

$$\equiv M[T^2,T^1], \text{ symmetry} \tag{22b}$$

$$\text{Min}[T^1,T^2] \leqq M[T^1,T^2] \leqq \text{Max}[T^1,T^2] \tag{22c}$$

$$M[T,T] \equiv T \tag{22d}$$

The $M[T^1,T^2]$ function is thus an *internal unweighted mean* of the temperatures – unweighted because the two masses are specified to be equal and identical.

Suppose we had four such equal masses, with respective temperatures of $(T^1,T^2,T^3,T^4)$. We would get a *mean* of their temperatures if we brought them all together in one step. It is a verifiable law of nature that this final temperature could also have been found by either of the following two-stage procedures:

**Procedure I:** Combine the $T^1$ and $T^2$ items to get $M[T^1,T^2] = T^{12} = T^{21}$; simultaneously combine the $T^3$ and $T^4$ items to get $M[T^3,T^4] = T^{34} = T^{43}$. Next combine the $T^{12}$ and $T^{34}$ items to get $M[M[T^1,T^2],M[T^3,T^4]]$, which will yield numerically exactly what the direct mixture of all four would have yielded.
**Procedure II:** This is the same as I above, but now $T^1$ and $T^3$ are initially paired along with the initial pairing of $T^2$ and $T^4$.

It is not a law of arithmetic that makes the two procedures give the same result: rather it is a testable law of nature, connected with the First and Second Laws of Thermodynamics, that entails the functional identity:

$$M[M[T^1,T^2],\ M[T^3,T^4]] \equiv M[M[T^1,T^3],\ M[T^2,T^4]] \tag{23}$$

As shown in Aczél (1966), this Abel-like identity puts a strong restriction on the $M[T^1,T^2]$ function, which is required to be an *associative mean*, of the form:

$$m(M[T^1,T^2]) \equiv m(T^1)/2 + m(T^2)/2 \tag{24a}$$

$$M[T^1,T^2] \equiv m^{-1}\{m(T^1)/2 + M(T^2)/2\} \tag{24b}$$

where m(x) is a determinable function, arbitrary only with respect to origin and scale parameters – and where

$$m(x) = y, \; x = m^{-1}\{y\}$$

It is well known that empirical measurements of temperature can be made in a variety of ways: thus, if the Ts in (22) were lengths of mercury columns, then lengths of alcohol columns might replace T by the stretching $\tau\{T\}$, $\tau'\{T\} > 0$. Clearly the function that specifies m(T) in (24) would have to be a different function from the $\mu(\tau)$ function that would appear in (24) if we had begun measuring temperatures by τs: by $\tau_1$ and $\tau_2$; by $\tau_1,\tau_2,\tau_3,\tau_4$. Because of the law of nature expressed in (23) we can know that there is a universal temperature scale – a Kelvin-like scale – that employs the *invariant* m(T) or $\mu(\tau)$ functions, where

$$a + bm(t) \equiv \mu(\tau\{T\}), \; a \gtreqless 0, \; b > 0 \tag{25}$$

where a is an arbitrary *origin* constant and b is an arbitrary *scale* constant.

All the above deals with *un*weighted, or *equal*-mass, mixtures. The point of the present section is to *deduce* from known behaviour of *un*weighted means what has to be the form of the following kind of *weighted* mean:

> What equilibrium temperature results ultimately when we mix two identical substances of respective temperatures $T^1$ and $T^2$, but where the latter has (say) three times the mass of the former?
> What equilibrium results when the $T^1$ item has mass of $Q^1$ and $T^2$ item has mass of $Q^2$?

For $Q^1/(Q^1 + Q^2) = 1/4$, we know the answer. Combine one-third of the larger-mass $T^2$ item with all of the $T^1$ item – a combination that involves equal-mass mixtures. The new mixture has half the original total of mass and has for its temperature $M[T^1,T^2]$. Combine this half of the mass with the amount of the $T^2$ item not used, which is the other half of the original total. This gives a result in which *all* the mass now has settled down to a common temperature:

$$M[T^1,M[T^1,T^2]]=T^{1222} \tag{26}$$

This result, pure deduction shows, could also be arrived at if we possessed knowledge of (24)'s m(T) function, namely

$$\begin{aligned} T^{1222} &= m^{-1}\{m(T^1)/4+3m(T^2)/4\} \\ &\equiv M[T^1,M[T^1,T^2]] \end{aligned} \tag{27}$$

Similarly, by pure deduction, we can in principle work out *any* weighted mean temperature:

$$\begin{aligned} M[T^1,T^2;Q^1,Q^2] &\equiv M[T^1,T^2{:}Q^1/(Q^1+Q^2),\ Q^2/(Q^1+Q^2)] \\ &\equiv M[T^1,T^2;q],\ 0\leqq q=Q^1/(Q^1+Q^2)\leqq 1 \end{aligned} \tag{28}$$

from prior knowledge of (24)'s m(T) function, namely as

$$M[T^1,T^2;q]\equiv m^{-1}\{qm(T^1)+(1-q)m(T^2)\} \tag{29}$$

It might be a tedious task to deduce m(T) numerically for a wide range of Ts; and this task would not be worth doing just in order to calculate a few $M[T^1,T^2;q]$ evaluations. The whole point of the present exercise is to elucidate how, from knowledge of the single bivariate $M[T^1,T^2]$ function alone, we can deduce to any desired degree of accuracy the value of $M[T^1,T^2;q]$ for *any* real value of q on the (0,1) interval. (Of course, $M[T^1,T^2]$ is what we mean by $M[T^1,T^2;1/2]$.)

The requisite algorithm turns out to involve the chaotic motions of the breadbaker's algorithm plotted in Figure 5.2 and defined in equation (16). The Appendix summarises how all this applies in economics, applies not to temperatures but to utilities people use in betting or in other stochastic investment decisions.

The desired general algorithm for evaluating unweighted means from a succession of weighted means is simple. Of any two masses, combine the smaller with an equal part of the larger. That gives a new temperature already betwixt the two original ones; and it leaves one mass with an old temperature.

Again we face two masses of unequal temperature. Repeat the process with them, getting two new masses and two temperatures or whichever one is nearer the final equilibrium.

Repeat so long as you don't face equal masses (in which case you would be home in a single final step). Almost always, the algorithm will never come to such a happy end: but always it will be the case that each whirl of the algorithm lowers the temperature differences of the two masses you have left; and always with enough whirls, you can bring the temperature as near to the true equilibrium as any pre-assigned degree of accuracy requires. Equation (16)'s baker's transformation is precisely what is involved here in the form of $q_t \rightarrow f[q_t] = q_{t+1}$.

$$\begin{aligned}
&[q_{t+1}, T^1_{t+1}, T^2_{t+1}] \\
&= [2q_t, M[T^1_t, T^2_t], T^2_t] \text{ if } 0 < q_t < 1/2 \\
&= [2q_t - 1, T^1_t, M[T^1_t, T^2_t]] \text{ if } 1/2 < q_t < 1 \\
&= [1/2, M[T^1_t, T^2_t], M[T^1_t, T^2_t]] \text{ if } q_t = 1/2
\end{aligned} \tag{30}$$

$$\lim_{t \rightarrow \infty} [T^1_t, T^2_t] = m^{-1}\{q_0 m(T^1_0) + (1 - q_0) m(T^2_0)\} \tag{31}$$

The reader is referred to the self-contained Appendix. In it, we see how *all* stochastic bettings for *any* probabilities can be axiomatised in terms of knowledge of 'even-odds-bettings' (equal-masses, so to speak).

## 5.8 CONCLUDING OBSERVATIONS ON CHAOS

Suppose a scientist perceives what looks to be a pattern of periodicity in business-cycle data, or sun-spot data, or extinction-of-species data. Some of the familiar statistical tests – as with the old-fashioned Schuster periodogram, or R. A. Fisher's more stringent test, or Wiener–Kolmogorov generalised-harmonic analysis – may seem to be satisfied by the scientists's data.

Surely, however, caution is called for. Such periodicities may still be 'spurious', in the sense that the data may have been generated by deterministic-chaos models that are prone to stay for a long time near an (unstable) periodic motion and yet are bound to move indefinitely away from this accidental pattern.

It will take very large samples of time-series data to enable the scientist to refute the hypothesis of chaos or to provisionally accept it. History – relevant history – is what we economists are short on, making us perhaps as unlucky as weathermen, geologists, paleontologists and cosmologists.

Oh well.

## APPENDIX: CALCULATING ANY-ODDS CERTAINTY EQUIVALENTS IN TERMS OF CHAOS DYNAMICS OF EVEN-ODDS EQUIVALENTS

### Even-Odds revealed preferences

It is well known that, if there exists a utility function whose expected value I am always maximising, it can in principle be identified from my observed reactions to even-money bets alone. Thus, Gerard Debreu (1959) as a sixtieth-birthday offering to Jacob Marschak provided a topological analysis of this problem, thereby independently paralleling the discussion in Ramsey (1930, Ch. VII).

What will be spelled out here is how, solely from knowledge of the even-odds certainty-equivalent function, one can infer complete knowledge of the any-odds certainty-equivalent function.

Begin by considering two alternative money wealths, $x_1$ or $x_2$. (Although these could be vectors of goods, the scalar case suffices to make the essential points.) There is some intermediate wealth, y, which if it were available with certainty, would be deemed by me to be just as desirable as the option [$x_1$ with probability 1/2 or $x_2$ with probability 1/2]. For any feasible pair $(x_1,x_2)$, I could reveal to you my even-odds certainty-equivalent function, $f(x_1,x_2)$, with its following assumed properties:

$$y = f(x_1,x_2) \leftrightarrow (\text{y with certainty}) \sim (x_1 \text{ or } x_2 \text{ at } 1/2 \text{ probabilities}) \tag{A.1a}$$

$$\equiv f(x_2,x_1)\text{: symmetry} \tag{A.1b}$$

$$< f(x_2+h,x_1) \text{ for } h>0\text{: monotonicity} \tag{A.1c}$$

$$x \equiv f(x,x)\text{; a general mean} \tag{A.1d}$$

$f(x_1,x_2)$ to be a *continuous* function (perhaps even smoothly differentiable with well-defined

$$\delta f(x_1,x_2)/\delta x_1 = f_i(x_1,x_2) \tag{A.1e}$$

It is well known that, if and only if f satisfies the following Abel-like functional equation, there does exist for me a utility-of-wealth function, F(x), whose *expected value* I do maximise in choosing among stochastic alternatives:

$$f(\,f(x_1,x_2),f(x_3,x_4)) \equiv f(\,f(x_1,x_3),f(x_2,x_4)) \qquad \text{(A.2a)}$$

As in Aczél (1966), the functional equation of (A.2a) implies, as is implied by the fact that my f(x,y) is an *associative* (or *quasi-linear*) *mean*, of the form

$$f(x,z) = F^{-1}[(1/2)F(x) + (1/2)F(z)] \qquad \text{(A.2b)}$$

$$z = F(x) \leftrightarrow x = F^{-1}[z]$$

$$F(x+h) > F(x) \text{ for } h > 0 \qquad \text{(A.2c)}$$

$$-F''(x)/F'(x) \text{ an observable invariant of} \qquad \text{(A.2d)}$$

$$a + bF(x),\ a \gtrless 0,\ b > 0$$

where a is an arbitrary parameter of origin and b is an arbitrary positive scale parameter. In stochastic contexts of economics, F(x) is the von Neumann or Bernoulli utility function. Aczél (1966) shows how it can be constructively defined without needing differentiability properties. Thus, we can replace (A.2d)'s *derivative* expression by the difference expression:

$$[F(x) - F(z)]/F(y) - F(z)] \qquad \text{(A.2d')}$$

which is an invariant for $y \neq z$ and any x.

In terms of partial derivatives of f, $\delta f/\delta x_i \equiv f_i(x_1,x_2)$, the following quadrature formulation is useful:

$$F(x) = b^0 \int_{x0}^{x} [f_1(X,x^0)/f_2(X,x^0)]dX + a^0 \qquad \text{(A.3a)}$$

$$F(x^0) = a^0,\ F'(x^0) = b^0$$

**Any-odds certainty-equivalents**

Even-money gambles are special cases of any-odds gambles. One can define, from observations of my choices, generalisations of the previous section's $f(x_1,x_2)$ function. What y wealth offered to me with certainty will I reveal to you I find just exactly as desirable as the option [$x_1$ with probability q or $x_2$ with probability $1-q$]? Observable is the following asymmetric function, defined for any real fraction q:

$$(\text{y with certainty}) \sim (x_1 \text{ with q prob or } x_2 \text{ with } 1-q \text{ prob}) \quad \text{(A.4)}$$

$$\leftrightarrow$$

$$y = f(x_1,x_2;q),\ 0 \leqq q \leqq 1 \quad \text{(A.5a)}$$

$$\equiv f(x_2,x_1;1-q)\text{: notational symmetry} \quad \text{(A.5b)}$$

$$f(x_1+h,x_2;q) > f(x_1,x_2;q) \text{ for } q>0 \quad \text{(A.5c)}$$

$$\text{Iff } f(x_1,x_2;q+h) > f(x_1,x_2;q) \text{ and } h>0, \quad \text{(A.5d)}$$

then

$$x_1 > x_2 \text{ and } f(x_1,x_2;1) > f(x_1,x_2;0) \quad \text{(A.5e)}$$

$f(x_1,x_2;q)$ continuous (and perhaps smoothly differentiable) in its three arguments. (A.5f)

Clearly, what was earlier called $f(x_1,x_2)$ is just the same as $f(x_1,x_2;1/2)$ in (A.5a). It can be shown by detailed reasoning that, if $f(x_1,x_2;1/2)$ is an *associative mean* in the sense of (A.2b) then $f(x_1,x_2;q)$ will be an *associative mean* of the form:

$$f(x_1,x_2;q) = F^{-1}[qF(x_1)+(1-q)F(x_2)] \quad \text{(A.6)}$$

The reader may verify various special relations, such as

$$f(\ f(x_1,x_2;q_1),f(x_1,x_2;q_2);\ q_3) \quad \text{(A.7)}$$
$$\equiv f(x_1,x_2;q_1q_3+q_2[1-q_3])$$

Also

$$f(\ f(x_1,x_2;q_{12}),f(x_3,x_4;q_{34});\ q_{12.34})$$
$$\equiv f(\ f(x_1,x_3;q_{13}),f(x_2,x_4;q_{24});\ q_{13.24}) \quad \text{(A.8)}$$
$$\equiv F^{-1}[\sum_1^4 p_jF(x_j)] \quad \text{(A.9)}$$

where

$$[p_1\ p_2\ p_3\ p_4] \qquad \text{(A.10)}$$
$$=[q_{12}q_{12.34},\ (1-q_{12})q_{12.34},\ q_{34}(1-q_{12.34}),\ (1-q_{34})(1-q_{12.34})]$$

$$q_{13}=q_{12}q_{12.34}/[q_{12}q_{12.34}+q_{34}(1-q_{12.34})] \qquad \text{(A.11)}$$
$$q_{24}=(1-q_{12})q_{12.34}/[(1-q_{12})q_{12.34}+(1-q_{34})(1-q_{12.34})]$$
$$q_{13.24}=q_{12}\ q_{12.34}+q_{34}(1-q_{12.34})$$

## A dynamic algorithm of chaotic type

All the above is by way of review. The present note shows how, if one has knowledge only of the even-odds function, $f(x_1,x_2)$ – which is $f(x_1,x_2;1/2)$ – and even without going to the labour of calculating out its associated F(x) function, one would be able to calculate to any desired degree of accuracy the $f(x_1,x_2;q)$ function for any specified q. The dynamic sequence whose limit gives the needed answer is an interesting species of the genus of *chaos* motions, with strange attractors, being precisely of the form of (16)'s breadbaker's transformation.

The algorithm suggested here was shown above (p. 52) to be closely related to writing q and $1-q$ as binary fractions and then approximating them by lower and upper bounds that involve binary fractions with a finite number of digits, namely successively 1, 2, 3, . . . numbers of such digits.

### *Examples*

To indicate the general idea, I first give a Santa Claus case where in two steps we arrive at an exact answer.

Consider $f(x_1,x_2;3/4)$. First calculate $f(x_1,x_2;1/2)$. Then calculate the required answer as

$$f(x_1,f(x_1,x_2;1/2);1/2)=f(x_1,x_2;3/4) \qquad \text{(A.12)}$$

Of course, two-step convergence almost never happens – even though we do also encounter the case

$$f(x_1,x_2;1/4)=f(\ f(x_1,x_2;1/2),\ x_2;1/2) \qquad \text{(A.13)}$$

In 3 steps we can calculate $f(x_1,x_2;2^{-3})$. The reader can calculate $f(x_1,x_2;2^{-n})$ in exactly n steps; and calculate $f(x_1,x_2;1-2^{-n})$ in n steps. Likewise, for $q=\sum_1^n a_j 2^{-j}$ and $n<\infty$.

Almost never will the algorithm give us the exact answer in a finite number of steps. But always it is closing in on the correct answer, and we can achieve whatever precision of accuracy we desire by taking enough steps.

*General procedure*

Here is how the successive rows of the algorithm are to be determined.

1. In the initial row, write to the left of the semicolon $(q,1-q)$ and call this $(q[0],1-q[0])$. To the right of the semicolon, write $(x_1,x_2)$ and call this $(x_1[0],x_2[0])$.
2. The $(t+1)$th row will be written as follows

$$\{q[t+1],\ 1-q[t+1];\ x_1[t+1],\ x_2[t+1]\}$$

   and it will be determined by the same nonlinear causal law(s) as appeared in (22) – but of course with $(x_1,x_2)$ taking the place of $(T^1,T^2)$ and $f(x_1,x_2)$ the place of $M[T^1,T^2]$.
3. Should a t be reached at which q[t] first equals 1/2, the algorithm will terminate at $t+1$, with equal correct answers to the right of the semicolon. When q[1] fails ever to equal 1/2, the algorithm goes on forever. At every stage $x_1[t]$ and $x_2[t]$ are in the same order as $x_1$ and $x_2$ were, and the following bounds hold

$$\mathrm{Min}(x_1[t],x_2[t]) \leqq f(x_1,x_2;q) \leqq \mathrm{Max}(x_1[t],x_2[t]) \qquad \text{(A.14)}$$

The special case of $f(x_1,x_2;1/3)$ is illuminating. It yields a periodic q[t], $q[t]\equiv q[t+2]$: 1/3, 2/3, 1/3, 2/3, . . . .

It will be found that

$$\lim_{2k\to\infty} x_1[2k]=\lim_{2k\to\infty} x_2[2k]=f(x_1,x_2;1/3) \qquad \text{(A.15)}$$

The case of $f(x_1,x_2;1/\pi)$ is even more interesting. Here q is an irrational number and the algorithm for q[t] neither converges to 1 in a finite number of steps nor does it cycle periodically. Still the Césaro limit holds:

$$\lim_{t\to\infty}\{q[1]+q[2]+\ldots+q[t]\}/t=1/2 \qquad \text{(A.16)}$$

$$\lim_{t\to\infty} x_1[t]=\lim_{t\to\infty} x_2[t]=f(x_1,x_2;1/\pi) \qquad \text{(A.17)}$$

For almost all values of the real fraction q, the motion will be chaotic and q[t] will eventually come indefinitely close to any real number on the interval (0,1). In the longest run, there will be an ergodic probability distribution that governs the appearance of q values – and, in this case, makes all points on the unit interval have the same (rectangular) probability density.

## Pure deduction

Provided $f(x_1,x_2;q)$ is continuous in its arguments, it suffices for $f(x_1,x_2;1/2)$ to satisfy (A.2)'s Abel functional relationship for $f(x_1,x_2;q)$ to satisfy the more general Abel relation of (A.6). To see this, freeze $(x_1,x_2)$ in f so that it can be thought of as a continuous function of q alone; $\bar{f}(q)$. At all q points that have a finite number of digits in the binary representation $\sum_1^\infty a_j 2^{-j}$, (A.6) is certainly implied. However, a continuous function must have its behaviour at *all* real arguments determined by its behaviour at the subset of arguments of the form $(\sum_1^n d_j 2^{-j}\colon n<\infty)$. Therefore, for all real q, the basic axiom of (A.6) will have to hold.

## Notes

1. I owe thanks for my Gordon Y. Billard Postdoctoral Fellowship to the Sloan School of Management and to the MIT Center for Real Estate Development for partial support. Aase Huggins and Ruth Pelizzon provided appreciated editorial assistance.

## References

ACZÉL, J. (1966) *Lectures on Functional Equations and Applications* (New York and London: Academic Press).

COLLET, P. and J.-P. ECKMANN (1980) *Iterated Maps on the Interval as Dynamical Systems* (Boston: Birkhauser).

DAY, R. H. (1983) 'The Emergence of Chaos from Classical Economic Growth', *Quarterly Journal of Economics*, vol. 98, no. 2, pp. 201–13.

DEBREU, G. (1959) 'Cardinal Utility for Even-Chance Mixtures of Pairs of Sure Prospects', *Review of Economic Studies*, vol. XXVI, no. 71, pp. 174–8.

FEIGENBAUM, M. (1978) 'Quantitative Universality for a Class of Nonlinear Transformations', *Journal of Statistical Physics*, vol. 19, no. 1, pp. 25–52.

GRANDMONT, J. M. (1983) 'Periodic and Aperiodic Behaviour in Discrete One-dimensional Dynamical Systems', in W. Hildenbrand and A. Mas-Colell (eds), *Contributions to Mathematical Economics in Honour of Gerard Debreu* (Amsterdam: North-Holland).

LORENZ, E. N. (1963) 'Deterministic Nonperiodic Flow', *Journal of Atmospheric Science*, vol. 20, no. 2, pp. 130–41.

LOPEZ, A. (1961) *Problems in Stable Population Theory* (Princeton: Office of Population Research, Princeton University Press).

MAY, R. M. (1976) 'Simple Mathematical Models with Very Complicated Dynamics', *Nature*, vol. 261, pp. 459–66.

POINCARÉ, *Les Méthodes Nouvelles de la Mecanique Celeste*, I, II, III, 1892, 1893, 1899; reprint New York: Dover, 1957.

POTTS, R. B. (1982) 'Nonlinear Difference Equations', *Journal of Nonlinear Analysis* vol. 6, pp. 659–65.

PRIGOGINE, I. (1980) *From Being to Becoming* (San Francisco: W. H. Freeman).

RAMSEY, F. P. (1931) *The Foundations of Mathematics and other Logical Essays*, ed. R. B. Braithwaite (London: Kegan and Paul).

RÖSSLER, O. E. (1981) 'Chaos and Chemistry', in C. Vidal and A. Pacault (eds), *Nonlinear Phenomena in Chemical Dynamics* (Heidelberg: Springer-Verlag).

THOM, R. (1975) *Structural Stability and Morphogenesis* (Reading, Mass.: W. A. Benjamin, Inc.).

# 6 A Model of Cyclical Growth

Richard Stone

This paper was originally written for a festschrift planned to coincide with Richard Goodwin's retirement from Cambridge in 1980. This plan miscarried and so, with the agreement of Professor Velupillai, the paper was published, slightly amended, in 1984 in vol. 1, no. 1 of *Economic Modelling*, whose editor has kindly agreed to its republication in the present book.

## 6.1 INTRODUCTION

Of Richard Goodwin's many ingenious and insightful contributions to economics, a particular favourite of mine is his note 'A Growth Cycle' which was presented at the First World Congress of the Econometric Society in 1965, and later appeared in the Festschrift for Maurice Dobb (Goodwin, 1967). In it Goodwin takes a number of familiar building blocks, such as a steady growth of the labour force, a constant capital–output ratio and so on, but puts them together in a new way so that he ends up with the nonlinear predator–prey equations of Volterra. For wolves and sheep, however, Goodwin substitutes the share of wages in the national income and the rate of employment. The point representing these two variables moves round a closed phase-trajectory corresponding to an endless series of waves in their separate time-paths. Interesting extensions of Goodwin's model are made in Desai (1973).

Models of cyclical growth are discussed in Bergstrom (1967), where reference is made to Goodwin's earlier work on trade cycles. In what follows I shall undertake some more explorations of cyclical growth but I shall use a different model from either Goodwin's or Bergstrom's and adopt a different form of presentation.

My model in its simplest form was described in Stone (1980). Here I shall develop it by: (i) distinguishing the incomes received by the two factors of production, capital and labour, and the propensity to save out of these incomes; (ii) separating the demand for labour from the supply, so that unemployment makes its appearance; (iii) showing the rate of change in the demand for labour as dependent on a comparison between the value of the marginal product of labour and the wage rate; (iv) connecting the rate of change of the wage rate with the unemployment rate; (v) allowing for money illusion in wage formation; and (vi) introducing the growth of knowledge resulting in exogenous technical progress.

The model is nonlinear and expressed in continuous time. The rate of population growth is not constant but time-dependent. From given initial conditions, the equations are solved computationally for 150 time periods. These periods are not explicitly defined but since, in the standard run, the upper bound of the capital–output ratio is 2, they can hardly be longer than a few years and I shall refer to them as 'years'. Thus the calculations might be considered to relate to a few centuries but not to a few millennia. The results are set out in a series of simulation diagrams.[1] Readers who do not like my economic assumptions will find in the diagrams that follow illustrations of a method that could be equally well applied to different assumptions more to their liking.

## 6.2 THE FORM OF THE MODEL

Variables taken from the national accounts, such as capital or income, appear in the model divided by the population, n say. Thus, if total income is denoted by Y, the income variable in the model is $y \equiv Y/n$. Since there is only one product, with price p, money income will appear as py, but initially I shall ignore price variations and assume that $p = 1$. I shall only abandon this simplification when I wish to discuss the possibility that price responds to cost and that wage formation is subject to money illusion.

Each of the following subsections contributes to the model one equation, which carries the same number as the subsection; subsidiary equations are distinguished by a letter following the number. In all the equations, variables are denoted by roman and parameters by greek letters. Subsidiary equations are distinguished by a letter following the number.

### 6.2.1 Population growth

It is convenient to be able to consider a stationary population, a population growing exponentially and a population growing sigmoidally. If we denote the size of the population by n and choose the Gompertz form of sigmoidal growth, then we can write

$$\dot{n}/n = \nu_1 e^{-\nu_1 t} + \nu_2 \tag{1}$$

In (1) the population is stationary if $\nu_1 = \nu_2 = 0$; grows exponentially at rate $\nu_2$ if $\nu_1 = 0$; and, if $\nu_2 = 0$, grows along the Gompertz path

$$n = n^* \exp(-e^{-\nu_1 t}) \tag{1a}$$

where as $t \to -\infty$, $n \to 0$; and as $t \to \infty$, $n \to n^*$, its upper bound, passing through a point of inflection, $n^*/e$, at $t = 0$. In the standard run I shall assume that the population grows along a Gompertz path with $\nu_1 = 0.05$ and $\nu_2 = 0$ in (1). With $n^* = 1$, the course of the population over the 150 'years' appears as in Diagram 6.A.

The use of a Gompertz function for population growth carries the absurd implication that as $t \to -\infty$, $\dot{n}/n \to \infty$, but in the present context this is not a disadvantage. It does something to counteract the fact that my simple saving function, in (7) below, implies that the proportion of income saved tends to be high when the wealth–income (capital–output) ratio is low. Had I used a logistic rather than a Gompertz function for population growth, the main difference would have been that more of the variation of the economic series would have been concentrated in the early stages, with the result that the curves would soon have become relatively flat.

### 6.2.2 The production account

Since the model relates to a closed economy, the economic flows can be set out in the usual three national accounts. If we write y for income (or value added or net unduplicated output), c for consumption and v for net investment, each expressed per head of the population, then from the production account we obtain the identity

$$y \equiv c + v \tag{2}$$

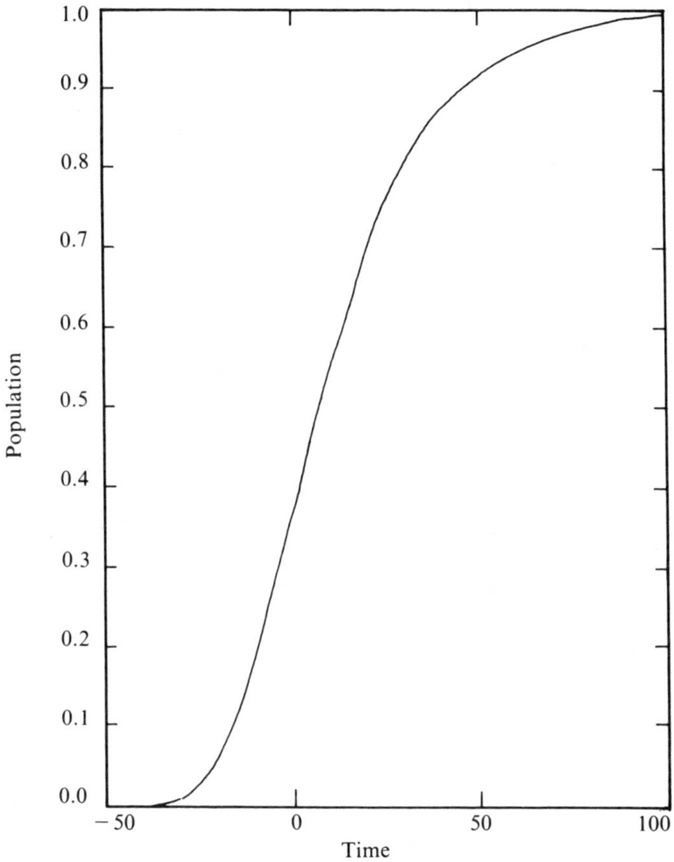


DIAGRAM 6.A *The course of the population over the simulation period*

### 6.2.3 The income and outlay account

This account shows how income is allocated to consumption and saving. If we write s for saving per head of the population, then from this account we obtain the identity

$$y \equiv c + s \tag{3}$$

### 6.2.4 The capital account and the balance sheet

The capital account provides the identity $v \equiv s$; but this adds nothing new since it is already implied by (2) and (3). There is, however, a relationship between the entries in the capital account and the entries in the balance sheet, namely the identity

$$\dot{K} \equiv V \tag{4a}$$

or

$$\dot{k} \equiv v - k\dot{n}/n \tag{4}$$

where $\dot{k}$ denotes the rate of change over time of the net capital stock of tangible assets per head of the population.

From the balance sheet we could obtain another identity, namely that the community's wealth (or net worth) was equal to its net capital stock of tangible assets, since in a closed economy issues and holdings of financial claims cancel out. However, there seems no point in introducing a separate symbol for wealth per head which, accordingly, I shall denote by k.

### 6.2.5 Production

Output y depends on the inputs of capital and labour, k and m say, and on the incorporation of new knowledge into the productive process. New knowledge arises the whole time and with various delays comes to be applied. I assume that output is related to inputs by a Cobb-Douglas function with labour-augmenting technical progress, that is

$$y = \alpha\, k^{\theta}\, m^{1-\theta}\, e^{\omega(1-\theta)t} \tag{5}$$

In the standard run the parameter $\theta$ is set at 0.25, $\omega$ is set at 0 and $\alpha$ is set at 0.5, so that in equilibrium $k/m = 1$.

### 6.2.6 Income shares

If we denote the real wage rate by r, then the income of labour is rm.

The remaining income, $y_1$ say, which goes to the owners of capital, is given by

$$y_1 \equiv y - rm \tag{6}$$

### 6.2.7 The supply of capital

New capital is supplied by saving and I assume: first, that saving depends positively on income and negatively on wealth; and, second, that the propensity to save out of wages may be different from the propensity to save out of profits. Thus

$$s = \sigma_1 y_1 + \sigma_2 rm - \gamma k \tag{7}$$

I shall sometimes make the assumption, in conformity with a common convention, that $\sigma_2 = 0$ so that all the savings are made and all the capital is owned by the recipients of profits; but I shall also examine the case where saving is made out of wages. In the standard run I shall assume that $\sigma_1 = 0.8$, $\sigma_2 = 0$ and $\gamma = 0.1$.

### 6.2.8 The supply of labour

I assume that the supply of labour per head of the population, $l$ say, would be a constant, $\pi$ say, but for the fact that as wealth per head of the population increases, the supply of labour per head may fall along an exponential decay curve. Thus

$$l = \pi\, k^{-\mu} \tag{8}$$

where $\mu$ denotes the coefficient of exponential decay. If $\mu = 0$, then the supply of labour per head is unaffected by wealth per head. In the standard run I shall assume that $\mu = 0.05$, indicating a tendency to work less hard with increasing wealth, and in all runs I shall assume that $\pi$ is such that $l = 1$ initially.

### 6.2.9 The demand for labour

I assume that there will be an increase in the demand for labour, m, if the marginal product of labour, $(1-\theta)y/m$, is greater than the wage, r, and that there will be a decrease in the demand if the inequality is reversed. If we normalise the difference by dividing through by the wage then we can express the proportionate rate of change of m as

$$\frac{\dot{m}}{m}=\beta\left[\frac{1-\theta y}{rm}-1\right]-\frac{\dot{n}}{n} \tag{9}$$

where the larger the parameter β the more quickly does the adjustment take place. It is not obvious *a priori* what value is appropriate for β but, as we shall see, the stability of the system depends on β being sufficiently large.

### 6.2.10 The unemployment ratio

This ratio, u say, is given by

$$u\equiv(l-m)/l \tag{10}$$

### 6.2.11 Wage formation

I assume that the proportionate rate of change of the real wage rate, $\dot{r}/r$, is connected to u by a relationship of the form

$$\dot{r}/r=\kappa u^{-\rho}-\lambda \tag{11a}$$

which implies an equilibrium unemployment ratio, $\bar{u}$ say. By putting $\dot{r}/r=0$ we see that

$$\bar{u}=(\lambda/\kappa)^{-1/\rho} \tag{11b}$$

and by combining (11a) and (11b) we can write (11a) in the form

$$\dot{r}/r=\lambda[(u/\bar{u})^{-\rho}-1] \tag{11}$$

In the standard run I have put $\kappa=0.01585$, $\lambda=0.9$ and $\rho=1.4$, implying that $\bar{u}=5.584$ per cent.

### 6.2.12 Money illusion

In the preceding section I assumed that wage formation could be described in terms of the real wage. It may be better to work in terms of money wages and make provision for money illusion. If we denote the money wage rate by w so that $w \equiv rp$, then we could replace (11) by

$$\dot{w}/w = \lambda[(u/\bar{u})^{-\rho} - 1] + \psi\dot{p}/p \tag{12}$$

If we put $\psi = 1$, (12) reduces to (11), but if $\psi < 1$ we shall give expression to some degree of money illusion.

### 6.2.13 Price formation

If we are to use (12) with $\psi \neq 1$, we must have some means of forming $\dot{p}/p$. I shall assume that the price desired by producers, $p^*$ say, can be represented as a mark-up on money unit costs, that is

$$p^* = \zeta(wm/y) \tag{13a}$$

and that

$$\dot{p}/p = \xi[\zeta(wm/py) - 1] \tag{13}$$

I assume that $\xi = 1$, implying that producers revise their prices once a 'year', and that $\zeta = 1.4$, thus giving an equilibrium rate of inflation of 5 per cent a 'year'.

## 6.3 AN ALTERNATIVE REPRESENTATION

Let us begin with a simplified version of the model, restricting ourselves to equations (1) through (11) above and putting $v_2 = 0$ in (1) and $\omega = 0$ in (5). These equations can be reduced to a state-space model in the three variables k, m and r. Thus

$$\dot{k} = \left[(\sigma_2 - \sigma_1)\left(\frac{rm}{k}\right) + \alpha\sigma_1\left(\frac{m}{k}\right)^{1-\theta} - (\gamma + v_1 e^{-v_1 t})\right]k \tag{14}$$

$$\dot{m} = \left\{\beta\left[\frac{\alpha(1-\theta)}{r}\left(\frac{k}{m}\right)^{\theta} - 1\right] - v_1 e^{-v_1 t}\right\} m \tag{15}$$

$$\dot{r} = \lambda\left[\left(\frac{1 - \pi^{-1} m k^{\mu}}{\bar{u}}\right)^{-\rho} - 1\right] r \tag{16}$$

From these equations we can form the system Jacobian, that is the matrix of the partial derivatives of $\dot{k}$, $\dot{m}$ and $\dot{r}$ with respect to k, m and r. If we denote this matrix by J, then

$$J = \begin{bmatrix} \alpha\theta\sigma_1\left(\frac{m}{k}\right)^{1-\theta} - \gamma - \nu_1 e^{-\nu_1 t} & (\sigma_2-\sigma_1)r + \sigma_1\alpha(1-\theta)\left(\frac{k}{m}\right)^{\theta} & (\sigma_2-\sigma_1)m \\ \frac{\alpha\beta\theta(1-\theta)}{r}\left(\frac{m}{k}\right)^{1-\theta} & \frac{\alpha\beta(1-\theta)^2}{r}\left(\frac{k}{m}\right)^{\theta} - \beta - \nu_1 e^{-\nu_1 t} & -\frac{\alpha\beta(1-\theta)m}{r^2}\left(\frac{k}{m}\right)^{\theta} \\ \frac{\lambda\mu\rho r m k^{\mu-1}}{\pi\bar{u}}\left(\frac{1-\pi^{-1}mk^{\mu}}{\bar{u}}\right)^{-(1+\rho)} & \frac{\lambda\rho r k^{\mu}}{\pi\bar{u}}\left(\frac{1-\pi^{-1}mk^{\mu}}{\bar{u}}\right)^{-(1+\rho)} & \lambda\left[\left(\frac{1-\pi^{-1}mk^{\mu}}{\bar{u}}\right) - 1\right] \end{bmatrix} \qquad (17)$$

In equilibrium, J reduces to a simpler form, J* say, given by

$$J^* = \begin{bmatrix} -\frac{(1-\theta)\gamma\sigma_2}{\sigma} & \sigma_2 r & (\sigma_2-\sigma_1)m \\ \beta\theta\left(\frac{\gamma}{\alpha\sigma}\right)^{1/(1-\theta)} & -\beta\theta & -\frac{\beta m}{r} \\ \frac{\lambda\mu\rho r}{l\bar{u}}\left(\frac{\gamma}{\alpha\sigma}\right)^{1/(1-\theta)} & \frac{\lambda\rho r}{l\bar{u}} & 0 \end{bmatrix} \qquad (18)$$

where $\sigma \equiv \theta\sigma_1 + (1-\theta)\sigma_2$.

## 6.4 STABILITY

The system I have been describing will be locally stable if the real parts of the roots of J are negative. Let us now examine this question by setting all but one of the parameters of the system at plausible values and see what happens when we vary the remaining one. Specifically, let us adopt for our standard runs the parameter values listed in Table 6.1, leaving β to be varied at will. I have omitted π from the list since it is a scale parameter which varies from one analysis to another.

In the present case, J has one real root and a conjugate pair of complex roots. We can picture the position of these on a root-locus diagram which is simply Argand's diagram, in which the real axis is along the abscissa and the imaginary axis is along the ordinate. In the present case the relevant part is shown in Diagram 6.B.

TABLE 6.1 *The standard values*

| | |
|---|---|
| $\alpha = 0.5$ | $\nu_1 = 0.05$ |
| $\gamma = 0.1$ | $\nu_2 = 0$ |
| $\theta = 0.25$ | $\rho = 1.4$ |
| $\kappa = 0.01585$ | $\sigma_1 = 0.8$ |
| $\lambda = 0.9$ | $\sigma_2 = 0$ |
| $\mu = 0.05$ | $\omega = 0$ |

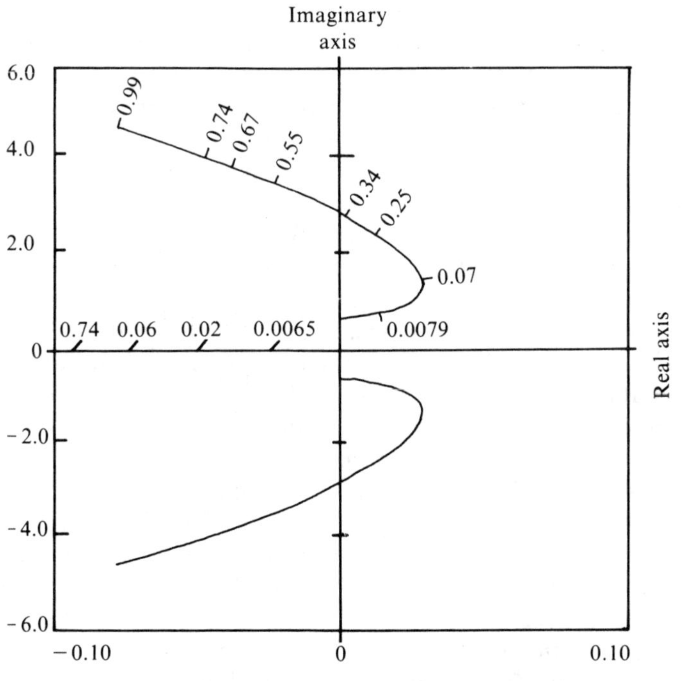


DIAGRAM 6.B *The position of latent roots of J for O⩽β⩽1*

For $\beta > 0$, the real root is always negative and in Diagram 6.B its position on the real axis is shown for $\beta = 0.0065$, 0.02, 0.06 and 0.74. The two curves show the position of the complex roots for different values of $\beta$ (marked in the diagram along the upper curve). Starting from the imaginary axis with $\beta = 0$, the curves move first to positive values on the real axis, but at about $\beta = 0.07$ they turn round, and at about $\beta = 0.35$ they cross the imaginary axis to negative values on the real axis. For all higher values of $\beta$ they remain in the negative real zone. In fact the size of $\beta$ determines the speed of response of the demand for labour (employment) to a discrepancy between the marginal product of labour and the wage rate. Its reciprocal, $1/\beta$, is the time-constant of the lag in adjustment. As $\beta \to \infty$, $1/\beta \to 0$ and there is no lag; and as $\beta \to 0$, $1/\beta \to \infty$ and no adjustment takes place.

Thus, given the values of all the parameters other than $\beta$, the system cannot be characterised as either stable or unstable. For $0 < \beta < 0.35$ approximately it is unstable, but for all higher values it is stable.

This feature is illustrated in the first three diagrams of the appendix, which show the time paths of a number of variables for $\beta = 50$, 0.5 and 0.25. The calculations for all the diagrams are based on the following initial conditions, which hold at time $t = -50$: (i) the population is very small, $n = 5.12 \times 10^{-6}$, compared with its upper bound of 1; (ii) capital per worker is low, $k/m = 1$ per cent of its equilibrium value; (iii) the wage is equated to the marginal product of labour; and (iv) unemployment is at the equilibrium level.

It is convenient to start with a high value of $\beta$, since then adjustment is quick and the paths of the variables are smooth and easy to follow. The standard run with $\beta = 50$ is shown in Diagram 6.1. With this high value of $\beta$, the wage and the marginal product of labour are kept together, as can be seen from Panel 4. Labour is always paid its marginal product and so receives $(1 - \theta) = 0.75$ of total income. The remainder, 0.25, goes to capital and appears as the horizontal line, $y_1/y$, in Panel 1. As capital is built up, as shown in the curve for k in Panel 3, the return on capital $y_1/k$ falls rapidly to begin with but later slows down and approaches its equilibrium value of 0.125, as shown in Panel 1. The reciprocal of the capital–output ratio, $y/k$ in Panel 1, moves similarly and eventually approaches its equilibrium value of 0.5. The supply of labour per head of the population, l in Panel 2, falls from its initial value of 1 towards its equilibrium value; and the demand for labour per head, m in Panel 2, moves similarly, since the unemployment ratio, u in Panel 1, remains at its equilibrium value. The capital–labour ratio, $k/m$ in Panel 1, moves upwards towards its equilibrium value of 1. The paths of capital, income, wages, profits, consumption and saving per head are shown in Panel 3. In equilibrium, consumption is equal to income and saving falls to zero.

Let us now see what happens if $\beta=0.5$, a value still in the stable zone but not high enough to keep the wage and the marginal product of labour continuously adjusted to one another. The result is shown in Diagram 6.2. We now get damped cyclical growth. In the early stages the wage rate, though highly fluctuating, tends to be below the marginal product of labour. As a consequence the share of profits in the national income is initially far above its equilibrium value and the proportion of income saved is very high. The capital stock grows much faster to begin with than it did in Diagram 6.1 but in the end all the variables tend to the same stationary values.

Not surprisingly, the amplitude of the oscillations in the different series varies greatly even when allowance is made for the different scales used in the different panels of the diagram; for instance, the marginal product of labour moves along a fairly steady path whereas the wage rate fluctuates widely. The realist may object that the cycles seem very short. This is due, no doubt, to the simplicity of the model and to the fact that it contains no time delays. A mixture of difference and differential equations would seem more appropriate in modelling an economic system; but it would be more complicated and in this paper I have tried to keep things simple.

Though fluctuating, the economy represented in Diagram 6.2 is stable; in the end the variables approach their equilibrium values and the oscillations die away. Let us now reduce $\beta$ further until it passes into the unstable zone. Diagram 6.3 shows the catastrophic results of putting $\beta=0.25$. The wage rate fluctuates widely, remaining for a time below the marginal product of labour, profits and saving are high and the capital stock grows. After a time the wage rate, fluctuating ever more widely, climbs above the marginal product of labour and the capital stock begins to fall with increasing fluctuations. In response to this, the supply of labour begins to rise but there is no answering call from the demand and the unemployment ratio tends to increase.

Matters would be much worse if $\beta$ were smaller still. I have a diagram for $\beta=0.16$ but I have not included it in the appendix since the fluctuating paths of the different series run into one another to such an extent that many of them cannot be separated out. The capital stock climbs to quite a high level but by $t=0$ it has begun to fall and by $t=25$ the economy may be said to have broken down, with the unemployment ratio at 15 to 20 per cent and rising.

If we use the term exploitation to describe the situation in which a factor of production is paid less than its marginal product, then we can state the conclusions of this section as follows. If $\beta$ is sufficiently high there will be no exploitation and the variables will follow smooth paths to their equilibrium values. As we reduce $\beta$, keeping it still within the stable zone, damped oscillations will appear, labour will be exploited in the early stages, each factor will tend to be exploited alternately in the later stages and only as equilibrium is approached will all exploitation tend to disappear. Finally, as we reduce $\beta$ still further so that it gets into the unstable zone, labour will again be exploited in the early stage but after a time this state of affairs will be reversed and it will be capital that tends to be exploited. Since, by assumption, the economy depends on capitalists for saving and therefore for the possibility of accumulating further capital, this reversal of exploitation brings to an end the growth of the capital stock and sets it on a downward path.

Thus my first example might be likened to a highly simplified version of the workings of an ideal economic system. My second example is reminiscent of what Keynes says in *The Economic Consequences of the Peace* about the psychology of society in nineteenth-century capitalist England. My third example has something in common with the distracted state of the British economy in the late 1970s.

The exploitation of labour may be bad; but, if an economy depends on capitalists for its saving, the exploitation of capital may be much worse. However, the economy may not be dependent in this way; and if we make other assumptions about the parameters we may expect to obtain different results. Let us now look at the sensitivity of the model to various changes of this kind, beginning with the propensities to save in equation (7).

## 6.5 SENSITIVITY

### 6.5.1 Saving propensities

If we assume that capitalists not only do all the saving but also save the whole of profits and not only 80 per cent of them, the system becomes more unstable though I shall not present a diagram to show this. On the other hand if, with $\beta = 0.5$, we put $\sigma_1 = 0.5$ (instead of 0.8) and $\sigma_2 = 0.1$ (instead of 0) the system becomes more stable as shown in Diagram 6.4.

### 6.5.2 Equilibrium income shares

In the model the marginal productivity of capital is equal to θ divided by the capital–output ratio. If, with $\beta = 0.5$ and the other parameters as in the standard run, we increase θ, we shall find that the system is greatly stabilised. The outcome if $\theta = 0.6$ is shown in Diagram 6.5. The change has other consequences: the equilibrium capital–output ratio is now 4.8 instead of 2 and equilibrium labour income is more than twice as high as in the standard run despite the fact that the share of profits in the national income always exceeds the share of labour.

### 6.5.3 Wealth and the supply of labour

Another factor making for stability is the tendency to offer less labour as wealth increases. If we put $\mu = 0.2$ instead of 0.05 in the standard run with $\beta = 0.5$, we obtain Diagram 6.6. In this version, k/m follows the same path as in Diagram 6.2 despite the much greater fall in the labour supply. But for this very reason the equilibrium values of k and y are much lower than in Diagram 6.2, tending to 0.44 and 0.22 respectively in place of 0.75 and 0.375. The equilibrium unemployment ratio is unaffected. The lack of effective demand, if that is what it is, does not throw the economy out of gear; it simply enables people to get what they want, namely more leisure, at the cost of a lower material standard of living.

### 6.5.4 Money illusion

The presence of money illusion, represented here by substituting (12) for (11) with $\psi < 1$ and using (13) with $\zeta = 1.4$ and $\xi = 1.0$, exercises a strong stabilising influence. This involves a change in the system Jacobian compared with the version given in section 6.5.3 above, but I do not propose to elaborate on this. The result with $\psi = 0.5$ is shown in Diagram 6.7. The equilibrium values are the same as in the standard run.

### 6.5.5 Technical progress

The final development that I shall discuss is the introduction of technical progress. This I shall treat as labour-augmenting, as can always be done with a Cobb-Douglas function, and redefine the capital–labour ratio as k/m* where $m^* \equiv me^{\omega t}$ from which it follows that $\dot{m}^*/m^* = (\dot{m}/m) + \omega$. Without going further into details, the result with $\omega = 0.01$ in (5) is shown for $\mu = 0$ in Diagram 6.8 and for $\mu = 0.05$ in Diagram 6.9. The picture is now radically altered. The ratios in the first panel of the tables tend to stationary values as before, the capital–labour ratio being calculated in terms of labour augmented by technical progress rather than in terms of employment. But this is no longer true of the variables themselves, shown in the third and fourth panels, all of which, including saving which no longer tends to zero, eventually reach a state of steady growth. The position in the second panel depends on μ: if $\mu = 0$, then $l = \pi$ and $m \rightarrow (1 - \bar{\bar{u}})\pi$, where $\bar{\bar{u}}$, the equilibrium unemployment ratio with the kind of technical progress I am assuming, cannot exceed $\bar{u}$; but if $\mu = 0.05$, then l and m continue to fall since k continues to rise. If we want an economy with technical progress to be fully stable, we must assume that the contribution of new knowledge to production grows sigmoidally rather than exponentially. This corresponds to the idea of technological stages, leaving open the question of whether there will ever be further stages more efficient than the one we are now in.

## 6.6 CONCLUSIONS

Many years ago Roy Allen warned economists against the difficulties of obtaining general solutions to problems and urged the advantages of computing many particular solutions. In Allen (1956, p. 304) he wrote:

> As economic models become more complex, and have greater empirical content, to make them applicable to the real world, the answers to general questions become less possible. The economist may need, therefore, to shift his ground from the general to the particular, and to follow the methods and the experience of the engineer.

I think this is correct and the purpose of my paper is to illustrate the advantages of building quantitative models which can only be handled computationally and to show how much can be learnt about them by modern simulation methods. The model I have chosen as an illustration is theoretical and simplified but similar methods can equally well be applied to realistic models once the basic econometric work has been done. The methods are not new though they are still developing. They could be useful to economists at all stages of their work, that is to say in devising, constructing, testing and controlling their models.

**References**

ALLEN, R. G. D. (1956) *Mathematical Economics* (London: Macmillan).
BERGSTROM, A. R. (1967) *The Construction and Use of Economic Models* (London: The English Universities Press).
DESAI, MEGHNAD (1973) 'Growth cycles and inflation in a model of the class struggle', *Journal of Economic Theory*, vol. 6, no. 6, pp. 527–45.
FEINSTEIN, C. H. (ed.) (1967) *Socialism, Capitalism and Economic Growth* (Cambridge: Cambridge University Press).
GOODWIN, R. M. (1967) 'A Growth Cycle', in Feinstein (1967) pp. 54–8.
STONE, RICHARD (1980) 'A simple growth process tending to stationarity', *Economic Journal*, vol. 90, no. 359, pp. 293–7.

## APPENDIX: THE MAIN DIAGRAMS

The results of this paper are set out in the following nine diagrams. The variables illustrated are in each case grouped together in one of four panels. The contents of a panel are the same in each diagram but their scales may vary from one diagram to another. The same diagrams are reproduced in larger format in *Economic Modelling*, vol. 1, no. 1 (1984).

**Panel 1**

This panel shows the course of the following ratios:

the capital–employment ratio, $k/m$ (or $k/m^*$ in Diagrams 6.8 and 6.9)
the income (output)–capital ratio, $y/k$
the ratio of profits to total income, $y_1/y$
the return on capital, $y_1/k$
the unemployment ratio, $u$

**Panel 2**

This panel shows the course of two variables each expressed per head of the population:

the supply of labour, l
the demand for labour (employment), m

**Panel 3**

This panel shows the course of the following variables from the national accounts and balance sheet, all expressed per head of the population:

capital (the net stock of tangible assets), k
total income (output), y
consumption, c
income from wages, rm
income from profits, $y_1$
saving, $s \equiv v \equiv \dot{k} + k(\dot{n}/n)$

**Panel 4**

This panel shows the course of two variables:

the marginal product of labour, $(1-\theta)y/m$
the real wage rate, r

### Note

The simulation diagrams were prepared for me by my friend and colleague Rick van der Ploeg. I wish to thank him here not only for putting his knowledge of these matters at my disposal and for carrying out the simulations but also for many interesting discussions on the possibilities of applying simulation methods in economics.

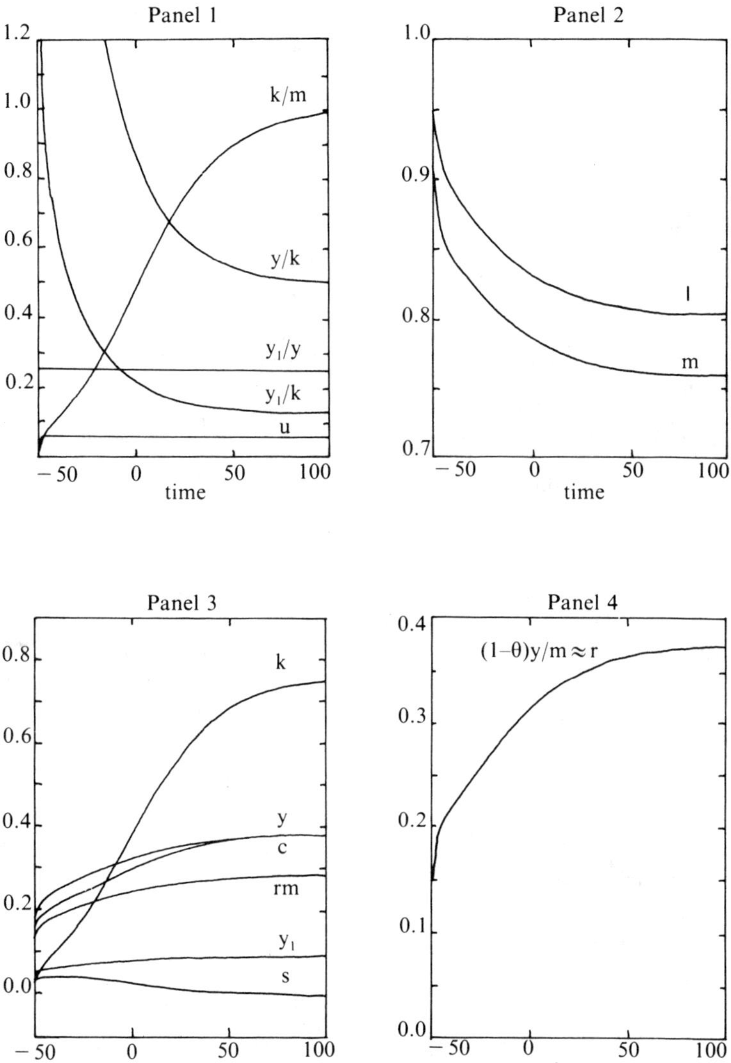


DIAGRAM 6.1 *A highly stable version of the standard run*
*$\beta = 50$; other parameters = standard values*

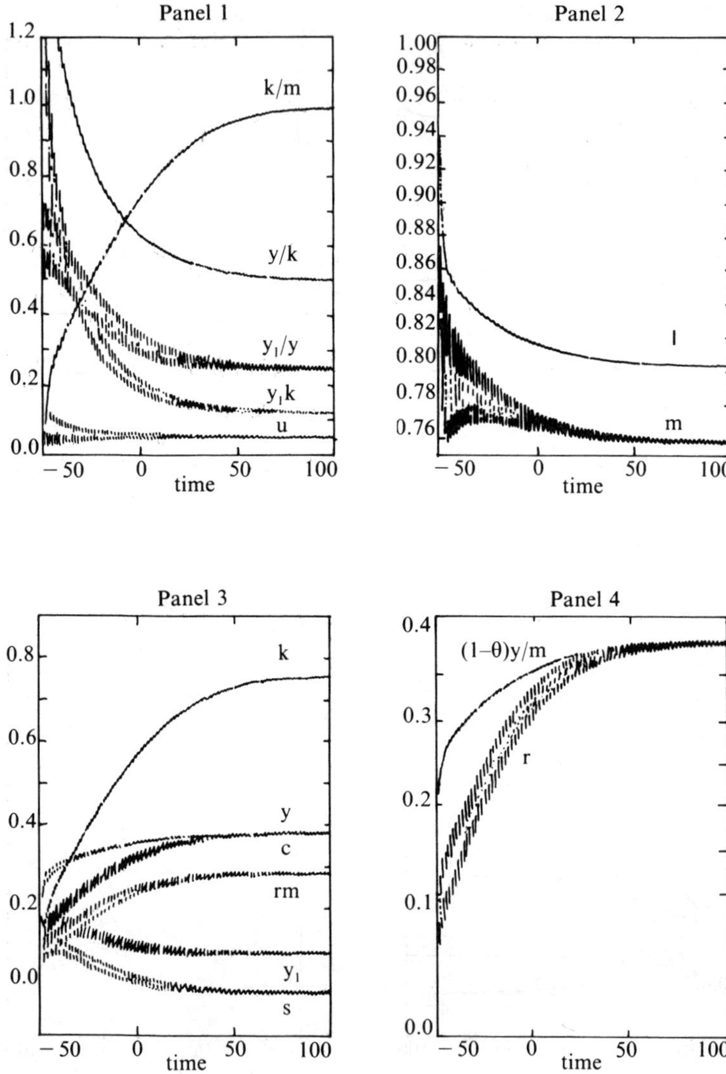


DIAGRAM 6.2 *A stable version of the standard run with damped oscillations* $\beta = 0.5$*; other parameters = standard values*

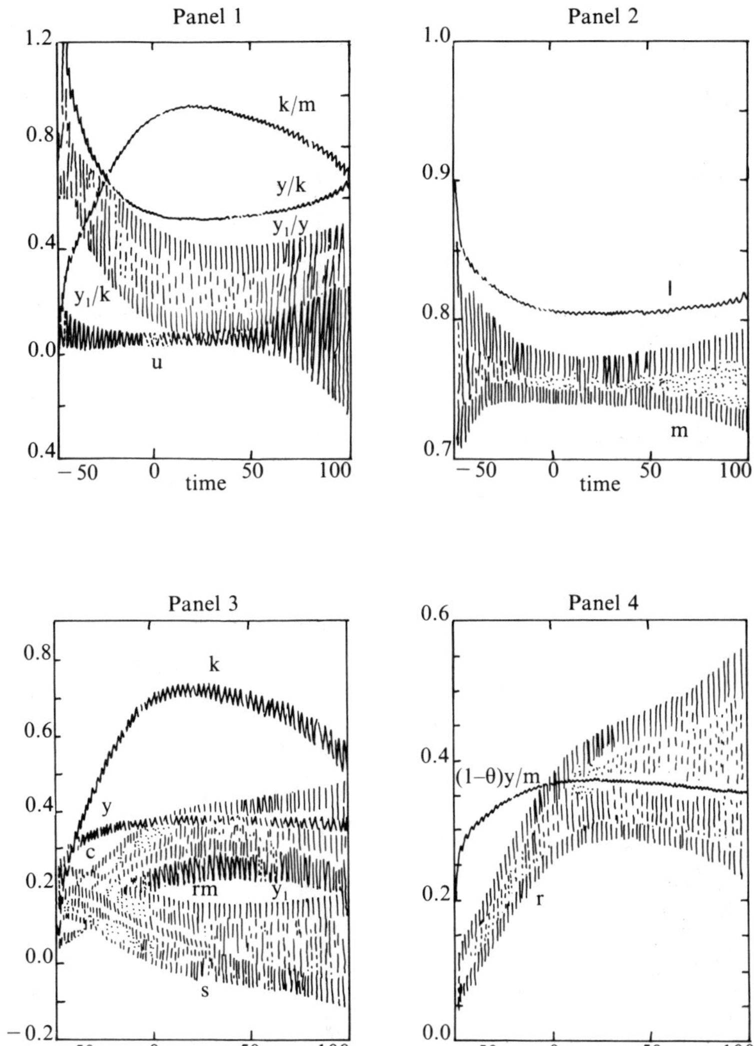


DIAGRAM 6.3 *An unstable version of the standard run*
$\beta = 0.25$; *other parameters = standard values*

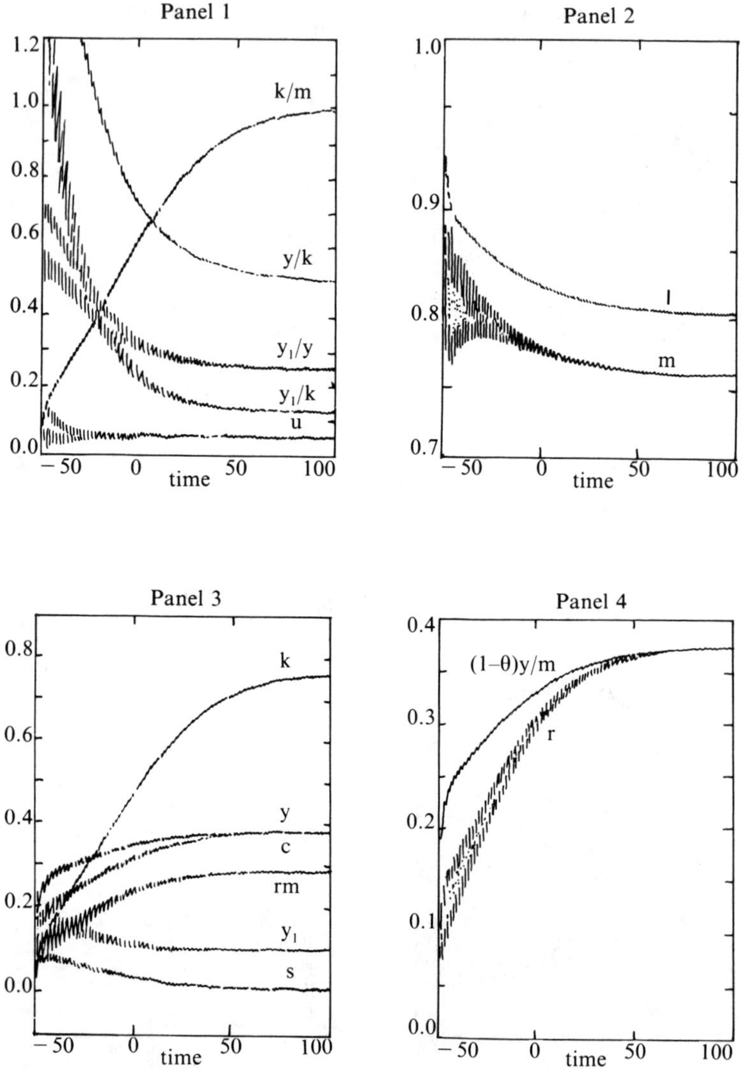


DIAGRAM 6.4 *Some saving out of wages, reduced saving out of profits* $\beta = 0.5$, $\sigma_1 = 0.5$, $\sigma_2 = 0.1$; *other parameters = standard values*

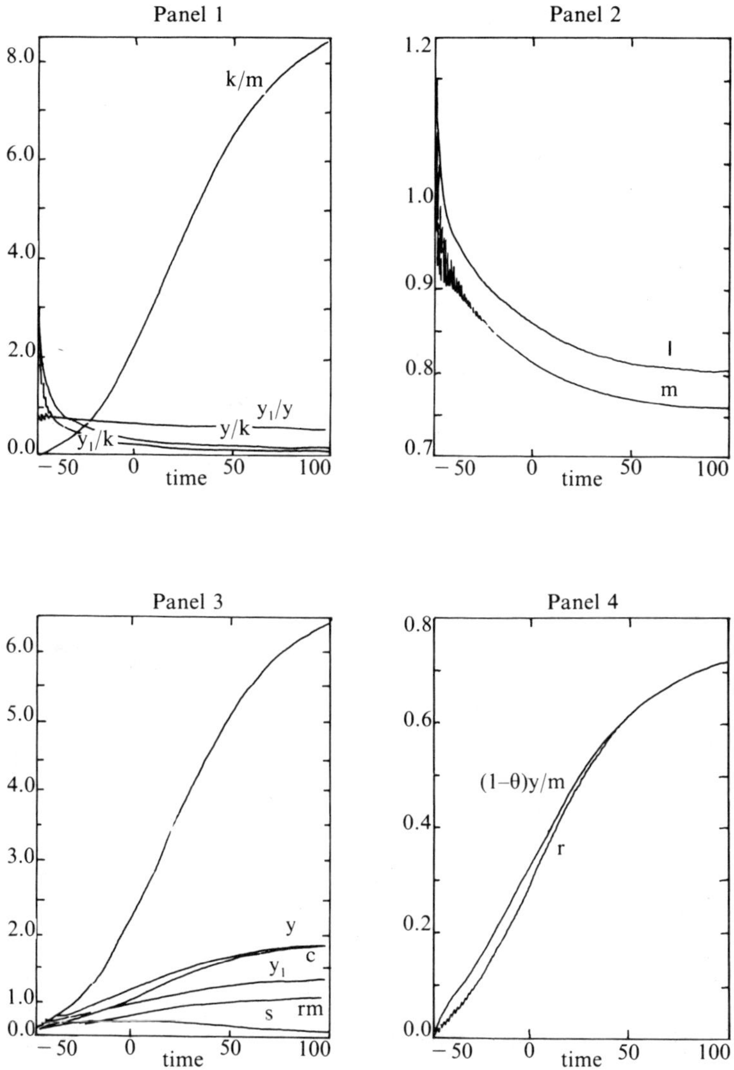


DIAGRAM 6.5 *A larger role for capital, a smaller role for labour*
*$\beta=0.5$, $\theta=0.6$; other parameters = standard values*

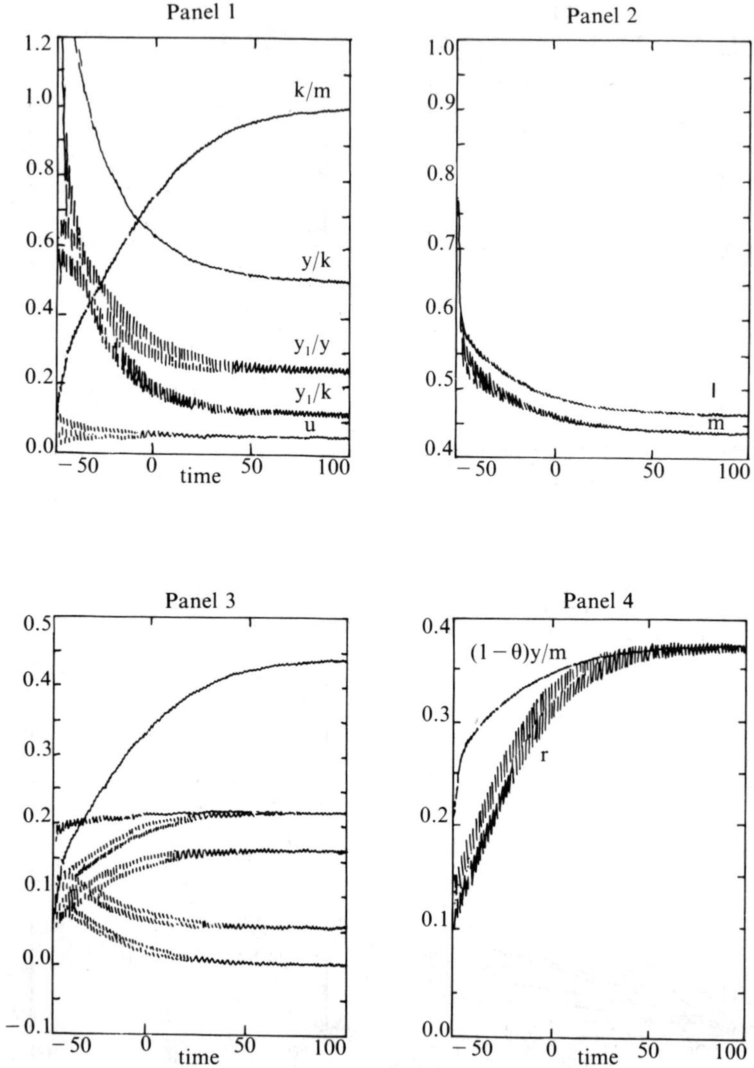


**Diagram 6.6** *The labour supply greatly reduced by increasing wealth $\beta=0.5$, $\mu=0.2$; other parameters = standard values*

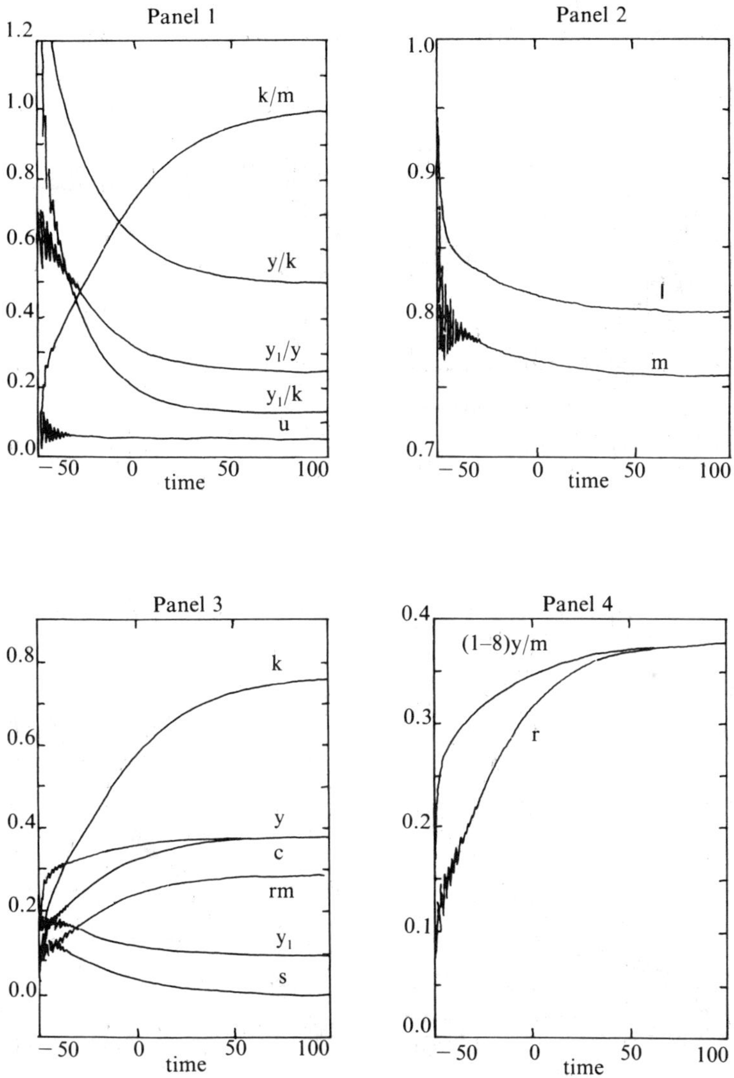


DIAGRAM 6.7 *Some money illusion in wage formation*
*$\beta=0.5$, $\psi=0.5$, $\xi=1.4$, $\xi=1$; other parameters = standard values*

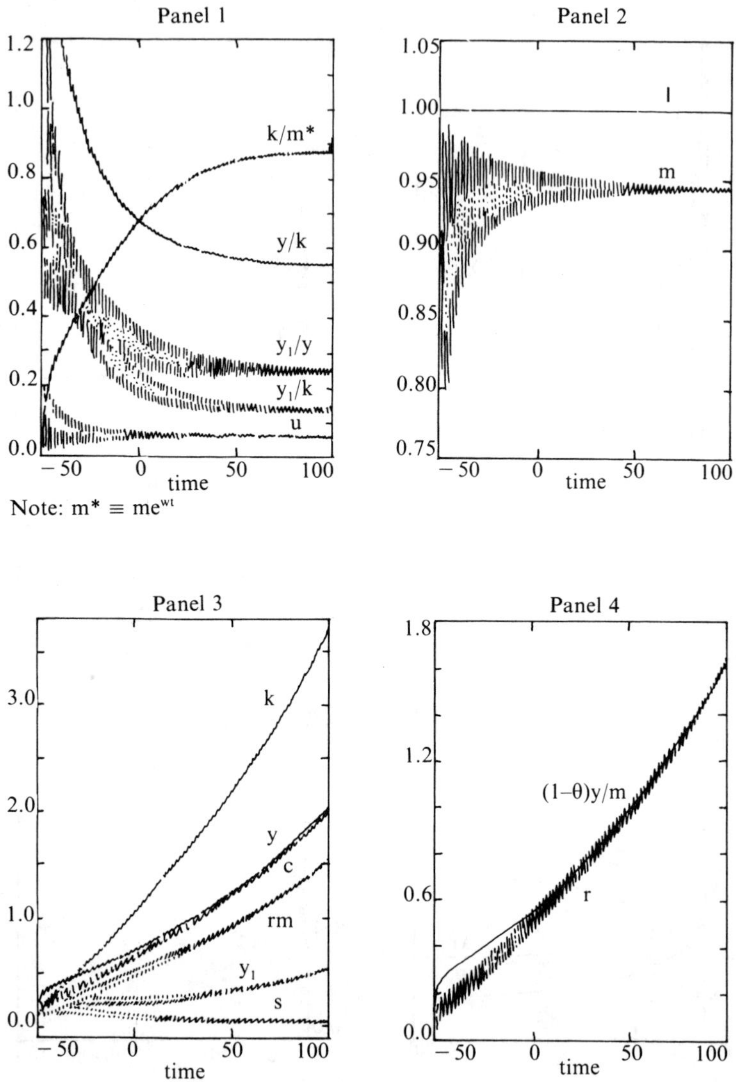


**DIAGRAM 6.8** *The effect of technical progress with a constant supply of labour $\beta=0.5$, $\mu=0$, $\omega=0.01$; other parameters = standard values*

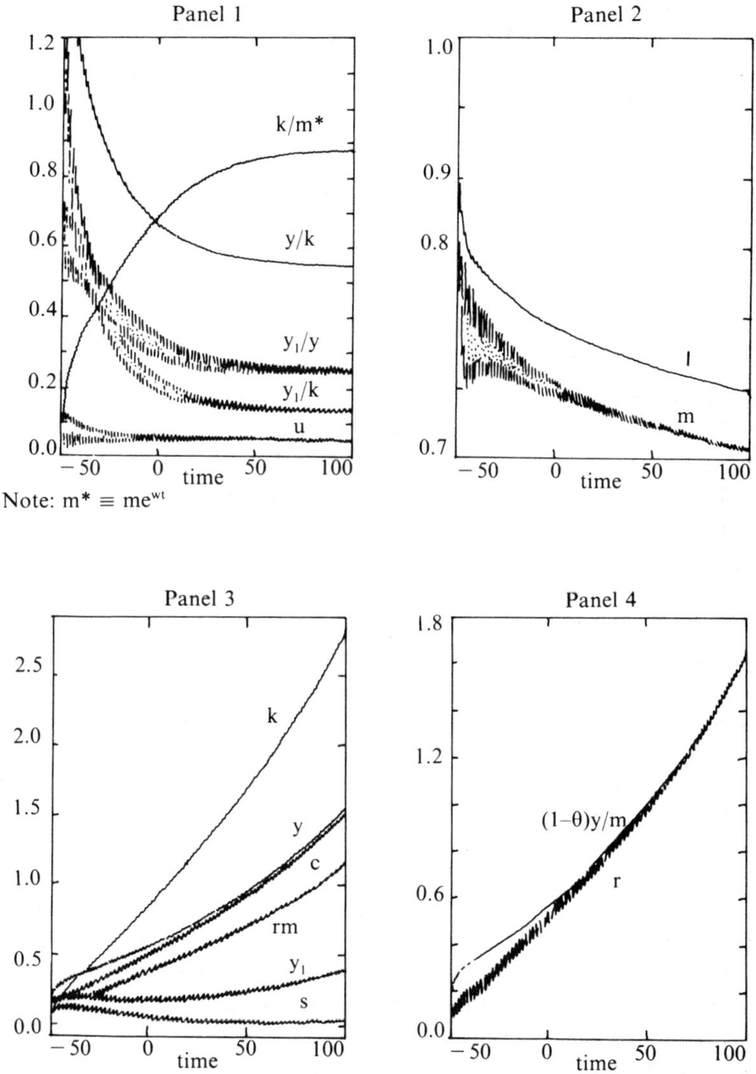


DIAGRAM 6.9 *The effect of technical progress with a falling supply of labour* *$\beta=0.5$, $\omega=0.01$; other parameters = standard values*

# 7 Observations Concerning the Growth Cycle

Andrew Brody

Whatever exists does so in a periodic manner. Whether this manifests itself as electromagnetic waves with their approximately 300.000 km/sec velocities, sound waves or trajectories of heavenly bodies with 1 km/sec velocities, or chemical, geochemical and biological processes with velocities around 0.1 to 10 millimikron/sec, the world seems to be nicely ordered into three or four strips with widely differing velocities of oscillations (Acta Geologica, 1980).

Economic fluctuations belong probably to the strip with modest velocities though it is impossible to place our subject unequivocally. We do know something about the time parameters involved, yet only the relative amplitude of economic cycles, the relative 'speed' of propagation allows closer analysis. Economics lacks a well-defined 'measuring rod'. Most of the economists are sceptical even about the possibility of constructing a suitable scale with a proper zero point and unit element.

Be it as it is, cycles have angular frequencies and so must have time parameters. The angular motion is described by an imaginary number: $e^{i\omega} = \cos\omega + i\sin\omega$, derived usually from differential equations. Worldly interdependencies contain only real proportions; thus we look for the square of the angualr frequency which is real. Therefore we require something of the dimensionality of $[T^2]$ or $[T^{-2}]$, where T stands for *tempus*.

The simplest oscillation, that of the pendulum, contains this dimensionality by dint of gravitation, represented in the equation as causing acceleration. The proper unit to measure acceleration is, of course, cm $sec^{-2}$, being the second time derivative of the displacement. Its dimension is $[LT^{-2}]$ where L stands for *longitudo*.

Economic models are mostly reticent about the inherent units of measurement. The supplementary introduction of dimensional constants often spoils and upsets the equations, indicating a dimensionally incorrect approach, as for instance with CD and CES production functions.

The Kaleckian model of economic cycles stands half-way. It did, indeed, introduce two important time parameters. The first has been capital intensity or capital–output ratio. This has to be measured in years, because stocks are accumulated flows, that is, time integrals. Alas, if we define a flow as 'value per year' and then integrate, the result is pure value. So the time parameter is seemingly lost. Yet value itself possessed the dimension of time in the classical labour theory of value. As Marx put it: 'value is labour *time* necessary to reproduce a given commodity.' Let us therefore consider flows as 'intensities', dimensionless streams, pure numbers. Stocks then have the dimension of time and so do capital–output ratios.

The second time parameter in the Kaleckian model has been the gestation period, the amount of time elapsing between deciding and finishing an investment – or any other process of production. To the chagrin of our profession these basic notions were coupled in a somewhat foggy fashion – even in the latest version proffered by Lange (1965). In the Kaleckian model oscillation times and even the existence of oscillations are hardly connected to the time parameters involved. This is the penalty for writing out equations without care for dimensional homogeneity.

Happily we now have a deeper and basically correct set-up with Professor Goodwin's growth cycle (Goodwin, 1965). Its first equation, governing the logarithmic derivative of the rate of employment, v, has a consistent dimension of $[T^{-1}]$.

$$\dot{v}/v = 1/\sigma - (\alpha - \beta - u)/\sigma \qquad (1)$$

where $\sigma$ stands for the capital–output ratio, $\alpha$ and $\beta$ respectively for the growth rates of labour productivity and of labour supply. Finally u stands for labour's share. The latter is a pure number, designing a proportionality. It is the classical concept of real wages, as defined by Ricardo: that part of newly-created value the worker may purchase back with his wages.

The second constituent equation is less clearcut – but Professor Goodwin clearly indicated its heuristic character:

$$\dot{u}/u = -\alpha - \gamma + \rho v \qquad (2)$$

The logarithmic derivative on the left side and also the growth rate of productivity, $\alpha$, on the right evidently indicate again the dimensionality of $[T^{-1}]$. The same dimensionality should be expressed – and it is correctly indicated by the Greek font – by $\alpha$ and $\rho$, the intercept and slope for the linear approximation of the Phillips curve. Yet how to attribute the correct dimension $[T^{-1}]$ to the latter quantities?

I am unable to solve this question in an entirely satisfactory manner. To do so would need applied theoretical work bearing on the theory of wages and being of the lucidity of the Harrod–Domar model. Still, relying on the insight and approach suggested by the equations I may propose the following line of reasoning:

> The 'real wage rate ... rises in the neighbourhood of full employment' (Goodwin, 1965, p. 54). This phenomenon may be due to the fact that augmenting the supply of labour requires a definite stretch of time – a 'gestation period'. There may be two distinct time periods and attached outlays to be considered here. The first is of a relatively short duration, a couple of months, implied in training a person, previously not in the labour force, to enable him or her to participate in the production process. The second time span is distinctly longer a sort of demographic constant: the time needed to produce a new offspring, able to participate in the labour supply after 16 to 24 years of being nursed, reared, educated and polished. These two kinds of magnitudes may be reflected in the values of $\gamma$ and $\rho$.

With these explanatory magnitudes in mind let us now drastically simplify the equations to obtain some qualitative and quantitative answers. Let us assume $\alpha=\beta=0$, that is absence of technological change and constant supply of labour. Let us also assume, for mathematical convenience, $\gamma=\rho$. Then the former equations become quite transparent:

$$\dot{v}/v = 1/\sigma(1-u) \tag{1*}$$

$$\dot{u}/u = \rho(v-1) \tag{2*}$$

In equilibrium the right sides must equal zero, this entails $u=v=1$. Equilibrium is achieved with zero profit and full employment. The latter conclusion is acceptable only with reservation. My plea for accepting it is the following: full employment does not necessarily mean that every person in the population, theoretically able to perform some work, is actually part of the labour supply. Thus a 'more than full employment' is conceivable – and is conspicuous in time of war or national calamities.

These simplified equations exhibit the known features of the original ones. There is a particular solution $v_t = v_0 \exp(t/\sigma)$ for $u=0$, exponential growth with zero wages, along the v axis; and a second particular solution $u_t = = u_0 \exp(-\rho t)$ for $v=0$, exponential decay with no work performed, along the u axis. All trajectories of the solutions, started in the positive orthant, must remain there because no trajectory can cross over the two axes, being particular solutions themselves.

For trajectories close to the equilibrium point $u=v=1$, we may compute approximate solutions. Let $\varepsilon$ be a small scalar, say $\varepsilon \leqslant 0.1$. Then

$$u_t = \exp(\varepsilon\rho^{\frac{1}{2}}\sin \rho^{\frac{1}{2}}\sigma^{-\frac{1}{2}}t)$$

$$v_t = \exp(\varepsilon\rho^{-\frac{1}{2}}\cos \rho^{\frac{1}{2}}\sigma^{\frac{1}{2}}t)$$

will solve our equations approximately. This is so, because

$$\dot{u}/u = \varepsilon\rho\sigma^{-\frac{1}{2}}\cos \rho^{\frac{1}{2}}\sigma^{-\frac{1}{2}}t$$

and

$$(v-1) = \varepsilon\sigma^{-\frac{1}{2}}\cos \rho^{\frac{1}{2}}\sigma^{-\frac{1}{2}}t + 0(\varepsilon^2) \qquad \text{satisfying (2*)}$$

while

$$\dot{v}/v = -\varepsilon\sigma^{-1}\rho^{\frac{1}{2}}\sin \rho^{\frac{1}{2}}\sigma^{-\frac{1}{2}}t$$

and

$$(1-u) = -\varepsilon\rho^{\frac{1}{2}}\sin \rho^{\frac{1}{2}}\sigma^{-\frac{1}{2}}t + 0(\varepsilon^2) \qquad \text{satisfying (1*)}$$

The period of the cycle can be computed as $T = 2\pi\rho^{-\frac{1}{2}}\sigma^{\frac{1}{2}}$, which can be expressed verbally as:

Time period $= 2\pi\sqrt{}$(capital intensity × gestation period)

Capital intensity being roughly of the order of 3 years, the short training period, say of two months, we obtain a cycle of $2\pi\sqrt{(3 \times \frac{1}{6})} = 2\pi\sqrt{(0.5)}$, which is approximately 4.4 years.

With an average time of rearing and educating from birth onward, say, 20 years duration, the period will be $2\pi\sqrt{(3 \times 20)} = 2\pi\sqrt{60}$, which is approximately 49 years. These two cycles do bear resemblance to the well-known business cycle and the Kondratiev cycle, which is once again fashionable.

The fact that the solution has the qualitatively intricate character exp $(\varepsilon \sin \omega t)$ explains why econometricians searched in vain for sinusoidal components in economic time series. The above form of motion, particularly when an exponential trend is added, will exhibit just that characteristic spectral shape reported by Granger (1966). The cyclic components, though present in the time series, are extinguished rather than found by up-to-date methods of time-series analysis. To remedy the situation we better return to ancient methods. Instead of analysing the original economic series let us consider its logarithmic derivative, its yearly or monthly growth rates. The latter, by the way, usually form a stationary series while neither the original data nor their logarithms are of a stationary character.

Acknowledging a period T, the integral of equation (1*), taken from 0 to T, will vanish. Its left side yields $\ln v_T - \ln v_0 = 0$ (because of the periodicity $v_T = v_0$) and therefore the integral of the right side must also equal zero. Hence

$$\int_0^T 1/\sigma \, dt = 1/\sigma \int_0^T u dt \text{ whence } 1/T \int_0^T u dt = 1 \tag{3}$$

In a similar fashion the integral of equation (2*) leads to

$$1/T \int_0^T v dt = 1 \tag{4}$$

Thus the *average* values of u and v, taken through a period, are equal to their *equilibrium* values.

The same is true for the original equations (1) and (2). Their average and equilibrium values are

$$u = 1 - \sigma(\alpha + \beta) \text{ and } v = (\alpha + \gamma)/\rho \tag{5}$$

Comparing different stationary solutions – considering different values for $\alpha$ and $\beta$ – we see that employment will be *augmented* by an increase of productivity. Workers' share will be *decreased* both by an increase of productivity and growth of labour supply.

When productivity increases, the small increase in employment will be more than counterbalanced by the fall of the workers' share. Thus it is no wonder that in modern industrial societies population growth is hampered and trade union movements usually resist technological improvements. This paradoxical result does not controvert the fact that an increase of productivity may improve the workers' lot. The real wage, measured by some index number as the amount of commodities at the workers disposal, may increase, even if the real wage, in the Ricardian sense, decreases. The classical and the modern definition of 'real wage' coincide only in absence of technological change. If productivity is rising, they may become contradictory. The worker may be better off in a physical sense nevertheless in a worse situation socially.

**References**

*Acta Geologica* (1980) Academiae Scientiarum Hungaricae, Budapest, Akadémiai Kiadó, vol. 23, nos 1–4.

GOODWIN, R. M. (1965) 'A Growth Cycle', in C. H. Feinstein (ed.) (1967) *Socialism, Capitalism and Economic Growth* (Cambridge: Cambridge University Press) pp. 54–8.

GRANGER, C. W. J. (1966) 'The Typical Spectral Shape of an Economic Variable', *Econometrica*, vol. 34, no. 1, pp. 150–61.

LANGE, O. (1965) *'Wstep do cybernetyki ekonomicznej'* (Warszava: Panstwowe Wydawnictwo Naukowe), chs 3 and 5.

# 8 A Reconsideration of Frisch's Original Cycle Model

Björn Thalberg*

## 8.1 INTRODUCTION

To comprehend how and why the economy bumps up and down, and continues to do so 200 years after the start of the Industrial Revolution, is a recurring task in a number of Richard Goodwin's famous essays collected in his book *Essays in Economic Dynamics* (Goodwin, 1982). In a volume to honour Richard Goodwin it may thus be pertinent to discuss the problem of the basic explanation of the cycle phenomenon. In this essay we shall return to one of the possible starting points when Goodwin first began his research, i.e. to Ragnar Frisch's classic Casselfestschrift essay in 1933 'Propagation Problems and Impulse Problems in Dynamic Economics'.

The basic idea developed by Frisch was the 'rocking-horse analogy' of Wicksell,[1] i.e. that while the solution of the deterministic or undisturbed part of a realistic model of the economy as a rule may be *damped*, cycles which are undamped and more or less regular may still be generated as a result of the impact of exogenous random shocks. The shocks can then be said to solve what Frisch called the 'impulse problem', as they provide energy to maintain the cycle. They strongly influence the amplitude of the generated cycles, while the length is mainly determined by the propagation mechanism given by the intrinsic structure of the economy.

Cycle theory has of course been advanced in several main directions since Frisch's 1933 essay. The contributions of Goodwin, for example, did not build on the Wicksell–Frisch approach. In fact, in the Preface to *Essays in Economic Dynamics* Goodwin writes that he did not find Frisch's solution very helpful. Nonlinearities provided a more fruitful answer. Goodwin then describes how he gradually sought to arrange an indissoluble union of growth and cycle, how he formulated a one-sided oscillatory economic model, i.e. an elastic system bumping repeatedly against a rising 'ceiling', and also how such a model can be rendered structurally stable and yield a single, stable limit cycle.

We may, however, point out several more or less distinct links between Frisch and Goodwin. Both operate with a 'carry-on-activity' function in the production of capital goods, and studying Frisch's model closely, one finds that it also contains a ceiling on expansion. Goodwin also operates occasionally with exogenous random shocks in his cycle models.[2] However, while these *exogenous* elements are essential in Frisch's approach, Goodwin's basic explanation is more genuinely *endogenous*: shocks are not necessary to explain recurrent cycles in his model. The two different approaches initiated the long endogenous/exogenous debate in basic cycle theory.

The 1933 essay of Frisch has thus never ceased to be part of the current theoretical discussion. Studies of the dynamic properties of relatively large econometric models, particularly the work by the Adelmans on the Klein–Goldberger model of the United States,[3] did lend support to Frisch's assertion that the exact part of such models would tend to be stable and that random disturbances are essential elements in the generation of business cycles. But his approach is also often questioned. For example, in an article as late as 1980, J. M. Blatt concludes that 'all Frisch-type econometric models of the economy are in contradiction to the facts'.[4]

In this essay, only occasional reference will be made to the endogenous/exogenous debate. The intention is primarily to discuss the 1933 essay of Frisch, to supplement his attempts to demonstrate the properties of his model, and also to attempt to analyse more thoroughly its limitations. This may yield some results. For one thing, while Frisch made great and pioneering efforts to illustrate the properties of his model by attempting to simulate numerical examples, 50 years ago, this could only be done in a very rudimentary manner. With the aid of a modern computer, it is now easy to continue where Frisch had to stop. Thus, we may be able to demonstrate more effectively his model's attributes, as well as weaknesses not observed by Frisch himself. In fact, looking at the results of the simulations described below, we may assert that if Frisch had had access to modern technical facilities, he would have reformulated his model and also, to some extent, his conclusions. (Needless to say, he would have been overjoyed by today's technical possibilities.)

In the introduction to his 1933 essay, Frisch emphasises firstly that the economic oscillations 'seem to be explained most plausibly as free oscillations' (p. 171). Thus, the periodicity of the cycle should be explained by the intrinsic structure of the economy, and not be linked to some exogenous periodic or quasi-periodic phenomenon.[5] Moreover, Frisch stresses that a model to explain the cycle should be determined and truly dynamic.[6] Furthermore, it ought to be a *macro*dynamic type of model where one tries to give 'an account of the whole economic system taken in its entirety', and 'deliberately disregards a considerable amount of the details of the picture' (p. 173). (Incidentally, this passage shows Frisch as a great coiner of names as it was probably the first time the terms 'macro' and 'micro' were used in this by now standard sense in economics.[7])

## 8.2 THE MODEL OF THE PROPAGATION MECHANISM

Turning now to Frisch's undisturbed model, i.e. his 'propagation mechanism', he (tacitly) assumes a *closed* economy, and considers the following three real variables:

y: 'production starting' of capital goods
z: production of capital goods
x: production of consumption goods

To explain the time-paths of these variables, he operates with the following relationships:

$$y_t = mx_t + \mu\dot{x}_t \tag{1}$$

$$z_t = \int_0^{\varepsilon} D(\tau) y_{y-\tau} d\tau; \text{ where } D(\tau) = 1/\varepsilon, \text{ i.e.:} \tag{2}$$

$$\dot{z}_t = (y_t - y_{y-\varepsilon})/\varepsilon \tag{2'}$$

$$\dot{x}_t = c - \lambda(rx_t + sz_t) \tag{3}$$

The parameters m, $\mu$, $\varepsilon$, c, $\lambda$, r and s are all positive constants.

Equation (1) explains the order inflow and at the same time the production starting of capital goods (i.e. Frisch disregards the possibility that new orders are at times stocked because of lack of capacity in the capital goods producing industry).[8] The first term $mx_t$ expresses the level of replacement investment in both lines of production;[9] while the term $\mu\dot{x}_t$ expresses the acceleration principle, which in this model works solely through variations in consumption.

Equation (2) is what Frisch denotes the 'carry-on-activity' equation. The production or value added of the capital goods producing sector depends upon the intensity with which the industry is working to complete the production of capital goods whose production was started at earlier times. In order to simplify, Frisch assumes that the 'advancement-function', $D(\tau)$, is constant and equal to $1/\varepsilon$, i.e. each unit of capital is given a constant amount of carry-on-activity per unit of time over its production period, which is $\varepsilon$ years. For certain purposes, Frisch differentiates (2) and employs (2′). (3) is called the 'consumption equation'. It explains, however, the time derivative and not directly the level of consumption. The idea is that during the upturn, when x and z increase, the need for cash also increases while as a rule the money supply is not expanded *pari passu*. This creates a tension which counteracts further expansion. According to Frisch, a plausible outcome would be that consumption would be the first to yield to the cash pressure, whereby $\dot{x}$ would decline and perhaps become negative. In contrast, when x and z decline during the downturn, the term $(rx + sz)$, which expresses the *encaisse désirée*, becomes small in relation to money supply, wherefore $\dot{x}$ may again be positive. Equation (3) is, however, a conspicuously weak part of the model. The liquidity pressure may become effective but it is surely not the prime mover of consumption demand.

With the aid of various ideas developed in the literature, Frisch has formulated in equations (1)–(3) a small and instructive linear model capable of generating cycles. Frisch ascribes the acceleration principle (1) to Clark, the distinction between production starting and carry-on-activity in the production of capital goods to Aftalion, and the idea of the variable *encaisse désirée* and its significance to Walras. The generation of cycles by the model can be outlined as follows: assume, to begin with, that $\dot{x}$ and according to (1), y, increase. Then, given (2), z will also increase after a while. But then $(rx + sz)$ increases which according to (3) implies that $\dot{x}$ declines and may easily become negative. Then y, and subsequently z, will also decline, whereby according to (3), $\dot{x}$ sooner or later again turns positive.

The model (1)–(3) is mathematically fairly complicated since it is a mixed system of differential and difference equations. Frisch is, however, able to sketch the form of the general solution analytically. To be able to say something definite about the length of the fluctuations and the degree of dampening, he inserts as a numerical example certain values for the parameters 'that may in a rough way express the magnitudes which we would expect to find in actual economic life' (p. 183).

Frisch's standard numerical example:

$$\varepsilon=6,\ m=0.5,\ \mu=10,\ \lambda=0.05,\ r=2,\ s=1,\ c=0.165 \tag{4}$$

Hence the length of the period required for the completion of capital goods is assumed to be as long as 6 years. It includes time needed for planning and organisation of the work, but seems anyhow extremely long. The value of $\mu$ may also seem exaggerated, indicating a very high capital–output ratio. Frisch stresses, however, that these guesses are very crude.

The values given in (4) imply that in a possible stationary state where all time derivatives are zero, we have: $\bar{x}=1.32$ and $\bar{y}=\bar{z}=0.66$; i.e. the level of (gross) production of capital goods is 50 per cent of that of consumption goods.[10]

The solution of the model (1)–(3) contains a number of components. As sketched by Frisch, it is of the form;

$$x(t)=\bar{x}+\Sigma a_k \exp \rho_k t$$
$$y(t)=\bar{y}+\Sigma b_k \exp \rho_k t$$
$$z(t)=\bar{z}+\Sigma c_k \exp \rho_k t$$

where $\rho_k$ are complex and/or real constants. Besides the stationary values, Frisch finds that, given (4), the solution contains a primary cycle ($k=1$) with a period of about 8.5 years, and a secondary and a tertiary cycle ($k=2, 3$) with periods of 3.5 and 2.2 years respectively, as well as shorter cycles. All cycles are heavily damped. The relative importance of the various components depend upon the constants $a_k$, $b_k$ and $c_k$ which depend on initial conditions.[11] Thus, depending on these conditions, i.e. on how the system is assumed to start, the model may generate primarily a damped cycle of periodicity of about 8.5 years or a mixture of this and other components. Frisch finds this result of 'considerable interest' since a primary cycle of 8.5 years 'corresponds nearly exactly to the well-known long business cycle' (Frisch, 1933, p. 188), while a secondary cycle of 3.5 years corresponds to the observed short cycle. In his discussion Frisch concentrates on the primary cycle.

Frisch asserts that the length of the cycle is mainly dependent on the value of $\varepsilon$. He attempts a sensitivity analysis,[12] but does not vary $\varepsilon$ (probably for technical reasons). In several numerical calculations he varies in turn m and $\lambda$. The variation of m is found to leave the generated cycle almost unchanged while a reduction of $\lambda$ from 0.05 to 0.001 leads to a modest increase in the length of the cycle but markedly increases its dampening tendency.

For all cycle components Frisch finds, furthermore, a distinct pattern of lead–lag relations. Production starting y is the leading variable. When it reaches its peak early in the upturn, $\dot{x}$ is at its maximum while x is still relatively low. When x reaches its peak, y has fallen off considerably. The carry-on-activity z is a typical laggard which reaches its turning points relatively late.

In order to examine Frisch's conclusions, I have made a number of simulations with the aid of a modern computer. In the undisturbed case, the results of these simulations agree fairly well with Frisch's analysis. Firstly, by applying the parameter values (4) and by choosing appropriate initial values (i.e. which ensures that the longest cycle component is predominant[13]) it is possible to demonstrate the highly damped 8-year cycle which Frisch emphasised (cf. Figure 8.1) also illustrates the effects of variations in the parameter $\lambda$. An increase of $\lambda$[14] is seen to reduce the dampening tendency and to some extent the length of the cycle. Moreover, also in accordance with Frisch, the length of the cycle varies strongly with the production period for units of capital, $\varepsilon$. For example, in the simulations given in Figure 8.2, where $\varepsilon$ is reduced from 6 to 4 years, the length of the cycle declines from 8–8.5 to 5.5–6 years.

Figures 8.3a and 8.3b illustrate the lead–lag relations between the fluctuations of x, y and z. (To reduce the dampening effect and thus make the picture clearer, we assume $\lambda = 0.2$, $\varepsilon = 4$ and $c = 0.66$ but otherwise (4).) Comparing the two figures, it can be seen that the upturns and downturns of y precede those of x, and that z is very much a laggard (or at least the time-paths, in accordance with Frisch's analysis, can be interpreted in this way).

The dampening tendency is, as mentioned, sensitive to variations of $\lambda$.[15] Moreover, the lower the values of the acceleration parameter $\mu$ and the depreciation factor m, the stronger the dampening (cf. equation (1) which shows that the tendency for y to fluctuate is then potentially weaker). Reducing the values of these three parameters one easily obtains an exponential path towards the stationary state

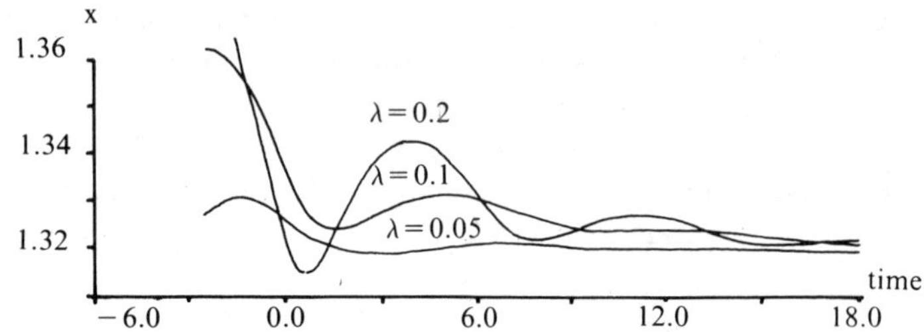


FIGURE 8.1 *Frisch standard; λ=0.05, 0.1, 0.2; c=0.165, 0.33, 0.66*

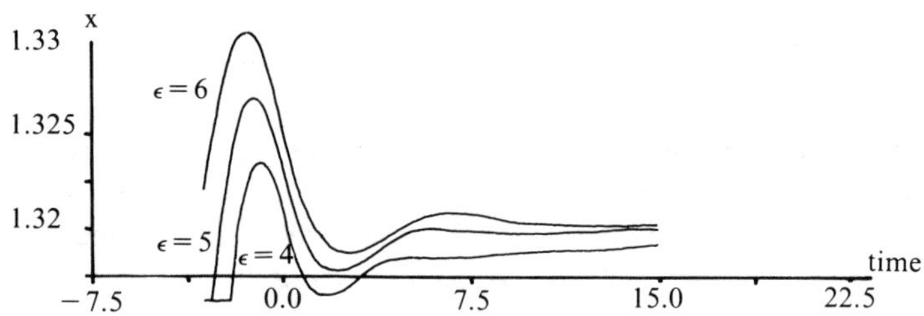


FIGURE 8.2 *Frisch standard: ε=6, 5, 4*

instead of a damped cycle. However, as shown by for example, Haavelmo, [16] the *disturbed* model may also produce persistent cycles in such cases (of, we may say, extremely stable 'rocking-horses').

It is of course difficult to assess what may be realistic values of the parameters of Frisch's model. However, as suggested we may safely assert that his values of $\varepsilon$ and $\mu$ are too high. Even 50 years ago, half that level would have been more realistic.[17] Also m seems somewhat high, while the value of $\lambda$ seems rather low (if one believes in the significance of the *encaisse désirée* effect).

As a more realistic alternative to (4), we may therefore specify, for example:

$$\varepsilon=3,\ \mu=5,\ m=0.4,\ \lambda=0.2,\ r=s=1,\ c=0.3696 \qquad (4a)$$

The model still generates heavily dampened cycles when modified Frisch values (4a) are used. (Note, incidentally, that $\bar{y}$ and $\bar{z}$ are now 0.528 while $\bar{x}$ is 1.32 as before.)

In retrospect, a crucial result of Frisch's numerical and general

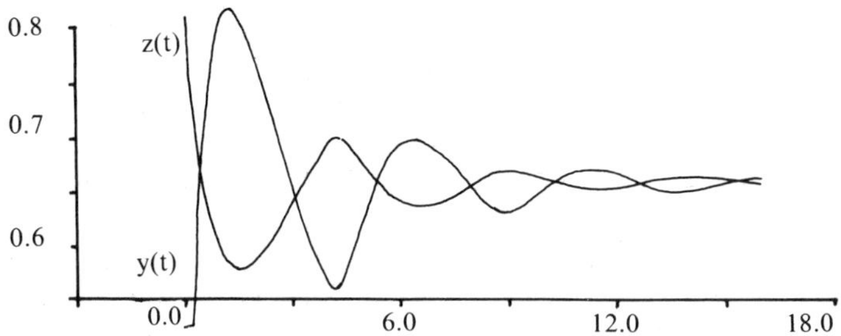


FIGURE 8.3a *Frisch standard: $\lambda=0.2$; $c=0.66$; $\varepsilon=4$*

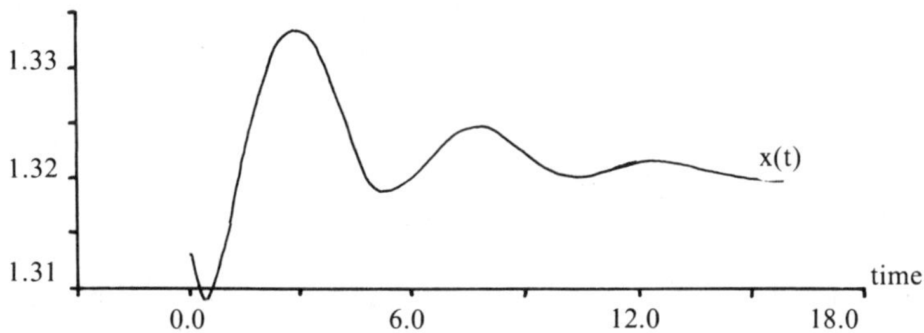


FIGURE 8.3b *Frisch standard: $\lambda=0.2$; $c=0.66$; $\varepsilon=4$*

analysis of his model of the propagation mechanism is that it produces *damped* cycles. This is, Frisch believed, very typical. When economic models give rise to fluctuations these will, given realistic values of the parameters, 'most frequently be damped'.[18] This might, Frisch remarks, at first seem a disturbing observation. But deterministic models should not be taken as a complete theory for the oscillating phenomena that we observe. 'They only form *one* element of the explanation: they solve the propagation problem. The impulse problem remains.' The full explanation is to be found in a *synthesis* 'between the stochastic point of view and the point of view of rigidly determined dynamical laws'.[19]

It is worth noting that in a linear model it is generally difficult to point out any immediate or particular cause of a turning-point, the explanation of each turn being in principle the whole model. This is in contrast with analyses by means of nonlinear cycle models where it often seems natural to link, for example, the upper turning-point to the existence of a kind of 'ceiling'. However, in the simple and very transparent model of Frisch (1)–(3), the restriction on the expansion of money supply and the subsequent liquidity pressure, as expressed by equation (3), plays virtually the same role as a 'ceiling' against which the expansion rebounds. This suggests that the borderline between linear and nonlinear models, from the point of view of the economic content, may not be very sharp.

Frisch obviously expected that some main results of his analysis of the undisturbed model would be retained in the disturbed case, while others would not. For example, he certainly expected that the production time of capital goods, $\varepsilon$, would have a bearing on the length of the cycle also in the disturbed model (cf. his assertion that the length of the cycle is largely explained by the structure of the propagation mechanism). Moreover, the characteristic lead–lag structure of the model (1)–(3), by which the ordering of capital goods leads consumption which again leads investment, was seen as a realistic feature which should be preserved in the final explanation, at least as part of the normal (average) picture.

A feature which obviously should not be, and is not, retained in the final analysis is the strict regularity which implies invariable time-lags between peaks and troughs. However, the regularity also implies that the upturns and downturns look unrealistically alike (with opposite signs). This feature is also part of Frisch's disturbed solution, which is the basis of Blatt's (1980) criticism.[20]

## 8.3 THE DISTURBED CASE. A 'FULL' EXPLANATION OF THE CYCLE

Frisch argues that, regarding the undisturbed model, we should be prepared to accept any degree of damping which a set of realistic parameter values will entail, and then explain the maintenance of the swings by erratic shocks. However, for technical reasons he was not able to demonstrate this principle by means of his own model but applied instead a simple model of an oscillating pendulum which produces a damped sine curve. Imagining that the pendulum was hit by a series of erratic shocks he computed a curve displaying persistent and quasi-regular cycles.[21]

To perform the same sort of experiment on Frisch's model (1)–(3), the first question is how to account for the erratic shocks formally. How are they to enter the model? As suggested by Frisch, we operate with additive erratic terms in (1) and (3) only.[22] We add in (1) a term $u_t$ implying that for some exogenous reasons the intensity of the order-inflow y is at time t increased by an amount $u_t$ per year. This is in agreement with Frisch's pendulum example where the velocity of the pendulum, and not its ordinate, is changed by the shocks.

Thus the model is:

$$y_t = mx_t + \mu\dot{x}_t + u_t \tag{1'}$$

$$z_t = \int_0^{\varepsilon} D(\tau)y_{t-\tau}d\tau, \text{ where } D(\tau) = 1/\varepsilon \tag{2}$$

$$\dot{x}_t = c - \lambda(rx_t + sz_t) + v_t \tag{3'}$$

Regarding the erratic terms $u_t$ and $v_t$ we assume:

$$u_t = \alpha_1 u_{t-1/h} + e_{1t} \tag{5a}$$

$$v_t = \alpha_2 v_{t-1/h} + e_{2t} \tag{5b}$$

where the terms $e_1$ and $e_2$ are normally distributed and serially uncorrelated stochastic variables with zero expectation and standard deviation equal to respectively $\sigma_1$ and $\sigma_2$. The first term on the right-hand side expresses a possible autocorrelation in $u_t$ and $v_t$.

There are also the questions regarding the durations of the shocks and the intervals between them. I have, alternatively, assumed (a) continuous, and (b) discontinuous shocks. In the first case each shock, ($e_{it}$), asserts its direct influence during a period of (1/h)-th of a year, whereafter a new shock is active, i.e. without any interval between them. In case (b) we assume that there is a constant interval between the shocks.[23]

Frisch explicitly discusses the nature of the solution of the disturbed case, i.e. how irregular shocks are formally transformed into cycles. The system of weights in the cumulation of the effects of the disturbances is, he shows, given by the shape of the solution of the model of the propagation mechanism. Thus, the structure of this mechanism must have a profound influence on the final result.

Turning now to some experiments on the model (1′)–(3′), we first imagine that there are only disturbances in the ordering of capital goods. Using Frisch's standard values (4) and assuming a modest value of $\sigma_1 = 0.0132$ (i.e. 2 per cent of y) while $\alpha_1$ is zero, the result is maintained fluctuations in z of an amplitude of about half a per cent of z, but no fluctuations in x. When $\sigma_1$ is raised to respectively 0.033 (5 per cent of y) and 0.066, the amplitude of the fluctuations of z increases to respectively about 1 to 2 per cent and 3 to 4 per cent. The fluctuations in z resemble observed series in that they are positively autocorrelated but they show no distinct periodicity. Only when $\sigma_1 = 0.066$ are there some small fluctuations in x of an amplitude of less than half a per cent. Thus, fluctuations on the investment side have very small repercussions on consumption. The path of y looks in all cases quite erratic (obviously, y must be dominated by u since x is nearly constant).[24]

In the case where, by contrast, there are disturbances only on the consumption side, i.e. in equation (3′), we find that even for small values of $\sigma_2$, while $\alpha_2$ is zero, there are sizeable maintained fluctuations in both x, y and z. For example, when $\sigma_2$ is 0.032, i.e. only 1 per cent of x, the amplitude is about 3 to 4 per cent for x, about 15 per cent for z, and as high as 60 to 70 per cent for y. When $\sigma_2$ is increased to 0.0264, the amplitudes increase to about 6 to 7 per cent and 30 per cent for, respectively, x and z, while for y it is more than 100 per cent. Further increases of $\sigma_2$ soon lead to meaningless results. The violent fluctuations in capital ordering as a result of moderate disturbances on the consumption side may be ascribed to Frisch's unrealistically high value of $\mu$. (Note that by inserting (3′) in (1′), the disturbance term becomes $10v + u$.)

To study cases with disturbances both on the investment and consumption side we first have to ask whether $e_{1t}$ and $e_{2t}$ are dependent or not. It seems implausible to assume that they are wholly independent, i.e. that investors are often discouraged at the same time as consumers are stimulated. For simplicity, we assume that $e_{1t}$ and $e_{2t}$ are perfectly correlated (which obviously exaggerates the dependency somewhat).

Since disturbances in the ordering of capital goods have little effect on consumption, while there are very strong repercussions in the opposite direction, increasing $\sigma_1$ while holding $\sigma_2$ constant has little effect on the path of consumption, but increasing $\sigma_2$ while keeping $\sigma_1$ constant has a strong effect on all three time paths. This is seen in a number of simulations, and it was also observed by Frisch who in his mimeographed notes remarked that the amplitudes of the generated fluctuations are more affected by the disturbances on the consumption side than by those on the investment side. In the same notes Frisch displayed a single computed time-path of consumption (as deviation from $\bar{x}$),[25] which is reproduced in Figure 8.4. It is possible, Frisch asserted, to distinguish in this time-path the 8.5-year cycle component but also to some extent the 3.5-year component.[26] He did not, however, seek to substantiate this assertion.

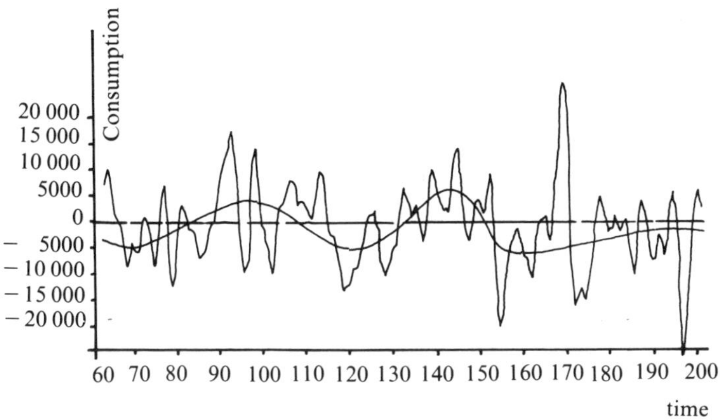


FIGURE 8.4

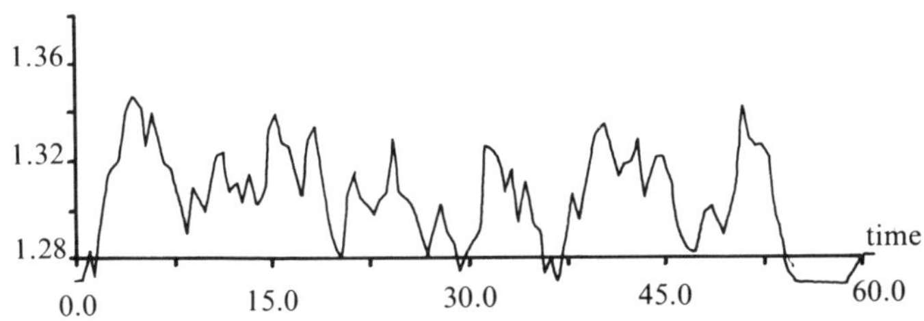


FIGURE 8.5a

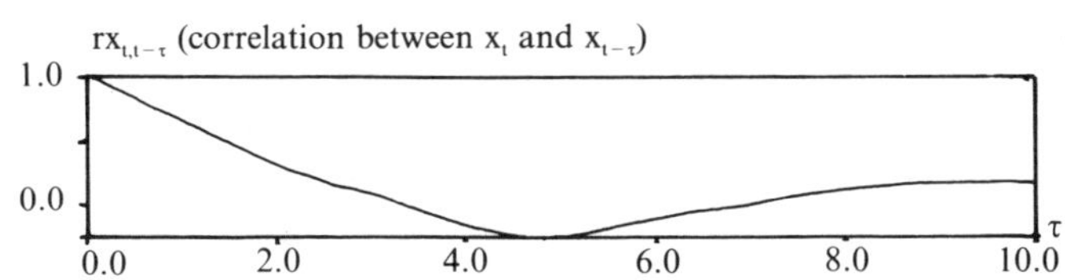


FIGURE 8.5b

In this numerical example Frisch assumed serially uncorrelated disturbances in (1′) and (3′), but he did not in his notes specify $\sigma_1$ and $\sigma_2$, etc. For comparison we show in Figure 8.5 a simulation of the path of consumption, where the values of the parameters are the same as in Frisch's example, i.e. (4), and moreover $\sigma_1 = 0.033$, $\sigma_2 = 0.0264$, and the duration of the shocks is one quarter. It is seen that the path of x in Figure 8.5a resembles that of Figure 8.4. However, the correlogram in Figure 8.5b does not indicate any distinct periodicity.

Since Frisch himself suggested that his stipulated value for $\mu$ was extreme, it may be of interest to look at some simulations with our modified Frisch-values (4a). An example with the same assumptions regarding the disturbances u and v as used in Figure 8.5 is shown in Figure 8.6. The lengths of the generated quasi-cycles are now smaller and the correlogram gives a weak indication of a cycle of about 4 to 4.5 years length (which is about the same length as in the undisturbed case).

We have so far only operated with parameter values which imply a strong degree of dampening. It remains to look at cases with only weak dampening, and/or with serially correlated disturbances. In such cases, which were not discussed by Frisch, the periodicity of the generated cycles may be more distinct. Still, let us at this point pause to consider what has been learned so far, and also to reflect on how Frisch would have reacted if he had today's technical facilities. Our simulations clearly demonstrate Frisch's main idea that disturbances keep fluctuations alive even when the degree of dampening is very strong. Moreover, the simulations demonstrate that the amplitude of the fluctuations increases with the variances of the disturbances, while the length of the fluctuations is more or less strongly tied to the propagation mechanism. Also, it is seen that when erratic disturbances are taken into account, the generated fluctuations become irregular and highly unpredictable. Thus, the Frisch type of model explained a certainly old experience so that it seems almost futile to make forecast of the phase of the cycle for more than say one or two years from now. A confidence interval for a forecast of the phase say five years ahead would include nothing less than the whole amplitude.

These are, I think, the main laudable results of Frisch's original analysis. However, the results of our simulations are in at least one respect very unrealistic and in disagreement with Frisch's vision. His model contains, as pointed out, no repercussions running from the investment to consumption, except the negative one through the liquidity pressure. This seems unrealistic *per se*, and it has distressing consequences. In all our simulations with relatively large disturbances on the investment side, i.e. $\sigma_1$ is large in relation to $\sigma_2$ (which may seem plausible), there are relatively large quasi-cycles in z, but only slight and as a rule considerably longer quasi-cycles in x, while the path of y looks very erratic; i.e. the three variables do not keep company in the way we usually observe during the cycle, but display

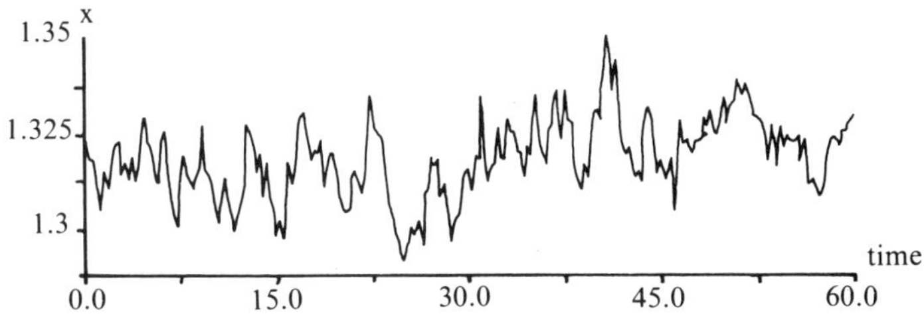


FIGURE 8.6a

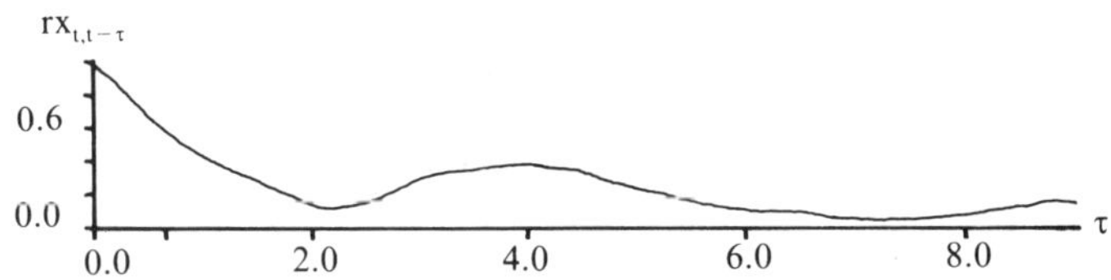


FIGURE 8.6b

different and seemingly fairly independent fluctuations. Only in cases where $\sigma_1$ is zero or extremely small in relation to $\sigma_2$, does the result contain traces of the typical lead–lag structure which was illustrated in Figure 8.3. Frisch obviously wanted to see the lead–lag structure, where y leads x and z is a laggard, as part of the disturbed solution, or at least he expected to find some fair degree of synchronism of the variations of y, x and z over the cycle. Thus, most probably Frisch would have been partly dissatisfied with the outcome of the simulations, and would have looked for amendments.

To get the variables to keep better together during the course of the cycle Frisch would have had to reconsider his structural equations. In general, if a model of the propagation mechanism does not knit the variables pretty firmly together, the disturbed solution may diverge sharply from the undisturbed one. Confronted with this problem Frisch would, I think, probably have stumbled across the 'multiplier'. Naturally the link between the investment activity and consumption should be strengthened, and it seems difficult to think of a better solution than to incorporate some form of a Keynesian multiplier. Moreover, he could easily have taken the idea from Clark, who in his discussion with Frisch on cycle models had recently given a very clear verbal exposition of a multiplier–accelerator model.[27]

## 8.4 INCLUSION OF THE MULTIPLIER

We assume that the growth of investment, $\dot{z}$, affects the growth of income and thereby, with a certain lag, the growth of consumption, $\dot{x}$. Also, we assume as in (3) above that $\dot{x}$ is affected by a possible liquidity pressure. We thus get:

$$\dot{x}_t = c - \lambda(rx_t + sz_t) + h\dot{z}_{t-\theta} + u_t \qquad (3b')$$

Our extended version of the Frisch model now consists of equation (3b′) together with (1′) and (2).

Frisch's cycle model is as a rule characterised as pre-Keynesian. It is, however, Keynesian in the sense that investment and consumption are restricted from the demand side, but it is pre-Keynesian in that it neglects the income-generating effect of investment. By the formally simple extension of adding the term $h\dot{z}_{t-\theta}$ in (3b′), we have arrived at a more modern multiplier–accelerator type of cycle model.

If an undisturbed linear model generates cyclical fluctuations, these are usually damped for some sets of parameter values but explosive for other sets. The very possibility of explosive fluctuations may be considered as a deficiency of linear cycle models, i.e. if we are not prepared to assert stability as an empirical hypothesis, or to otherwise reject explosive solutions on *a priori* grounds. However, considering again the original Frisch model (1)–(3), the problem of exploding fluctuations does not seem to arise in this linear model. The 'consumption equation' (3), contains, it seems, at the same time both a 'ceiling' and a 'floor' against which an upward, or downward, movement rebounds. In fact, if one draws the lines for $\dot{x}=0$ and $\dot{z}=0$ in an (x,z)-diagram and studies the movements of x and z from various points around the equilibrium point $(\bar{x},\bar{z})$, it appears, since the $\dot{x}=0$ curve must be steeper than the $\dot{z}=0$ curve, that the equilibrium point is stable for all deviations of x and z.

However, after the inclusion of the multiplier the system is no longer necessarily stable. A study of the positions of the curves $\dot{x}=0$ and $\dot{z}=0$ in the (x,z)-diagram reveals *inter alia* that a necessary condition for stability is that $h<\varepsilon/\mu$. High values of h and $\mu$ tend, as one would expect, to render the system unstable. For example, in both the case of (4) and of (4b), the value of h should not exceed 0.6.

Because of lack of repercussions running from the investment to consumption side the disturbed original model was in some cases seen to yield solutions with seemingly realistic quasi-cycles in z but with no or only slight, and much longer, fluctuations in x. This deficiency is now largely seen to be remedied. For example, in a case with the parameter values (4), $\sigma_1 = 0.066$ and $\sigma_2$, $\alpha_1$ and $\alpha_2$ all zero, the original model generated quasi-cycles in z of an amplitude of 3 to 4 per cent but only insignificant fluctuations in x. In a simulation on the model (1′)–(3b′) with the same parameter values, and where $h = 0.2$ and $\theta$ is zero, the model generated highly synchronised quasi-cycles in z and x with amplitudes respectively 5 to 7 per cent and about 1 per cent. In the case in which h was raised to 0.3, the amplitude was 12 to 14 per cent for z and 2 to 3 per cent for x.[28]

Moreover, after the inclusion of the multiplier, investment z is no longer such a typical laggard as in the original model. This is illustrated in Figure 8.7 which shows the simulated time-paths of x and z in a case with parameter values (4), $h = 0.25$, $\theta = 0.25$, $\sigma_1 = 0.033$, $\sigma_2 = 0.0264$, and $\alpha_1 = \alpha_2 = 0$. Figure 8.7 can be compared to Figures 8.3a and 8.3b. It appears that x and z keep fairly closely together over the cycle. The path of y is, however, somewhat more erratic. The undisturbed model generates in this case weakly damped cycles of a length of 11 years. However, as seen in Figure 8.7c, the correlogram shows no distinct periodicity for x (and neither for y and z) in the disturbed case.

## 8.5 FURTHER EXTENSIONS OF THE FRISCH MODEL

The inclusion of the multiplier in the original Frisch model seemed an important step to mend a certain shortcoming of the model. As we intend to retain the model's quality as a basic ('first-approximation') explanation of the cycle, we should of course hesitate to complicate it any further. Still, it is, I think, reasonable to operate with slightly different assumptions regarding equations (1) and (2).

In (1), Frisch assumes that investors are stimulated by an increase in consumption but not by an increase in investment. No arguments are offered to justify this asymmetry, and it may be considered a misspecification of the equation. We may therefore add a term $u\dot{z}$ in (1).

The other alteration concerns Frisch's simplifying assumption regarding his 'advancement function', $D(\tau)$, in the carry-on-activity equation (2). Frisch had to give $D(\tau)$ a very simple form. Today, with access to a modern computer, we may specify a more realistic mathematical form for $D(\tau)$.

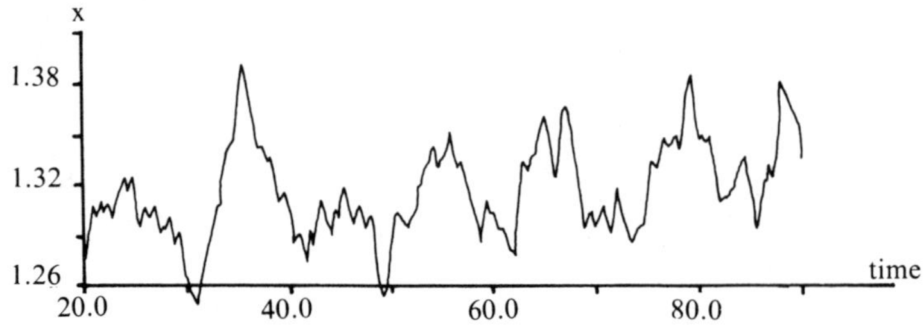


FIGURE 8.7a

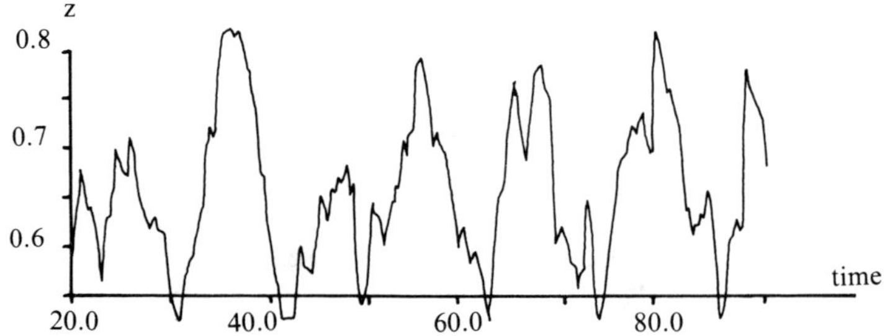


FIGURE 8.7b

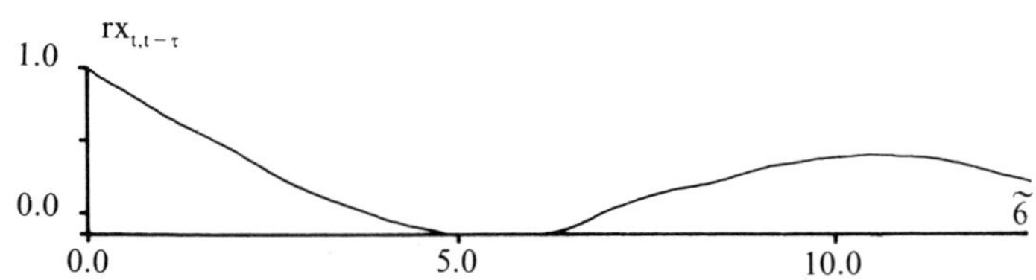


FIGURE 8.7c

The model may then be specified as:

$$y_t = mx_t + \mu_1\dot{x}_t + \mu_2\dot{z}_t + u_t \tag{6}$$

$$z_t = \int_0^\infty D(\tau)y_{t-\tau}d\tau \tag{7a}$$

where

$$D(\tau) = w^2\tau e^{-w\tau} \tag{7b}$$

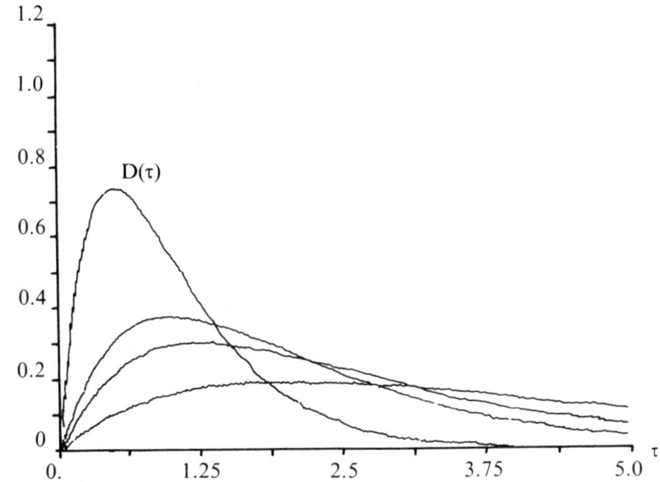


FIGURE 8.8 *w = 2, 1, 0.8, 0.5*

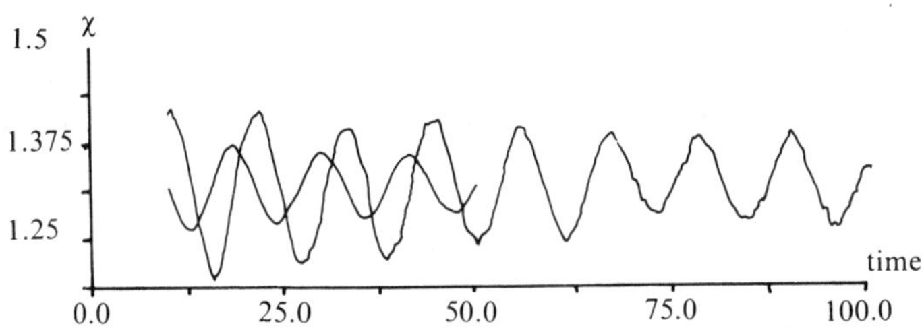


FIGURE 8.9

$$\dot{x}_t = c - \lambda(rx_t + sz_t) + h\dot{z}_{t-\theta} + v_t \tag{8}$$

Regarding the erratic terms u and v we assume, as above (5a and 5b).

The form of the 'advancement function' (7b), is illustrated in Figure 8.8. For example, if the value of the parameter w is 2, the work on a unit of capital is, as seen, concentrated to the first 1 to 1.5 years from the point of time the investment was decided. If w is 1, or lower, the work is much more evenly spread out over a fairly long period. A value of w above 1 seems realistic today (according to studies of D. Jorgenson, S. Almon and others).

Simulations on the model (6)–(8) reveal, as one would expect, that an increase of $\mu_2$ tends to make the solution less stable. The same is the case with an increase of w, i.e. when the work on capital units is more concentrated on a short period. An increase of w otherwise tends to shorten the length of the generated cycles, as does a decrease of $\varepsilon$ in Frisch's original model.

In Figure 8.9 we show an example of a simulation on the model (6)–(8). The path of x which runs from time $t=10$ to 50, is the undisturbed solution, and the path of x from 10 to 100 is the disturbed solution. Parameter values are: $w=0.7$ (which corresponds roughly seen to $\varepsilon=6$), $h=0.2$, $\mu_1=\mu_2=2.7$, $\theta=0.25$, otherwise the same values as in Frisch standard, i.e. (4). Regarding the stochastical variables it is assumed that $\sigma_1=0.033$ (5 per cent of y), $\sigma_2=0.0264$ (2 per cent of x) and $\alpha_1=\alpha_2=0$. Duration of shocks is 0.25 years. This example represents an extreme case of a degree of dampening close to zero. In such a case the model is seen to generate maintained cycles with a periodicity only slightly less regular than in the undisturbed case. The initial conditions are seen to affect the first cycles generated, but no the later ones.

Raising the values of w, $u_1$ and $u_2$ somewhat, which may seem quite realistic, would easily render the example unstable. Thus, it is seen that a stepwise elaboration of Frisch's original model, while keeping it linear, implies that the instability problem may become more and more relevant.[29]

However, in cases where the propagation mechanism generates damped fluctuations, the explanatory power of Frisch's disturbed model seems quite strong. Hicks's criticism that the Frisch theory is useful only when the degree of dampening is close to zero, while it leaves us with fluctuations which remain largely unexplained if the dampening is moderate or strong,[30] is, I think, not valid. In fact, if the degree of dampening is close to zero, the disturbed Frisch model generates cycles which look unrealistically regular. But for a wide range of other degrees of dampening his disturbed model generates quasi-cycles which look reasonably realistic. The main achievement of Frisch's 1933 essay is, however, in its methodological innovations. The mathematical apparatus, which he introduced, certainly contributed to move the discussion to a sharper and more productive level.

**Notes**

*The author wishes to thank Professor K. Velupillai for valuable comments and advice.

1. In a review of a business-cycle study by Karl Petander, Wicksell discusses the kind of theory needed to explain the cycle. He writes that, like Petander, he thinks that besides what may be considered 'causes' in the literal sense of the word one has also to consider the intrinsic structure of the system itself ('själfa samhällskroppen och dess psyke'). Then he gives in a footnote the admirable analogy: 'if you hit a rocking-horse with a stick, the movement of the horse will be very different from that of the stick. The hits are the cause of the movement, but the system's own equilibrium laws condition the form of the movements.' (Wicksell, 1918, pp. 70–1).
2. See for example, Goodwin (1983).
3. See I. and F. L. Adelman (1959), and I. Adelman (1960). For an example that yields a somewhat different result, i.e. where the *undisturbed* model together with the factual changes in the exogenous variables explain observed cyclical behaviour, see Evans (1969), p. 429.
4. Blatt (1980) pp. 467–79.
5. An example being Jevons' sunspot theory. Another example is that for small and open economies, the cycle may be linked to quasi-periodic fluctuations in export demand, the causation being largely one way in direction.
6. This was, 50 years ago, an appropriate remark, as witness the many studies discussed in Marshak (1954).
7. See Samuelson (1974).
8. Which is a matter of central importance in Goodwin's cycle theory.
9. The coefficient m accounts for both the direct depreciation of capital in the production of x-goods and the associated indirect depreciation of capital in the production of capital goods.
10. By (1) $\bar{y}=0.5\bar{x}$. Since by (2) $\bar{z}=\bar{y}$, (3) gives $\bar{x}=c/\lambda(r+ms)$.
11. However, the *relations* between $a_k$, $b_k$, and $c_k$ depend, for given k, upon the structural parameters. Moreover, the ρs depend only on the structural parameters.
12. Although very tentative, this analysis was a pioneering achievement from a methodological point of view.
13. Initial values were after a number of trials set at: $x=1.25$, and $z=y=0$ up to time $t=-\varepsilon$. Incidentally, the way to compute the primary cycle suggested by Frisch (1933), i.e. to let $y_t$, from $t=-6$ to 0, follow a path given by his equation (23b), did not work.
14. To keep the same stationary state values, i.e. $\bar{x}=1.32$ and $\bar{z}=\bar{y}=0.66$, the parameter c was changed proportionately.
15. As well as to r and s, since only λr and λs appear in the solution.
16. Haavelmo (1940), p. 312.
17. In Frisch (1934), p. 8535.1, Frisch actually remarks that $\mu=5$ would perhaps be a more realistic value. Otherwise he repeats here the analysis of his 1933 essay.
18. It is surprising that Frisch so strongly asserts that realistic models

produce damped fluctuations. Econometric studies were rare at the time, and he gives no references. One may speculate that his conviction originates from a general idea that most economic mechanisms and systems must imply stability because the reality we observe is as a rule stable (cf. the idea behind Samuelson's 'correspondence principle').

Moreover, it is interesting to note that Samuelson writes that the impact of Frisch's strong emphasis on dampedness was so overly strong as to have 'bad as well as good effects'. Samuelson, for one (but not Goodwin), fell into the dogma that all cycle models should have damped roots, a dogma which hampered his recognition of interesting nonlinear models (Samuelson, 1974).

19. Frisch (1933) p. 197.
20. It is true that Frisch's disturbed model does not provide a realistic picture of the differences between upturns and downturns. However, I consider this a task of the second order of approximation, i.e. a problem which need not be explained in a basic and very general explanation of the cycle, but later in elaborated and more specific versions of it. In fact, the last section of Frisch's 1933 essay, where Frisch comments on Schumpeter's theory of innovations, contains some ideas which may be used to explain why the lengths of upturns and downturns differ.
21. It had, Frisch mentions, already been established by Slutsky (1927) and others, that some sort of swings would be produced by the accumulation of erratic influences. But the relationship between a propagation mechanism and shocks had not been studied.
22. Frisch suggests in his lectures notes (Frisch, 1934, p. 8536.2), that in the first place it seems reasonable to disregard disturbances in the carry-on-activity.
23. Stochastic intervals may seem plausible, but not important. Moreover, whether we assumed continuous or discontinuous shocks, the main results were as a rule virtually the same.
24. In the reported cases we assumed continuous shocks with a duration of alternatively one quarter of a year and half a year. The main results were closely similar in the two cases. Also a simulation with an interval between shocks of one quarter gave roughly the same results.

    Initial conditions were the stationary state, or, alternatively, the same as reported in the undisturbed case above; the result being (after some time) about the same.
25. Frisch (1934), p. 8536.3.
26. Figure 8.4 also shows a moving average curve which has a periodicity of about 50 years.
27. Clark (1932), p. 629. Also, Frisch (1933, p. 180) mentions Keynes' concepts of saving and investment, which he did not use himself, but which would be 'exceedingly interesting' to develop.
28. The lag $\theta = 0.25$, and the duration of the disturbances also 0.25 years.
29. It may be noted that neither in his 1933 essay nor in mimeographed lectures notes (Frisch, 1934), does Frisch offer any principal argument in favour of linear models.
30. Hicks (1933), p. 90.

**References**

ADELMAN, I. and F. L. ADELMAN (1959) 'The Dynamic Properties of the Klein–Goldberger Model', *Econometrica*, vol. 27.

ADELMAN, I. (1960) 'Business Cycles – Endogenous or Exogenous?', *Economic Journal.*

BLATT, J. M. (1980) 'On the Frisch Model of Business Cycles', *Oxford Economic Papers*, vol. 32, 1980, no. 3.

CLARK, J. M. (1932) 'Capital Production and Consumer-taking: A Further Word', *Journal of Political Economy*, vol. XL, pp. 691–3.

EVANS, M. K. (1969) *Macroeconomic Activity. Theory, Forecasting and Control* (New York: Harper).

FRISCH, R. (1933) 'Propagation Problems and Impulse Problems in Dynamic Economics', in *Essays in Honour of Gustav Cassel* (London: George Allen & Unwin), pp. 171–205.

FRISCH, R. (1934) 'Forelesninger over makrodynamikk' ('Lectures on Macro-Dynamics'), mimeographed, Oslo.

GOODWIN, R. M. (1982) *Essays in Economic Dynamics* (London: Macmillan)

GOODWIN, R. M. (1983) 'Disaggrating Models of Fluctuating Growth', in R. M. Goodwin, M. Kouger and A. Vercelli (eds.): *Nonlinear Models of Fluctuating Growth: an international symposium, Siena, Italy, 1983* (Heidelberg: Springer-Verlag).

HAAVELMO, T. (1940) 'The Inadequacy of Testing Dynamic Theory by Comparing Theoretical Solutions and Observed Cycles', *Econometrica*, 4.

HICKS, J. R. (1950) *A Contribution to the Theory of the Trade Cycle* (Oxford: Clarendon Press).

MARSHAK, J. (1954) 'A Cross Section of Business Cycle Discussion', *American Economic Review*, vol. XXXV, no. 3, pp. 368–81.

SAMUELSON, P. A. (1974) 'Remembrances of Frisch', *European Economic Review*, vol. 5, no. 1, pp. 7–22.

SLUTSKY, E. (1927) 'The Summation of Random Causes as the Source of Cyclic Processes', *Econometrica*, vol. 5, no. 1, pp. 105–46.

WICKSELL, K. (1918) 'Karl Petander: Goda och dårliga tider', *Ekonomisk tidskrift*, vol. 19, pp. 66–75.

# 9 Social Rigidities, Growth Cycles and Development Planning

Amiya Kumar Bagchi

## 9.1 THE HOPES OF DEVELOPMENT PLANNERS IN THE 1950s

In 1956, Richard Goodwin constructed a model for drawing out an optimal growth path for an underdeveloped economy. This was published in the *Economic Journal* five years later (Goodwin, 1961). One novel feature of the model was that it used difference equations to solve a problem in the calculus of variations. Another feature was that it considered the whole growth path and not just two terminal points along the path and provided explicitly for 'life after planning' in the shape of a capital stock which would permit a certain minimum rate of growth of national (any per capita) income. Although many other economists became involved in drawing up optimal growth models later on, in 1967, Sen still considered Goodwin's model (and solution) to be 'more interesting' than the available alternatives. It still remains an illuminating construct because of the clarity of its assumptions, its method of exposition and the way the limitations of the basic model are laid bare.

Around the same time, Goodwin also became probably the first economist to draw up an input–output model for India. In their various mutations, with increasing structural complexity built into them and with explicit consumption functions and investment projections providing the vector of final outputs, input–output models have remained the backbone of Indian plan models.

Development planning and development economics have since then come under attack from many quarters. The left has attacked development planning as cynical exercises in self-deception and deception of ordinary people; the right has attacked the whole notion of development economics as a separate discipline. In particular, it has attacked the alleged tendency of this branch of economics to come out with recommendations for interference with the market to the detriment of real development. Some economists have already come out with spirited and effective replies against many such attacks (Sen, 1983; Toye, 1985). Moreover, a large number of governments use a variety of models to try and chart their paths of development. Even the World Bank, which cannot be called an enemy of free markets, has assisted many countries such as Sri Lanka, Turkey and the Republic of Korea (South Korea) in drawing up economic development plans.

However, it remains true that development planning does not evoke the same enthusiasm in the breast of the average social scientist as it did even 15 years earlier (cf. Chenery, 1971). Leaving aside the purely ideological objections of the New Right, what has caused this disenchantment with development planning on the part of perhaps a majority of economists? There is no single answer to this question: it will vary from country to country and with the phases of the business cycle. But I would group the more important reasons for the disenchantment under two major headings – growth cycles and structural, or more precisely, social rigidities.

In the analysis of growth cycles, again, Goodwin has made a pioneering contribution. The germs of much of the modern neo-Keynesian and neo-Marxian models of growth cycles are to be found as much in Goodwin's elegant essay in the Dobb festschrift (Goodwin, 1967) as in the work of Michal Kalecki. Many economists have modelled the causes of stagflation in the advanced capitalist countries from the 1970s onwards around the conflict between workers and capitalists over the share of the pie (Boddy and Crotty, 1975; Rowthorn, 1977; Weisskopf, 1979; Marglin, 1984; and Taylor, L., 1985). Goodwin's model is in real terms and does not explicitly tackle problems of price changes; but the growth cycle is caused by the predator–prey relationship between capitalists and workers. The growth cycles caused by such struggles lie at the heart of the disarray and recession in the advanced capitalist countries over the last ten to fifteen years.

In order to fully appreciate the responsibility of these growth cycles in bringing development planning into disrepute, we have to put them in an international perspective. We have to study, if you like, the nature and consequences of 'the dynamical coupling' (a significant concept in Goodwin's models) of the advanced capitalist economies (the 'first world') with their fix-price regimes and their financial and manufacturing clout, and the Third World countries with their flex-price regimes often at the mercy of the financial and political pressures exerted by the governments, firms and organisations based in the first world. But in order to appreciate why Third World countries make such a mess of development planning and appear to be feckless victims of influences stemming from the first world, we will have to discuss the typical rigidities in social organisation that hold up development in the Third World.

In the next three sections I take up three aspects of the problems that have bedevilled the development of the Third World during the last fifteen years. In the first section, I discuss how social barriers have held up agricultural growth, skewed the income distribution towards landlords and merchants, complicated the transfer and absorption of industrial technology and hampered industrialisation efforts. In the next section I take a brief look at the major features of the growth cycles that have caused widespread recession in the first world and have released financial and other forces that have impeded recovery in the core countries of the OECD. Then follows a brief résumé of the developments in the international economic order that have rendered life so difficult for so many Third World countries. In the final section, I revert to the question as to whether it still makes sense to draw up developmental plans, and in particular, to plan for industrialisation.

## 9.2 SOME SOCIAL BARRIERS AGAINST GROWTH OF PRODUCTIVE FORCES IN THE THIRD WORLD

An early analysis of the way social barriers hold up agricultural development in the Third World and thereby render the financing of development a tricky problem occurs in the work of Kalecki (Kalecki, 1955; cf. also Rao, 1952). This line of reasoning was elaborated into a model of inflationary stagnation by the Latin American school of structuralism.[1] According to one version of the theory, if the government, with an eye to expanding the productive base of the economy, attempts to raise public investment, the increased flow of expenditure will soon meet less and less elastic stretches of the supply curve of foodgrains and agricultural goods in general. The multiplier effect will then primarily express itself in a rise of prices rather than real outputs. If all the actors which have an access to monetary resources – the government with its central bank and its printing press; the capitalists and landlords with access to bank credit; traders or manufacturers who are able to raise their prices unilaterally – then try to realise their expenditure plans in *real* terms, they will all be, to some degree, frustrated and a price spiral will start. In some particular versions of the story, it is the resistance of the wage-earners against erosion of their real wages which becomes the main force propelling the inflationary spiral upward. The inflation will then lead to balance of payment crises, and development plans requiring imported inputs will be partially or totally aborted.

The food price-propelled inflation is, however, in a sense only a dramatically visible symptom of the deep-seated ills that plague agriculture and economic life in general in most Third World countries. In many African countries and in many parts of south and south-east Asia, shifting cultivation and dry farming, with extensive dependence on forest resources, and natural or locally controlled irrigation and drainage systems were in vogue, until quite recently. The growth of population and the pressure for producing water-intensive cash crops without extensive investment in alternative systems of water and vegetation control have led to a disastrous fall in productivity and caused famines in such areas, and whole communities have migrated in a struggle for survival. We will leave this genre of problems alone. We shall mostly deal with settled agriculture and the typical social structures found there.

Most rural areas in the non-socialist Third World (that is, all countries of the Third World except China, Cuba, Vietnam, Laos and Kampuchea) are dominated by landlords and rich peasants. One straightforward consequence of this is that often there is neither a free market in land nor an entirely free wage labour.[2] Landlords can use both market and non-market power to continue their domination; to put land to uses which are most convenient to them though not necessarily most profitable from a social or even a narrowly economic point of view; and to monopolise any public subsidies or other resources which are supposed to improve agricultural productivity and rural infrastructure. Thus in many Latin American countries vast areas are devoted to raising livestock while they have at the same time to import food from abroad. This can be very costly when the country is suffering from a chronic balance-of-payments crisis. This happens because the landlords find it more convenient to supervise land-intensive livestock production rather than labour-intensive foodgrain production. Moreover, the marketing costs of the former (since they are often sold to large exporting firms) can be lower from the landlords' point of view. Few have either the money or the political might to challenge the overlordship of the landlords over their domain. Even when agricultural innovations are introduced, they tend to be biased towards factors of production that landlords and rich peasants can use cheaply. For example, they tend to be capital-intensive at least partly because landlords can get cheap credit from banks and other financial bodies (Janvry, 1973). In other situations, also, where landlord domination is not so absolute, market expansion tends to be biased against food crops, especially those which are the staple diets of the poorer population. The market for sugar, wheat, and superior varieties of rice, and soya beans – commodities that are destined for the urban or export markets – expands and takes away land, water and other resources from the 'inferior' millets, pulses and root crops. The latter happen to be the major sources of nutrition for the poor in large areas of Africa, Asia and Latin America.

Under these circumstances, when a national government seeks to implement a development plan, and additional flows of money expenditure are directed towards foodgrains and agricultural goods – and in a poor country expenditure on such goods could easily form 60 per cent of new incomes – they are often met with an inelastic supply of foodgrains. Even if the outputs of superior varieties of foodgrains respond (and they have responded quite well in such countries as India or Indonesia), the outputs of the more 'traditional' and the inferior crops stagnate or even actually decline.

Absolute prices of food crops and other agricultural commodities then tend to rise. Since in these countries, the workers in small-scale enterprises, sweatshops and even in large-scale factories generally live on the margin of bare subsistence, there is an upward pressure on money wages, whether workers are unionised or not. When money wages rise, prices of industrial goods and services also increase, the extent of increase depending on the mark-ups charged by the industrial and marketing firms.

This is a familiar tale. A twist is added to the story when the government tries to stimulate the production of some favoured crops or agricultural commodities in general by supporting the prices of those commodities. These support devices are generally accompanied by policies to introduce new inputs such as HYY seeds, chemical fertilisers, and power tillers, or oil- or electricity-driven pumps for raising water. Many of these inputs are produced by the industrial sector. Naturally, the landlords and farmers take the costs of these purchased inputs in estimating their costs of production. They also impute opportunity costs or nominal market prices to inputs which are not purchased in the market. The government becomes committed to meeting these costs (including a normal return on capital). So when prices of industrial goods and money wages of workers rise, these increases are transmitted through government price-support policies to the prices of the favoured products of agriculture and to those of all related commodities.

Agriculture has been treated – and as far as most agricultural products in most Third World countries are concerned, rightly so – as a flex-price sector, or a sector in which prices are determined by the state of demand, rather than on a cost-plus basis (Kalecki, 1954; Morishima, 1984). However, government price-support policies have converted at least part of agriculture into more of a fix-price than a flex-price sector, at least as far as internal prices are concerned. Moreover, the monetisation of a large part of the agricultural surplus controlled by landlords and rich peasants as a result of public procurement operations imparts a permanent inflationary bias to the economy – independently of impulses of expansion transmitted by the non-agricultural sector.[3] Thus a set of policies which had been recommended for remedying the inelasticity of agricultural supplies and thereby removing a barrier against growth poses new problems for Third World countries. Moreover, the incomes of small peasants, agricultural workers and unskilled workers in most occupations are abysmally low in many Third World countries. So when the public policies and new technologies have led to a substantial rise in outputs of foodgrains, the government has often been unable to sell all food procured and has had to struggle with increasing stockpiles of grain. As we shall see later the drastic fall in primary commodity prices in the international market in recent years and the continued subsidisation of their agricultural sectors by the OECD countries have compounded these difficulties.

If the agricultural sector in Third World countries is hindered by these barriers against development, the non-agricultural sector is also bound in other shackles, some of which are linked to the constraints binding agriculture and rural areas in general. We can but touch on the following aspects of the problems holding up development of the non-agricultural sectors: (a) the role of mercantile capital in agriculture, trade and industry; (b) the restricted size of the home market because of low per capita incomes and the highly skewed nature of distribution of those incomes; (c) the limited nature of the access of most Third World exports to the markets of the OECD countries; (d) the swiftly changing character of the product spectrum; and (e) processes of production in the developed market economies and hindrances against the transfer and absorption of new technologies by Third World countries.

As we have noted above, markets in land and labour are very 'imperfect' in landlord-dominated rural areas in the Third World. The products of that land and labour have to be sold in the nearby villages, or towns or distant towns and countries. Where the peasants and workers are so poor, they need consumption loans to survive until the next harvest. In all these trading and credit operations, mercantile capital (including capital owned by landlords and rich peasants) plays a crucial role. Merchants, moneylenders and landlords advance consumption loans and loans for purchase of inputs to poor peasants (including share-croppers). The merchants buy up the crop at low post-harvest prices often from peasants who had borrowed from them and sell them at high pre-harvest prices. (Poor peasants are often unable to take advantage of public procurement operations or buy foodgrains at the fair price shops, even when such shops operate in rural areas.) Merchants also speculate in grain and other crops when the harvest is expected to be poor. In most cases, the landlords or merchants operate in all the markets and act locally as virtual monopolists or monopsonists as the case might be. The poor peasants and workers are generally left with bare subsistence or rather less than bare subsistence so that they are compelled to take consumption loans again from their landlords or other creditors. In these operations, the merchants and moneylenders expect the returns to be high and the pay-off periods to be short (normally less than a year).

In most Third World countries, it is the domestic merchants or transnational corporations who have been responsible for setting up large-scale manufacturing enterprises. When the merchants enter industry, they expect the same high rates of return as they earn in trade and moneylending. They also expect similarly short pay-off periods. When the pay-off periods are longer, they expect the returns to be correspondingly higher or virtually guaranteed for a long period. One way in which they try to ensure this is to obtain tariff or quota protection against foreign competitors. Many transnational corporations, (TNCs), which have obtained a stake in a particular country join up with local merchants in such tactics.

Paradoxically, the restricted size of the home market provides a strong plea for demanding protection against both internal and external competition. It is argued that only a few units at most can expect to make a profit by exploiting a narrow market. Pursuing this argument further, it is claimed that if competition is unrestricted, the country will continue to be supplied with goods produced by large firms located abroad, and no domestic enterprises worth the name will get off the ground. Once the domestic firms or subsidiaries of TNCs get established, their small number makes it easy for them to work out cosy restrictive or market-sharing arrangements that stifle competition.

One way in which this circle can be broken is to open up export markets. But markets in the most affluent group of countries in the world, viz. the OECD block, were rarely open in the proper sense. Various tariff and non-tariff barriers have restricted entry of both manufactured goods and agricultural goods in those markets. In some cases, TNCs have used such countries as Brazil or Mexico or enclaves such as Singapore and Hong Kong as platforms to export manufactured products to the USA or the EEC countries. But as the cases of Brazil and Mexico illustrate, where the export platforms are large, it is their home markets which prove to be the real magnets for the TNCs. When these countries get into trouble, the TNCs cut down their operations – thus proving to be true fair-weather friends. A privileged political relation such as that enjoyed by South Korea, Singapore, Hong Kong and Taiwan in relation to Japan and the USA, and often marketing links through TNCs – along with price competition – have proved to be crucial for these countries to penetrate OECD markets on a long-term basis. As the OECD countries have become more and more troubled by recession, their governments have tended to turn more and more protectionist and have been reluctant to shed those 'traditional', low-productivity but labour-intensive industries in which the industrialising Third World countries enjoy the greatest comparative advantage.

While a Third World country is industrialising, the technological base in the advanced capitalist countries is changing. 'Representative' consumption patterns change towards more sophisticated goods as incomes grow in the affluent countries (Linder, 1961), and a trade between the affluent countries grows in precisely these new bundles of commodities. As new products are innovated, they go through cycles in their locale of manufacture, as the innovating firm experiences rising manufacturing and delivery costs at the home base. The original innovators begin producing either in lower-cost locations or locations which are nearer the expanding markets and imitators follow them in the older locations and in new locations. Finally, the home country of the innovating firm begins to import the fabricated product (Posner, 1961; Vernon, 1966). As intercapitalist competition in the international arena becomes more intense, the different phases of the product cycle become syncopated, especially because TNCs resort to global sourcing for different stages of their production (including research) and different countries develop at different speeds so that there is an ongoing process of leapfrogging, catching up and falling behind (Vernon, 1979; Kindleberger, 1982, Ch. 7).

By and large, however, internationalisation of production has been truly pervasive within the charmed circle of the OECD countries. TNCs find it convenient to use some Third World countries as export platforms or to set up subsidiaries or affiliates as a means of getting round tariff and non-tariff barriers and beating down competition from potential challengers. Innovation has become more and more an activity requiring high levels of research and development (R. & D.) expenditure, a high degree of interaction between personnel engaged in such activities and, in many cases, massive government support in the form of defence contracts and subsidies for R. & D. related to arms production. Thus few Third World countries can aspire to be innovators except in minor products or processes. Some analysts have found it plausible, therefore, to treat the developed market economies as the sole producers of innovations and the less developed countries as producers of goods that the former have discarded (cf. Krugman, 1979).

The transfer of technology, however, is neither costless from the transferors' point of view, nor trouble-free from the point of view of the transferee. The transferors must carefully weigh the relative advantages of continuing to produce the commodity concerned in their home bases or in other OECD countries, setting up subsidiaries in Third World locations to produce the products partly or wholly, and licensing the knowhow to another firm or several other firms for producing the product partly or wholly for sale in specifically designated territories (a clause restricting the sale of products covered by a knowhow licensing agreement to specific regions is quite common). It has been found that by and large, the incidence of licensing of patents and knowhow by the original possessors of these 'knowledge goods' to other firms and organisations is highly and positively correlated with the degree of development of the country in which the licensee seeks to use the licence (Bosworth, 1980; Contractor, 1980).

The country which seeks to import new technology needs to possess certain favourable conditions in order to be able to absorb the technology successfully. A country may enjoy a favourable geopolitical situation so that a TNC seeking a low-cost base for some of its operations will choose it to set up business there. Such was the case, for example, with Brazil, Mexico, South Korea, Singapore, Hong Kong and Taiwan in the 1970s. The attitude of the TNCs is not, however, the decisive factor. The country must also have a suitable social structure so that workers and their supervisors are sufficiently educated, the merchants and industrialists consider industrial investment (rather than speculation in commodities, land or urban real estate) as their main source of profit, and the local capitalists have enough confidence in their ability to control the environment so that they invest heavily in adaptive R. & D. aimed at absorbing the technology effectively. Mexico and Brazil satisfied most of the other conditions, but their rural areas were still dominated by landlordism, so that for the capitalists speculation in land, real estate and commodities still remained lucrative activities. Moreover, the USA beckoned as a safe haven for placement of funds by capitalists when they found their home base racked by social conflicts and economic upheavals. In Taiwan and South Korea, for partly fortuitous reasons, the power of the landlords had been destroyed. Their governments, with their repressive labour policies and with the political backing of the US government, made certain that merchants would make money out of industrial investment. But authoritarianism promoted industrialisation in these countries also because it was utilising a highly literate working class and professional managers, and in Taiwan's case, a business community with knowledge and skills gained out of a long experience at its command. China, of course, followed quite a different policy. It destroyed landlordism and then pursued goals of universal literacy, egalitarianism and rapid industrialisation with remarkable success. The technologies she borrowed were absorbed through a meticulous integration of education, research and production (Bagchi, 1987, Ch. 4).

In other countries such as India, efforts to absorb borrowed technology were at best half-hearted. They were hampered by such problems as a low degree of literacy of workers; inadequate linkage of research with productive activities; a make-believe attitude of a section of policymakers who claimed more than was ever achieved; the constricted nature of the home market with a thin layer of rich people at the top and a teeming mass of very poor people at the bottom; and a mercantile community thriving on the mess. The net inflow of foreign private capital into India, in common with most Third World countries, has been almost uniformly negative. The foreign firms and their affiliates have always managed to send out more capital as profits and fees of various kinds than they brought in. India, in common with many other countries has followed a policy of encouraging domestic firms to import technology through an ever-increasing number of collaboration agreements with foreign firms. However, most firms entering into such collaboration agreements have contributed little to the growth of exports; nor have those agreements improved productivity, at least as measured by a positive change in the ratio of net value added to gross output. Indeed, foreign collaboration agreements in the second half of the 1970s led to an increasing net outflow of foreign exchange (Reserve Bank of India 1985; Bagchi, 1986a).

As we have noted above, in most Third World countries, when all the direct and indirect payments for the use of foreign capital and technology are taken into account, the contribution of foreign investment to the balance of payments turns out to be negative. What is even more disconcerting is that many Third World countries have witnessed a steady flight of domestic capital abroad over a long period of time. Some researchers at the World Bank have estimated that over the period 1974–82, capital flight amounted to US$ 10.8 billion[4] from Venezuela, $15.3 billion from Argentina, and $32.7 billion from Mexico. Over the same period, the external debts of Venezuela, Argentina and Mexico increased by $27 billion, $32.6 billion and $82.6 billion respectively (World Bank, 1985). More recently, the Morgan Guaranty Trust Company has estimated the capital flights from Venezuela, Argentina and Mexico over the ten-year period 1976–85 to be $30 billion, $26 billion, and $53 billion respectively. (Thus the capital flight from Mexico alone amounted to more than half the amount of external debt accumulated by that country.) For Brazil, over the same period, capital flight amounted to $10 billion (Morgan Guaranty Trust, 1986). Thus in the case of many Latin American countries a large proportion of the loans extended by transnational banks (TNBs) or other external agencies and governments almost at once ended up in US banks or other safe havens abroad (thus repeating a pattern which was witnessed widely in the nineteenth century, except that in the earlier period, it was the lenders or 'promoters' who kept back a large chunk of the loan). But the phenomenon was not confined to Latin America, nor could it be attributed just to exchange instability or to propinquity to the USA. Even for such a poor, and not-so-heavily-indebted country as India (whose external debt increased by $22 billion over 1976–85), capital flight amounted to $10 billion over the decade 1976–85, and accounted for a little less than half the increase in her foreign indebtedness.

At least three separate factors seemed to have prompted the capital flight from the major non-socialist Third World countries. One is the perception by domestic capitalists that the field of investment at home was narrow and uncertain and they could earn higher or more stable returns abroad. The social barriers against expansion of domestic market and the absorption of technology would have been a major ingredient in this perception. Fear of political instability in a country such as Brazil and even more, in a country such as South Africa (where over the period 1976–85 external debt increased by $16 billion and capital flight amounted to $17 billion) would have been an important push factor. Where such instability was caused by protests against a repressive and corrupt regime as in the cases of Iran under the Shah and the Philippines under Marcos, the rulers and their associates themselves would have hidden large amounts of their ill-gotten wealth abroad.

Second, because of both internal and external factors, practically all Third World countries have suffered from balance-of-payment crises and volatility in exchange rates, which have been controlled in most cases with various exchange and import control measures. When an exchange depreciation or more stringent exchange control measures seem likely, many merchants connected with the foreign-trade sector try to beat the gun and transfer part of their wealth, to hard currency areas, through various legal and illegal means. In trying to do so, these merchants will put a further strain on the balance of payments and exert a downward pressure on the effective exchange rate and on the prices of exportable goods (by underinvoicing and clandestine price-cutting) and an upward pressure on prices of importables (by overinvoicing of imports in collusion with foreign suppliers). This is yet another force causing a deterioration in the terms of trade of Third World countries, the reasons for which and the consequences of which we notice in some detail below.

To all these endemic forces causing a capital flight was added the high-interest regime maintained by the USA throughout the first half of the 1980s. The high-interest rate was a major support keeping up the exchange value of the US dollar. The high value of the dollar (and capitalists' faith in its sustainability) and the attractive rates of interest made the USA the world's biggest sink for capital flowing in from all countries including the capital-starved Third World.

In the next section, we turn to developments in the core countries of the OECD that led their top policymakers to take an increasingly jaundiced view of development planning and development aid for the Third World.

## 9.3 GROWTH CYCLES, INTERCAPITALIST COMPETITION AND CHOICE BETWEEN GUNS AND BUTTER FOR THE THIRD WORLD

Since the end of the Second World War until the beginning of the 1970s all the major OECD countries experienced an unprecedented prosperity: Japan and the Federal Republic of Germany (FRG) participated fully in this. In fact, once post-war reconstruction was over in the former, these two overtook most other countries in terms of rates of growth (Armstrong, Glyn and Harrison, 1984). Practically without any exception, all the major countries experienced rates of investment, growth of GNP and productivity growth higher than they had ever witnessed over a comparable period during the preceding 100 years. These 25 years or so were also characterised by the hegemony of the US dollar as the currency underpinning in the rates of exchange of all the major currencies (except for devaluations at long intervals of the weaker currencies such as the pound sterling), and relatively smooth operation of the system of adjustment of balance-of-payments disequilibrium devised at Bretton Woods. (This 'smooth' system of adjustment could still be pretty rough for many Third World countries with chronic deficits in their balance of payments, and could involve them as well as a lagging affluent country such as Britain in stop–go cycles. But the process of adjustment did not involve deliberate deflation on a long-term basis.)

During these years of growth and prosperity, the USA and her allies and, to a lesser extent, the Soviet bloc countries were prepared – in some cases, even eager – to extend grants and loans on soft terms to many Third World countries. The World Bank was accepted as an informal coordinator for the multilateral 'aid' or loan operations of the OECD countries, and was itself a dispenser of relatively large volumes of loans. (The soft loans provided by the IDA, the affiliate of the World Bank, were particularly welcome to the governments of such countries as India and Pakistan which had launched long-term development plans.) These years also witnessed the construction of theoretical models to test whether the *ex ante* gap between investment and savings or that between exports and imports was the dominant constraint holding up growth in Third World countries, and whether the donors should try to bridge the larger or the smaller of the two gaps; and to indicate the steps that would have to be taken during the period when a transition to a balanced growth path – aided by the inflows of foreign capital – was taking place (cf. Vanek, 1967; and Chenery, 1971).

From the 1970s, the secular boom of the advanced capitalist economies changed into bursts of increasingly short upturns followed by long troughs in output and productivity. Unemployment kept on rising to levels not witnessed since the 1930s. Inflation rates also tended to accelerate in many countries. Many economists attributed these changes to 'supply shocks', especially the 'oil shock' of 1973–74, when the price of oil was raised several-fold by the OPEC. However, other analysts traced the long recession in most of the developed capitalist economies to deeper-seated, endogenous problems which had already manifested themselves in the later part of the 1960s (Rowthorn, 1980; Armstrong, Glyn and Harrison, 1984). These problems centred on a tendency for the rate of profit and the share of profit in GNP to decline – especially in the USA and UK – the dislocations caused by intercapitalist competition between countries with different rates of growth of GNP and labour productivity, the further dislocations following on the breakdown of the Bretton Woods system, and the increasing dominance of finance over manufacturing interests in two major countries of the OECD, viz., the UK and the USA.

We shall try here only to recapitulate some typical conclusions by analysts interested in this area. For our purpose, it is not necessary to attach exact weights to the major factors adduced as explanations of the long recession following the long boom. Glyn and Sutcliffe (1972) had already pointed to profit squeeze as a major force causing business cycles in the post-war British economy and claimed that struggles between labour and capital were the major reasons for the profit squeeze. In a similar vein, Boddy and Crotty (1975) traced the apparent decline in the relative strength of US industrial capital to a fall in the rate of profit caused by the successful struggle of the workers to protect their absolute relative wages and their share of the output. Rowthorn (1977) linked up the emergence of secular inflation with the mutually inconsistent claims of the capitalists and workers to a share of the GNP. In a carefully argued paper, Weisskopf (1979) grouped the different theories explaining the cyclical and secular fall in the rates of profit earned by the US non-financial corporate business sector over the period 1949–75 into three variants, viz., those which stressed the rising organic composition of capital, those which centred on realisation or effective demand failures and those which emphasised the rising strength of labour as the main culprit. Weisskopf found the rising strength of labour to be the best explanation for both the secular and cyclical variations in the rates of profit. But according to his analysis, this was to be interpreted more as a successful defence of labour's own living standards in the face of a tendency of prices of wage goods to rise in relation to the prices of the final products produced by non-financial corporate business than as the outcome of an offensive struggle by labour to raise its share of the net product.

While struggles between capital and labour occupied the foreground of attention of economic analysts in the UK and the USA, there was also a major shift in the relative manufacturing prowess of the different OECD countries. The industrial outputs and GNP of both Japan and the FRG, in particular, advanced at a much faster pace than the corresponding magnitudes in the UK and the USA. Also associated with these differences in rates of growth were systematic differentials in rates of productivity growth, especially of labour. Economists have debated the causes of these differentials. Among the factors that have been cited are the diffusion of technologies from the higher-productivity to the lower-productivity countries, and in particular, the diffusion of US technologies to countries which had earlier lagged behind; the higher ratios of investment to national income devoted to private industry in the FRG and Japan; the beneficial effects of destruction of a large proportion of the capital stock in these two countries and the consequential youth and higher-productivity built into new capacity installed there; the lower relative and absolute defence burden shouldered by these countries compared with the UK and the USA; and the considerably higher proportion of R. & D. devoted to civilian production in the FRG and Japan, in comparison with most other countries. (By implication, military expenditure is seen to have insufficient spinoff effects to offset the relatively weak R. & D. position of civilian production in the UK and the USA.) Along with these factors, social scientists have stressed the greater degree of flexibility of labour and product markets in Japan (for example, Olson, 1982). Many economists have also emphasised the unique features of business–government coordination of plans and policies in Japan, which have led them to coin the phrase 'Japan Inc.' to characterise that system of coordination.

These shifts of comparative advantage in manufacturing and international competitiveness between the OECD countries became more visible as the 1970s wore on. However, already by 1971 the international monetary system which was overseen by the IMF and anchored to the use of the dollar as the universally accepted medium of international exchange (and store of value) had broken down. In that year the dollar was delinked from a fixed value of gold ($35 per ounce) against which the US government was committed to exchange it for all comers. As US manufacturing competitiveness declined internationally, the dollar became overvalued, and there was a tendency for capital to flow out of the USA. The delinking of the value of the dollar from that of gold was partly a response to this. After 1971 a system of floating exchange rates ruled. But this did not do away with the problem that while the degrees of international competitiveness continued to shift, there was virtually no coordination of economic policies among the major capitalist countries. Different countries tried to attain mutually incompatible objectives (such as a balance of trade surplus for all countries) and followed beggar-my-neighbour policies. The latter generally meant that deflation and high interest rates at home and protectionism against foreign goods came to be the norm in most countries.[5]

In the early 1970s the rise in oil prices coincided with a rise in the prices of primary commodities. This caused cost-push factors behind the inflation in the advanced capitalist countries to be stronger. (The oil-importing countries in the Third World experienced further difficulties in meeting their deficits but some such countries also gained in terms of exports of goods and labour services to the oil-exporting countries in the Middle East where an investment boom was unleashed for a time.) Several other factors, however, enabled the OECD countries to ride out the oil shock quite well and the USA appeared to acquire a new lease on its hegemony of world capitalism. First, the major TNCs engaged in extracting, refining and marketing oil were based in the USA and they shared handsomely in the increased revenues of OPEC. Secondly, the USA itself was a major producer of oil and other primary commodities and therefore its terms of trade did not deteriorate as much as those of other non-oil-producing OECD countries that had specialised more intensively in the production of manufactured goods. Thirdly, the US, and to a lesser extent, European TNBs became the major vehicles for the recycling of the foreign exchange earned by the OPEC and other oil-exporting countries. The financial sectors of both the UK and the USA gained enormously from the activities of their TNBs in collecting and lending out the extra oil revenues earned by the oil-exporting countries. (The UK itself joined the league of oil-exporters but that did not alter the continuing ascendency of finance over industry in that country.) Finally, the investment boom in the oil-exporting countries involved the import of enormous volumes of capital goods supplied mostly by the OECD countries and only to a much lesser extent, by such countries or enclaves as South Korea, Singapore, Taiwan and India. Indeed, many of the OPEC countries went in for purchases of armaments on a huge scale, and these again were supplied mostly by the USA, UK and France, among the OECD countries. (The Soviet Union is also a major supplier of weapon systems to some of the countries in West Asia.) The recycling of OPEC revenues through the OECD-based TNBs and the purchase of armaments on a huge scale are both traceable to the social and political problems of most West Asian countries. They are unable to expand their internal markets by absorbing the immigrant workers permanently (as for example, the USA did until the First World War) and their distrust of their own people and of neighbouring rulers induce their ruling classes to go in for huge armament expenditures.

In the longer term, the strategies pursued by the major OECD countries and the TNCs and TNBs based in those countries robbed the OPEC countries of most of the advantages they had gained through a rise in oil prices. (This loss of the gains obtained through a rise in oil prices occurred much more quickly after the second oil price rise of 1978–9 than in the wake of the first bout of price rise in 1973–4.) First of all, Japan and the FRG and following them, most other major capitalist countries, successfully brought down the use of oil and energy in general in most economic activities. With the oligopolistic structure of most of their major industries, the prices of manufactures produced and exported by them went on rising and soon the terms of trade turned against oil and primary products in general. Large conglomerate trading TNCs such as Cargill, Continental, or Louis Dreyfus handling grain, soya beans, and other related products,[6] Nestlé handling milk products and coffee, Lipton handling tea gained when the primary product prices rose. In many cases, it is these TNCs rather than the farmers in the Third World (and in the first world) producing the basic products who gained the lion's share of the increased revenues. But when the prices of the primary products crashed, the TNCs found it quite easy to pass on the losses to the producing peasants. The latter, after all could not match the financial and other resources, the information, and the power to manoeuvre and to collude that the TNCs possessed.

The OECD TNBs found themselves in possession of enormous OPEC funds which they were only too eager to lend to Third World enterprises and governments – especially those that were known to be favoured by Washington, London or Paris. The US administration and the World Bank came increasingly to profess the doctrine that all worthwhile projects should be bankable: the banks drew the (fallacious) corollary that all bank loans were worthwhile, particularly loans to those governments or projects which seemed to be blessed by the US government, the World Bank and the IMF. This naturally made the TNBs rather reckless in their lending policies, and the fruits of that recklessness are being reaped by the Third World countries.[7]

In the core countries of the OECD, the attention of most governments became centred on moderating inflation and improving the competitive position of their exports. The means chosen for doing this, first in the UK, then in the USA, and increasingly in other countries, was to try to moderate the rise of money wages, to keep real wages constant for some time, if possible, and to bring down the growth of money income. In many cases, such policies had the desired effect of bringing down the growth of real wages but they did not always improve competitiveness. For one thing, moderation of the rate of inflation and rise in the share of profits to national income attracted capital inflows and pushed up the external value of the currency, thus reducing international competitiveness. Moreover, there are several studies showing that regression of demand led to a slowdown not only of industrial growth but also of productivity growth – and in fact contributed considerably to a process of relative, if not absolute, de-industrialisation of such countries as the UK and even the USA (Singh, 1977; Helliwell, Sturn and Salou, 1985). These policies also contributed to rising unemployment. But the rising share of profits in a slowly growing GNP was welcomed by such bodies as the IMF and the OECD and clearly demonstrated the strength of aggressive capital trying to put down labour militancy. Such policies also merged naturally with the international stance of many governments and watchdog bodies such as the IMF and the World Bank that development aid that is meant merely to raise welfare levels by subsidising commercially unviable projects was to be discouraged, and only aid or rather loans that financed productive projects yielding profits to dynamic entrepreneurs would be welcomed. In effect, most development aid properly speaking was cut back in real terms, and the task of financing balance-of-payment deficits of major Third World governments was taken over by the TNBs, with disastrous consequences all round.

The deflationary objectives and policies of competitive devaluation of currencies within the core OECD region often ran counter to one another. Devaluation often produced higher rates of inflation in the short run, and unpredictable 'hot money' movements, and it took a long time for the desired effect to come through (Eltis, 1981; Buiter and Miller, 1981). In the UK and the USA as we have already noted, the strength of the financial sector created special problems. The interests of the financiers and the manufacturers (and in the case of the USA, the farmers as well) were often opposed in these countries. While financiers wanted a 'strong' dollar or a 'strong' pound to be supported, if necessary, with high interest rates, the manufacturers and exporters wanted a lower exchange value of the currency and lower interest rates. But, of course, if the domestic output contained a large fraction of imported inputs, devaluation did not at once produce an improved current balance (Buiter and Miller, 1981), and this acted as an additional argument in favour of the stance of the financiers.

The finding that devaluation often produced results which were contrary to traditional theory, viz., that it might worsen current account balance in the short run and the short run might get longer if expectations of further bouts of inflation and devaluation were entertained, was thought at one time to be applicable only to underdeveloped countries (cf. Cooper, 1973). In the higgledy-piggledy world of competitive jostling within the core OECD group, this disconcerting finding was found to be almost equally valid. But such findings did not lead to a real reversal of the 'monetarist' policies in those countries. Instead, the USA went on raising interest rates, running very large deficits (far exceeding $100 billion per year) and absorbing capital flows from all over the world, but especially from Japan, which emerged, along with the FRG, as the country with the largest current account surpluses. It is only in 1985–6 that the dollar began sliding against the yen and the continental European currencies and interest rates began to climb down as well. But unemployment remains at very high levels in practically all OECD countries except Japan. In spite of several favourable developments such as the moderation of the rate of inflation partly owing to the crash in primary product prices (see, for analysis of this link, Beckerman, 1985), and a considerable improvement in their terms of trade, in May 1986 the OECD projected an unchanged rate of unemployment in these countries for 1986 and 1987 (OECD, 1986). There is as yet no agreement about exchange rate parities, interest rate policies or policies to cut down the trade surpluses of the FRG and Japan.

It is unlikely, therefore, that in the near future there will be a radical change in the attitude of most OECD governments towards more developmental aid for the Third World, less protectionist policies against their exports or encouraging reflationary measures in countries reeling from balance-of-payments deficits and austerity measures imposed by the IMF and the TNB. The Third World countries have worse to reckon with than the *attitudes* of OECD governments in the international arena. It is to these other international problems damaging development efforts in those countries that we now turn.

## 9.4 THE INTERNATIONAL ENVIRONMENT FOR THIRD WORLD DEVELOPMENT IN THE 1980s

The drastic fall in primary product prices and the enormous external debt of many of the large Third World countries have rendered the international environment highly precarious for all but a handful of poor countries. The only exceptions are those few countries of East Asia which have already succeeded in changing their economic structure so that the contribution of manufacturing substantially outweighs that of primary products to their GNP. As we have noted already the second bout of raising of oil prices in 1978–9 was quickly nullified by the rise of prices of manufactured exports from the OECD countries. Moreover, since 1981, when the price of oil reached an all-time high at $36.3 per barrel, the price has inexorably slid downward. By the first quarter of 1986 it had fallen to $15 (OEC, 1986, pp. vii, 2) and it was still falling after that date. A decline in the price of oil by $11 per barrel between 1985 and 1986 is assumed to have benefited the OECD countries (after taking account of losses suffered by the oil producers in the OECD group) to the tune of $63 billion and impoverished the OPEC by $59 billion, thus effecting a major redistribution of income in favour of the advanced capitalist economies. The prices of non-oil primary commodities have also been sliding downward.

With the fall in the prices of primary commodities (including oil) the terms of trade of the OECD group are expected to improve in 1986 by between ½ and 1 per cent compared with 1985 (OECD, 1986, p. viii). For the group designated as 'industrial countries' (consisting mainly of the core OECD economies), the IMF staff have estimated that their terms of trade have improved every year from 1982 to 1986. The contributions of those improvements were 0.5, 0.4, 0.2, 0.4 and 0.8 percentage points of the aggregate national incomes of the industrial countries in 1982, 1983, 1984, 1985 and 1986 respectively (IMF, 1986, Table 2). Since these changes in terms of trade mean transfers of purchasing power from poorer countries, the adverse effects on the national incomes of the latter must be correspondingly magnified.[8]

The effects of the drastic fall in the terms of trade for most Third World countries (except for the tiny minority which chiefly export manufactured goods and import primary commodities) have been aggravated by several antecedent and concurrent factors. First, the Third World debt amounted to $800.5 billion at the end of 1985 and the service charges on that debt amounted to $114.4 billion. This has to be set against a continuous outflow of capital (as officially recognised, probably not including illegal private capital outflows) from these countries. This outflow came to $229.7 billion over the years 1981–5, *after* taking into account laboriously worked-out debt reschedulings so as to keep the countries from defaulting officially (Clairmonte and Cavanagh, 1986). That is, the debt has been prevented from growing even larger by forcing the heavily indebted countries to cut down on essential imports and forcing out an export surplus from them.

Second, and partly as a consequence of the debt servicing and debt rescheduling operations coupled with the decline in terms of trade, practically all the major Latin American countries have suffered negative rates of growth in their incomes per capita for several years running. So have most of the African economies. In the case of many of the poorest countries, rigidities of social structure and dislocations of ecology caused by sudden irruption of commercialisation had earlier stunted growth of production. The price fall of their main products and exportables has now further compounded the evil. Even what is produced cannot now be sold except at ruinously low prices. As we have noted, the pressure on primary producing Third World countries to export at whatever price they can get (because of their needs for importing essential goods and servicing their debt) tends to push their terms of trade further down. The continued subsidising of exports of farm products by affluent countries such as the USA or members of the European Community means that the produce of Third World countries has to take a further beating in world export markets. Subsidising of farm products by such a champion of 'free trade' as the US government has indeed provoked protests from even a relatively rich primary producing country as Australia.[9]

The IMF (increasingly followed by the World Bank as well) has preached policies of austerity, cutting down of public-sector deficits, and deregulation of economic activities. It has imposed such policies on the countries that have had to seek its assistance either for getting over balance of payments crises or meeting their debt obligations or rescheduling their debts. Such policies, when seriously pursued, have led to the actual shrinkage of national incomes in Third World countries along with a regressive redistribution of incomes towards the rich, thus compounding the problems of deficiency of demand for mass-consumption industries and for producer goods meant for equipping those industries.[10] One recurring complaint of the IMF–World Bank authorities and their advisors has been that Third World countries have favoured industry and discriminated against agriculture and that this has been one of the main causes of Third World ills. In such countries as India where many agricultural crops have long been supported by government subsidies for their inputs and price support policies, such complaints have never made such sense. It has been pointed out that even in the case of Africa, where agriculture has apparently fared very badly in most countries, the complaint has never been true for Kenya or Malawi, for example, and the economies of the latter have also suffered badly in the 1980s (Kydd and Hewitt, 1986; Mosley, 1986).[11]

Although the rates of inflation and interest have been coming down recently (as of August 1986) in the OECD countries, most Third World countries are too deeply mired in recession and balance-of-payment crises to be able to take advantage of such favourable developments. (To the extent that the decline in inflation rate is caused by the fall in primary product prices, primary producing Third World countries are really the sacrificial victims in this auspicious development!) In 1982, Mexico had to be 'rescued' from a situation in which she was about to default on her debt. Administration of the IMF medicine did nothing to lift up the economic condition in that country during the next four years. In June 1986, in the middle of another debt crisis, the Mexican Finance Minister resigned. The IMF agreed to 'more liberal' conditions which included a commitment to cut the budget deficit but not necessarily to zero; made provision for achivement of a positive rate of economic growth; and allowed the interest or debt service charges to be adjusted in accordance with the price of oil, which is now Mexico's biggest single export in terms of value.[12] However, such policies tinker only with the symptoms. They do nothing to remedy the rigidities of Mexican social structure nor to improve the bargaining position of primary producing countries *vis-à-vis* the affluent capitalist economies nor to ensure an uninterrupted process of industrialisation which will make Mexico less dependent on exports of primary products. In the case of Mexico, there is the special problem that the USA is just across the border, so that continued capital flight is almost a certainty. But with the best will in the world, structural adjustment loans extended by the IMF with the associated conditions of rational house management[13] will not do away with the debt problem of Mexico, Brazil, Peru or the Philippines, nor will they make them get on to a path of sustained industrialisation.

In the final section we turn to the success stories of development planning which in most cases also happen to be success stories of Third World industrialisation. We also make a case for defensive development planning as an alternative to the economy-shrinking policies preached and imposed by the IMF, TNBs and their backers among the governments of the advanced capitalist countries.

## 9.5 PRECONDITIONS AND IMPERATIVES OF DEVELOPMENT PLANNING

Development planning is not simply a matter of drawing up input–output tables, projecting consumption levels or juggling with social accounting matrices. It also requires right social institutions, flexibility in meeting external shocks, and an inducement mechanism that commits the main actors to long-term programmes of productive investment. The damaging of development plans by global recession, by the irresponsibility of many of the rulers of Third World countries and by the almost deliberate sabotaging of Third World efforts at achieving some degree of self-reliance by TNCs and TNBs has not negated the need for concerted action at a national level. Such action does require long-term development plans conceived in concrete terms but with sufficient flexibility built into the institutional structure. Even in a country which is as affluent as modern Japan, long-term projections and planning have been standard instruments of policy-making. As Morishima (1984, p. 252) has put it:

> In Japan it is frequently the Ministry of International Trade and Industry (MITI) which takes the lead in bringing together the Economic Planning Agency and other involved agencies from each government ministry, as well as banks, economic organizations and involved enterprises to look into and discuss which industries are to be developed as export industries, and what new industries are to be initiated. Such government-directed conferences of representatives of all sectors of the economy seem in the eyes of foreigners to be just like the board meetings of 'Japan Inc.' and are subject to severe criticism as joint conspiracies to give full play to 'Japan's egoism on the international state'. However, if these meetings are viewed, in the way in which *they should in essence be seen, as planning conferences*, to secure the most efficient use of capital, *such conferences are necessary to some degree or other in any country.* (Our italics)

Social rigidities and forcibly suppressed conflicts between classes and ruling groups in Third World countries lead to a situation where it becomes difficult to draw up a coherent plan and to implement it. If mercantile capital can thrive on shortages it can also play havoc with government plans by promoting speculative activities, by excess investment in particular sectors and by withdrawal of investment from other sectors. In the 1950s and 1960s economists often noted that many poor countries suffered from absorption problems. Social rigidities are indeed at the roots of their absorption problems. Long-term investment in mass-consumption goods is meagre, because the market for such goods is small; investment takes a long time to fructify because the needed inputs are not there, because suppliers try to obtain quasi-rents from artificially created shortages, because bureaucrats would not move without speed money. Technologies are not properly transferred because TNCs do not find it profitable to do so, because there is not adequate back-up investment in training and adaptive research, and because skilled manpower often migrates in response to the lure of lusher pastures in the USA or Europe.

Such problems do not negate the need for development planning. They underscore the fact that development planning requires as a precondition radical institutional reform – in particular, abolition of landlordism and the gearing of mercantile capital towards industrial investment rather than short-term speculation. Only those countries which have pursued the goal of rapid industrialisation effectively have been able to withstand the buffeting produced by international shocks during the last ten or fifteen years. China, South Korea and Taiwan are notable examples of countries where the industrialisation drive has been pursued with considerable success. China is a socialist society so it is not encumbered with mercantile capital, whereas South Korea and Taiwan are capitalist economies where merchants are very active indeed. There is moreover no parity between a country of continental dimensions such as China on the one hand and Taiwan and South Korea on the other, which are smaller than most provinces of China in both area and population.

In spite of these differences, the three countries share some important characteristics. First of all, in all the three countries, for very different historical reasons which we cannot go into here, landlordism was eradicated in the 1950s. Second, as already noted, all three countries adopted industrialisation as a major goal and set about purposely to attain it. Third, in spite of basic differences in property relations, class structures and political ideology, in all the three countries, the government has believed in coordinating and monitoring economic activities by using many direct instruments of guidance and control and has not left the pattern of economic activities to be directed by market forces alone. Taiwan and South Korea are no more shining examples of unfettered and unregulated market economies than China after Mao is an example of market socialism as envisaged in the Lange–Taylor model (Amsden, 1985; Chou, 1985; Bagchi, 1987).

South Korea, Taiwan and, to a lesser extent, China have been able to escape the effects of the adverse terms of trade of primary products, because they have emerged as major exporters of manufactured goods. Indeed, Taiwan is a major exporter of textiles and machine tools to the USA; South Korea of textiles, consumer electronics to the USA, and of cars to Canada; and China is an exporter of textiles and increasingly of other manufactured goods to the USA, the biggest single market in the world. For the small economies of South Korea and Taiwan, access to US and Japanese markets was crucial. But China developed as more or less a closed economy with rates of industrial growth of 10 per cent per annum even before the opening-up of the country in 1979. Since then she has used her developed economic base and her access to the US market to expand her exports rapidly not only to the USA but also to other markets. She has shopped widely for new technology but her social system and her widespread R. & D. network link industry or productive units in general with laboratories and universities to absorb imported technology on a wide front (Bagchi, 1987, Ch. 4). Similar comments would apply to the absorption of technology in South Korea.

What would be the place of development planning in countries where landlordism, illiteracy and non-market coercion of workers play important roles? Would it have to be scuttled in favour of 'free markets'? Fortunately or unfortunately, free markets cannot be obtained simply by abolishing all governmental regulations. Private regulations and private armies often take the place of State regulation and legal methods of coercion: they also, of course, supplement them. Abolishing controls might merely mean that landlords and merchants would take over. As we have argued in the second section, (pp. 120–3), in a society gripped by social rigidities mercantile activity often takes advantage of such rigidities rather than dissolves them in some miraculous fashion. Famines in many countries are as much the result of activities of merchants, of landlords diverting land to non-food cash crops, and of unbridled exploitation of the soil as of natural disasters or public bungling. Moreover, free markets without a firm basis in industrial development simply induce private domestic capital to fly abroad while TNBs acquire a stronger grip on an economy saddled with external debt. So in a world with frontiers and rigidities defensive development planning makes sense.[14] When that defensive development planning can be combined with a determined attack on landlordism and illiteracy, it can merge into real development planning. In a world of fast-changing technology and markets, if development planning aims at eventually absorbing the whole labour force in more productive activities as Goodwin (and many other leading economists) envisaged in the 1950s, more attention will have to be paid to stock-taking of technological options (cf. Ozawa, 1985) and to conscious design of institutions so that techniques are absorbed better and firms and markets operate in a competitive environment rather than thriving on restrictive practices and regulations. But doing away with development planning in poor countries may be a sure means of condemning millions of babies to an early death.

Balance-of-payment deficits have provided a major handle to the IMF, the TNBs and the OECD governments in general to interfere in the economic lives of Third World countries. One objective of defensive development planning would be to minimise such deficits, and to try to effect institutional changes within the economy so that merchants do not have either the power or the incentive to play on shortages and the poverty of ordinary people. If merchants can be induced to commit themselves to long-term investment projects, there will also be less tendency for capital to flow out. (We must remember that much of the outflow of capital from the Third World takes the shape of skilled manpower and the latter has been built up with considerable investment of scarce resources.) There will, of course, be situations where such institutional changes cannot be effected. Under those situations, market forces will also not produce economic growth but will produce the chaos that has been witnessed in many Latin American countries. Contemporary history does not support the IMF–World Bank view that the chaos is the product of efforts at development planning rather than the joint product of archaic social structures, TNB and TNC manipulations of Third World economies and the exertion of the power of the advanced capitalist countries in successfully turning the terms of trade and capital flows against the unwary Third World countries.[15]

**Notes**

1. For a convenient formalisation, see Cardoso, 1981.
2. In his *Capital*, vol. III, Marx had discussed the persistence of absolute ground rent as a barrier against the full development of capitalism in agriculture. But the practical consequences of landlord domination in perpetuating a situation of dependence of poor peasants and labourers on the landlords and rich peasants were brought by Lenin in the conquest of tsarist Russia. For a brief summary of Lenin's analysis and references to the literature see Bagchi, 1982, Ch. 6.
3. An analysis of some of these issues in the Indian context is presented in Patnaik, Rao and Sanyal, 1976; and Bose, 1985.
4. All $ figures mentioned from now on are US dollars.
5. On the problems caused by the use of the dollar as the dominant currency in face of a decline in US competitiveness, see Parboni, 1981. On the pursuit of incompatible goals in international economic policy and their consequences, see Taylor, 1985 and Vandenbrucke, 1985.
6. For vivid accounts of the activities of these TNCs and others, see George, 1977 and Morgan, 1980.
7. See Nunnenkamp, 1985, for a discussion of the so-called moral hazard problems posed for the TNBs lending to Third World countries.
8. Some doubts were raised earlier regarding the methodological and empirical basis of the Prebisch–Singer hypothesis of secularly declining terms of trade of Third World countries. But recent research by Spraos (1980, 1982) and Prabirjit Sarkar (1986a,b) has settled those doubts.

9. See, for example, *International Herald Tribune*, 26 August 1986.
10. For a critique of the theory and practice of IMF policy-making see Bagchi, 1986b.
11. It is ironical that India is currently being held up as a model of agricultural development, helped by multilateral aid, before the African countries. See *Economist*, 28 June 1986.
12. See *Economist*, 14 June 1986 and 19 July 1986; *International Herald Tribune*, 19 June 1986, and 3 July 1986.
13. For an analysis of the record of IMF-approved structural adjustment policies and their effects in the case of Malawi, see Kydd and Hewitt, 1986.
14. Cf. Ajit Singh's analysis of the Tanzanian development problem in Singh, 1986.
15. The author was a visitor at the Maison des Sciences de l'Homme, Paris, as Director d'Etudes Associe in the EHESS, when this paper was written.

**References**

AMSDEN, A. H. (1985) 'The State and Economic Development in Taiwan', in P. Evans, D. Rueschemeyer and T. Skocpol (eds), *Bringing the State Back In* (Cambridge: Cambridge University Press).

ARMSTRONG, P., A. GLYN, and J. HARRISON (1984) *Capitalism Since World War II: The Making and Breakup of the Great Boom* (London: Fontana).

BAGCHI, A. K. (1982) *The Political Economy of Underdevelopment* (Cambridge: Cambridge University Press).

BAGCHI, A. K. (1986a) 'Foreign Collaboration in Indian Industry', *Economic and Political Weekly*, vol. XXI, no. 2.

BAGCHI, A. K. (1986b) 'Theory and Practice of International Economic Policy: Implications of Sraffa's Prelude to a Critique of Economic Theory', *Economic and Political Weekly* (Review of Political Economy), 26 July.

BAGCHI, A. K. (1987) *Public Intervention and Industrial Restructuring in China, India and Republic of Korea* (New Delhi: ILO (ARTEP)).

BECKERMAN, W. (1985) 'How the Battle Against Inflation was Really Won', *Lloyds Bank Review* No. 155 (January).

BODDY, A., and J. CROTTY (1975) 'Class Conflict and Macro Policy: The Political Business Cycle', *Review of Radical Political Economics*, Spring, 1985.

BOSE A. (1985) 'Profit and Procurement' (mimeo.), unpublished paper presented at the seminar on State and Planning, Jawaharlal Nehru University, New Delhi, 6–8 December.

BOSWORTH, W. L. (1980) 'The Transfer of U.S. Technology Abroad', *Research Policy*, October.

BUITER, W. H., and M. MILLER (1981) 'Monetary Policy and International Competitiveness: The Problems of Adjustment' *Oxford Economic Papers* (New Series), vol. 33, July (Supplement).

CARDOSO, E. A. (1981) 'Food Supply and Inflation', *Journal of Development Economics*, vol. 8.

CHENERY, H. B. *et al.* (1971) *Studies in Development Planning* (Cambridge, Mass.: Harvard University Press).

CHOU, T.C. (1985) 'The Pattern and Strategy of Industrialization in Taiwan: Specialization and Offsetting Policy', *Developing Economics*, vol. XXIII, no. 2.

CLAIRMONTE, F. J. and J. CAVANAGH (1986) 'Third World Debt: The Approaching Holocaust', *Economic and Political Weekly*, vol. XXI, no. 31.

CONTRACTOR, F. J. (1980) 'The Composition of Licensing Fees and Arrangements as a Function of Economic Development of Technology Recipient Nations', *Journal of International Business Studies*, Winter.

COOPER, R. N. (1973) 'An Analysis of Currency Devaluation in Developing Countries', in M. B. Connolly and A. K. Swoboda (eds), *International Trade and Money* (London: Allen & Unwin).

ELTIS, W. (1981) 'The Fundamental Problem', *Oxford Economic Papers* (New Series), vol. 33, July (Supplement).

FEINSTEIN, C. H. (ed.) (1967) *Socialism, Capitalism and Economic Growth*, (Cambridge: Cambridge University Press).

GEORGE, S. (1977) *How the Other Half Dies: The Real Reasons for World Hunger* (Harmondsworth: Penguin).

GLYN, A. and B. SUTCLIFFE (1972) *British Capitalism: Workers and the Profit Squeeze* (Harmondsworth: Penguin).

GOODWIN, R. M. (1961) 'The Optimal Growth Path for an Underdeveloped Economy', *Economic Journal*, vol. 71, December.

GOODWIN, R.M. (1967) 'A Growth Cycle', in Feinstein, 1967.

HELLIWELL, J. F., P. H. STURM and G. SALOU (1985) 'International Comparison of the Sources of Productivity Slow-down 1973–1982', *European Economic Review*, vol. 28, no. 1–2.

IMF (1986) *World Economic Outlook April 1986: A Survey by the Staff of the International Monetary Fund* (Washington, D.C.: International Monetary Fund).

JANVRY, A. DE (1973) 'A Socioeconomic Model of Induced Innovations for Agricultural Development', *Quarterly Journal of Economics*, vol. 87, no. 3.

KALECKI, M. (1954) *The Theory of Economic Dynamics* (London: Allen & Unwin).

KALECKI, M. (1955) 'The Problem of Financing Economic Development', *Indian Economic Review*, February.

KINDLEBERGER, C. P. (1982) *Multinational Enterprises and Economic Analysis* (Cambridge: Cambridge University Press).

KRUGMAN, P. (1979) 'A Model of Innovation, Technology Transfer and the World Distribution of Income', *Journal of Political Economy*, vol. 87, no. 2.

KYDD, J. and A. HEWITT (1986) 'Limits to Recovery: Malawi After Six Years of Adjustment, 1980 to 1985', *Development and Change*, vol. 17, no. 3.

LINDER, S. B. (1961) *An Essay on Trade and Transformation* (Stockholm: Almquist and Wiksell).

MARGLIN, S. A. (1984) 'Growth, Distribution and Inflation: A Centennial Synthesis', *Cambridge Journal of Economics*, vol. 8, no. 2.

MORGAN, D. (1980) *Merchants of Grain* (Harmondsworth: Penguin).
MORGAN GUARANTY TRUST (1986) 'LDC Capital Flight', *World Financial Markets*, March (published by the Morgan Guaranty Trust Company).
MORISHIMA, M. (1984) *The Economics of Industrial Society* (Cambridge: Cambridge University Press).
MOSLEY, P. (1986) 'Agricultural Performance in Kenya Since 1970: Has the World Bank Got it Right?', *Development and Change*, vol. 17, no. 3.
NUNNENKAMP, P. (1985) 'Bank Lending to Developing Countries and Possible Solutions to International Debt Problems', *Kyklos*, vol. 38, no. 4.
OECD (1986) *OECD Economic Outlook May 1986* (Paris: Organisation for Economic Cooperation and Development).
OLSON, M. (1982) *The Rise and Decline of Nations* (New Haven, Conn.: Yale University Press).
OZAWA, T. (1985) 'Macroeconomic Factors Affecting Japan's Technology Inflows: The Postwar Experience', in N. Rosenberg and C. Frischtak (eds), *International Technology Transfer: Concepts, Measures and Comparisons* (New York: Praeger).
PARBONI, R. (1981) *The Dollar and its Rivals* (London: Verso).
PATNAIK, P., S. K. RAO and A. SANYAL (1976) 'The Inflationary Process: Some Theoretical Comments', *Economic and Political Weekly*, 23 October.
POSNER, M. V. (1961) 'International Trade and Technical Change', *Oxford Economic Papers* (New Series), vol. 13, October.
RAO, V. K. R. V. (1952) 'Investment, Income and the Multiplier in an Underdeveloped Economy, *Indian Economic Review*, February.
RESERVE BANK OF INDIA (1985) *Foreign Collaboration in Indian Industry: Fourth Survey Report* (Bombay: Reserve Bank of India).
ROWTHORN, R. E. (1977) 'Conflict, Inflation and Money', *Cambridge Journal of Economics*, vol. 1, no. 3.
ROWTHORN, R. E. (1980) *Capitalism, Conflict and Inflation* (London: Lawrence and Wishart).
SARKAR, P. (1986a) 'The Terms of Trade Experience of Britain since the 19th Century', *Journal of Development Studies*, October.
SARKAR, P. (1986b) 'The Singer–Prebish Thesis: A Statistical Evaluation', *Cambridge Journal of Economics*, December.
SEN, A. (1967) 'Terminal Capital and Optimal Savings', in Feinstein, 1967.
SEN, A. (1983) 'Development: Which Way Now?', *Economic Journal*, vol. 93, December.
SINGH, A. (1977) 'U.K. Industry and the World Economy: A Case of Deindustrialization?', *Cambridge Journal of Economics*, vol. 1, no. 2.
SINGH, A. (1986) 'Tanzania and the IMF: The Analytic of Alternative Adjustment Programmes', *Development and Change*, vol. 17, no. 3.
SPRAOS, J. (1980) 'The Statistical Debate on the Net Barter Terms of Trade Between Primary Commodities and Manufactures', *Economic Journal*, vol. 90, March.
SPRAOS, J. (1982) 'Deteriorating Terms of Trade and Beyond', *Trade and Development: An UNCTAD Review*, Winter.

TAYLOR, J. B. (1985) 'International Coordination in the Design of Macroeconomic Policy Rules', *European Economic Review*, vol. 28, nos 1–2.

TAYLOR, L. (1985) 'A Stagnationist Model of Economic Growth', *Cambridge Journal of Economics*, vol. 9, no. 4.

TOYE, J. (1985) '*Dirigisms* and Development Economics', *Cambridge Journal of Economics*, vol. 9, no. 1.

VANDENBRUCKE, F. (1985) 'Conflicts in International Economic Policy and World Recession', *Cambridge Journal of Economics*, vol. 9, no. 1.

VANEK, J. (1967) *Estimating Foreign Resource Needs for Economic Development* (New York: McGraw-Hill).

VERNON, R. (1966) 'International Investment and International Trade in the Product Cycle', *Quarterly Journal of Economics*, vol. 80, no. 2.

VERNON, R. (1979) 'The Product Cycle Hypothesis in a New International Environment', *Oxford Bulletin of Economics and Statistics*, vol. 41, November.

WEISSKOPF, T. E. (1979) 'Marxian Crisis and the Rate of Profit in the Postwar US Economy', *Cambridge Journal of Economics*, vol. 3, no. 4.

WORLD BANK (1985) 'The Outflow of Capital: For Some Countries it is Big', *The World Bank Research News*, vol. 6, no. 1.

# PART III
# Multisectoral Macrodynamics

# 10 Normalised General Coordinates and Vertically Integrated Sectors in a Simple Case[1]

Luigi L. Pasinetti

## 10.1 FOREWORD

Inter-industry economic analysis, whose roots go back to the works of François Quesnay and the classical economists (including Marx), has been recently rediscovered mainly through the works of Leontief (1951) and Sraffa (1960) – a rediscovery favoured by the development of computers in practical applications and by the spreading of matrix algebra in economic analysis. Inter-industry analysis has laid bare the interdependences among economic sectors, which are a basic feature of modern economic systems and at the same time are the source of endless analytical complications. For this reason, economic theorists have made several attempts at developing new analytical tools that may help to ease the complications.

In this paper I shall consider two of these new analytical tools, proposed by R. M. Goodwin (1974, 1976) and by myself (1973), respectively. They both aim at overcoming the difficulties of interdependence among the various sectors of an economy: in the case of Goodwin, by a transformation of the equation systems to normalised general coordinates, which eliminates interdependence completely; in my own case, by constructing vertically integrated sectors, which separate out and re-classify all processes, according to the final goods for which they are eventually working. The purpose of the paper is that of exploring connections and relations between the two approaches. This will be done by taking advantage of the properties of a particularly simple technology, which – while allowing the use of Goodwin's concepts – always maintains the analysis within the field of real nonnegative numbers, i.e. within a field where economic interpretation is intuitively obvious and immediate.

## 10.2 THE TWO USUAL SYSTEMS OF EQUATIONS FOR PRICES AND PHYSICAL QUANTITIES

Let us begin by supposing the usual (viable) economic system of the type represented by linear models, *à la* Sraffa (or *à la* Leontief), in which n commodities are produced by means of commodities and homogeneous labour. Following Goodwin we shall exclude the complications of joint production, which are not necessary for our purposes. We shall assume single production, i.e. we shall assume that each industry produces only one commodity. The price system may be represented by

$$\mathbf{p} = (1+\pi)\mathbf{p}\mathrm{A} + \mathrm{w}\mathbf{a} \tag{1}$$

and the physical quantity system by

$$\mathrm{q} = \mathbf{A}\mathbf{q}(1+\mathrm{g}) + \mathbf{y}\theta \tag{2}$$

Where A is the inter-industry coefficient (nonnegative, square) matrix; **a** is the (nonnegative, row) labour coefficient vector; **y** is the (nonnegative, column) per capita net income vector; **p** is the (row) price vector; **q** is the (column) per capita physical quantity vector; $\pi$, w, g, $\theta$ are scalars representing respectively, the rate of profit, the wage rate, the rate of population growth, and the proportion of the net income devoted to consumption.

Equation system (1) contains two degrees of freedom, which may be closed by fixing exogenously the rate of profits and by choosing a particular (single or composite) commodity, or the wage rate, as *numéraire*.

As far as the physical quantity system is concerned, it may be noticed that, by having defined the physical quantities in per capita terms (which allows us to drop all time subscripts, as per capita magnitudes remain constant on the steady-growth path, although the corresponding total magnitudes are growing), we have already implicitly introduced the employment equation:

$$\mathbf{a}\mathbf{q} = 1, \tag{3}$$

which, in each period of time, redefines the unit of measurement of labour in such a way as to equate total employment to unity, though employment is of course increasing through time. Moreover, the rate of growth of population g is taken as exogenously given.

But there is one further constraint. For simplicity we have made no distinction between labour force and population. Now population is exogenously given. From the employment point of view, this means in fact imposing full employment i.e. it means introducing an equality between the labour requirements of the system and the exogenously given labour force. (In other terms we may say that we consider the whole system of equations as a set of relations that must be satisfied in order to keep full employment over time.) The system is therefore over-determinate. One magnitude must give way; and this can be one of the components of vector **y**, which must be appropriately defined.

Now vector **y** is defined as expressing those per capita physical quantities that the average consumer chooses to consume in a stationary situation (defined as the one where $g=0$, and thus $\theta=1$, consumption coinciding with net national income). Obviously not all components of vector **y** can be arbitrarily chosen: at least one of them must be left free to be determined by the technical potential of the system, i.e. the *proportions* among the components of **y** are free to be determined by consumers' choices but not their absolute level. This makes the system of equations determinate at $g=0$ (where $\theta=1$). Once vector **y** has been determined at this point, the level of consumption at higher levels of g ($g>0$) will be expressed by $\theta$ decreasing below 1, within the interval:

$$0 \leqslant \theta \leqslant 1 \tag{4}$$

This also implies, to maintain economic sense, that g cannot be greater than that level (call it $g=G$), at which $\theta$ becomes zero.

## 10.3 GOODWIN'S REFORMULATION IN TERMS OF NORMALISED COORDINATES

Goodwin has proposed an interesting reformulation of the two systems of equations represented in the previous section. Suppose the coefficient matrix A to be such as to ensure the existence of n distinct eigenvalues $\lambda_1, \lambda_2, \ldots, \lambda_n$. This means that, for any given matrix A, we can immediately formulate:

(i) a diagonal matrix $\hat{\lambda}$, which has the n (distinct) eigenvalues on its main diagonal;
(ii) a square matrix E of the n linearly independent, right (physical quantity) eigenvectors;
(iii) a square matrix F of the n linearly independent, left (price) eigenvectors.
(iv) a normalisation rule by which $EF = I$, and therefore $F = E^{-1}$

The two equations systems (1) and (2) may therefore simply be re-written as follows:

$$\mathbf{p}' = w\mathbf{a}' + (1+\pi)p'\hat{\lambda} \tag{5}$$

$$q' = \hat{\lambda}\mathbf{q}'(1+g) + \mathbf{y}'\theta \tag{6}$$

where: $\mathbf{p}' = \mathbf{p}E$, $\mathbf{q}' = E^{-1}\mathbf{q}$, $\hat{\lambda} = E^{-1}AE$, $\mathbf{a}' = \mathbf{a}E$, $\mathbf{y}' = E^{-1}\mathbf{y}$.

The components of $\mathbf{p}'$ may be called eigen-prices; the components of $\mathbf{q}'$ eigen-quantities; the components of $\mathbf{y}'$ eigen-net products; the components of $\mathbf{a}'$ eigen-labour coefficients. They are all, clearly, linear combinations of the corresponding magnitudes in the original systems. The system has been transformed, from its own original coordinates, to another set of 'normalised general coordinates' – as Goodwin has called them – which are such as to make prices and quantities orthogonal to each other, since $E\,E^{-1} = I$.

There is of course the difficulty that we are no longer sure, on these coordinates, to be dealing with real numbers. In general only the highest of the eigenvalues and the two eigenvectors (left and right) associated with it surely contain real, nonnegative, numbers. All the others may contain complex numbers, to which it is hard to attribute any economic meaning.

But Goodwin points out that we may well use the normalised coordinates, when they are helpful, to carry out our elaborations. Then we can always transform these magnitudes back to their original coordinates, where they can be given their usual economic interpretation.

What is really remarkable is that, on the normalised coordinates, the technology matrix, which is usually so complex, is reduced to a simple diagonal matrix. In these terms, all interdependences disappear and each commodity (each eigen-commodity), besides entailing a labour (an eigen-labour) coefficient, is simply related to itself through one simple self-coefficient. All the eigen-commodities take up the analytical characteristics of Ricardo's 'corn' or, if we like, of Sraffa's 'standard commodity', with all well-known analytical simplifications attached to such concepts.

## 10.4 A REFORMULATION IN TERMS OF VERTICALLY INTEGRATED SECTORS

Another reformulation of the same system may be carried out by following another strand (see Pasinetti, 1973). This reformulation consists in logically constructing, behind each final good, a vertically integrated sector that resolves all intermediate goods simply in terms of one physical unit of capital and one physical unit of labour.

By defining:

$$H = A(I - A)^{-1} = (I - A)^{-1}A$$

$$\mathbf{v} = \mathbf{a}[I - A]^{-1}$$

$$\mathbf{z} = [I - A]^{-1}\mathbf{y}$$

equation systems (1) and (2) may be re-written as

$$\mathbf{p} = w\mathbf{v} + \pi\mathbf{p}H \tag{7}$$

$$\mathbf{q} = \mathbf{z}\theta + H\mathbf{q}g \tag{8}$$

This reformulation yields a few surprisingly compact concepts. Each equation of (7) expresses each price as a very simple sum of one physical quantity of labour (multiplied by the wage rate) and one physical unit of capital (multiplied by its price and the rate of profits), as vector $\mathbf{v}$ represents the vertically integrated physical labour coefficients and the n columns of matrix H represent the n physical units of vertically integrated productive capacities. The whole network of inter-industry relations behind the price system is thus collapsed into two physical magnitudes – labour and capital. Similarly, each equation (8) expresses each physical quantity produced simply as a sum of two addenda, representing respectively everything that physically goes (directly and indirectly) into final consumption and everything that physically goes (directly and indirectly) into the expansion of productive capacity (i.e. into net investments).

## 10.5 A VERY SIMPLE (DIAGONAL) TECHNOLOGY

It is not easy to put the two re-formulations considered above into relation with each other. Yet we can have a glimpse at the relations between the two if we take advantage of the properties of a particularly simple technology.

Suppose an economic system similar in all respects to the one considered so far, except that its coefficient matrix A has the particular form of containing zero elements everywhere, except on its main diagonal, i.e.:

$$A = \hat{\lambda} \tag{9}$$

This means that each of the n commodities in the economic system simply requires, to be produced, an input of itself, besides of course a labour input. The technology matrix (9), in this case, is real, nonnegative, nondegenerate, and shows explicitly, on its diagonal, all its eigenvalues (which are, by assumption, all real and positive). As may immediately be realised, this is a particular case in which the usual coordinates come to coincide with the normalised (or orthogonal) coordinates. The actual system is already on Goodwin's coordinates. Eigenvalues coincide with self-coefficients, eigenprices p′ coincide with usual prices p, eigenquantities q′ coincide with usual quantities q. Therefore we need not reformulate the two equation systems. Expressions (5) and (6) represent in this case the *actual* system (and of course also represents its orthogonal coordinate transformation, which coincides with it).

In this case, we can directly 'see', with reference to an actual system (albeit a simple one) all characteristics that Goodwin shows in general, but with reference to a hypothetical economic system represented by complex numbers. The economic system shows absolutely no interdependence. Each sector is self-sufficient. Each commodity though different from all the others, is a 'corn'-type commodity. Each of the n commodities produced in the economic system has the characteristics of Ricardo's 'corn' – there are, in fact n types of 'corn'. Each production process is simply represented by a self-coefficient and a labour coefficient. The 'surplus' is also 'corn', to be divided physically into two parts: 'replacement' corn and surplus 'corn', which in its turn can be physically divided in any proportion, between wages and profits (and between consumption and net investment).

## 10.6 THE SOLUTIONS

If we were to solve systems (1) and (2), after inserting the simple technology (9) we would immediately (i.e. without applying any transformation) obtain expressions in all similar to those of Goodwin (1974, 1976), with the important difference, however, that they would all be in terms of real, nonnegative, numbers, which have an immediate economic meaning.

But we can go one step further and find out the same solutions in terms of vertically integrated concepts.[2]

First of all, let us specify our basic matrices in details. Writing them up in extensive form, we have:

$$A=\hat{\lambda}=\begin{bmatrix} \lambda_1 & & & & & \\ & \lambda_2 & & & & \\ & & \cdot & & & \\ & & & \cdot & & \\ & & & & \cdot & \\ & & & & & \lambda_n \end{bmatrix}$$

$$[I-A]^{-1}=\begin{bmatrix} (1-\lambda_1)^{-1} & & & & & \\ & (1-\lambda_2)^{-1} & & & & \\ & & \cdot & & & \\ & & & \cdot & & \\ & & & & \cdot & \\ & & & & & (1-\lambda_n)^{-1} \end{bmatrix}$$

$$\mathbf{v}=\mathbf{a}[I-A]^{-1}=[a_1(1-\lambda_1)^{-1},\ a_2(1-\lambda_2)^{-1},\ \ldots,\ a_n(1-\lambda_n)^{-1}]$$

$$\mathbf{z}=[I-A]^{-1}\mathbf{y}=[(1-\lambda_1)^{-1}y_1,\ (1-\lambda_2)^{-1}y_2,\ \ldots,\ (1-\lambda_n)^{-1}y_n]$$

$$H=\begin{bmatrix} \lambda_1(1-\lambda_1)^{-1} & & & & & \\ & \lambda_2(1-\lambda_2)^{-1} & & & & \\ & & \cdot & & & \\ & & & \cdot & & \\ & & & & \cdot & \\ & & & & & \lambda_n(1-\lambda_n)^{-1} \end{bmatrix}$$

$$[I-\pi H]^{-1}=\begin{bmatrix} (1-\lambda_1)(1-\lambda_1-\pi\lambda_1)^{-1} & & & & \\ & (1-\lambda_2)(1-\lambda_2-\pi\lambda_2)^{-1} & & & \\ & & \cdot & & \\ & & & \cdot & \\ & & & & (1-\lambda_n)(1-\lambda_n-\pi\lambda_n)^{-1} \end{bmatrix}$$

By a straightforward substitution of these particular expressions into (7), (8) we obtain:

$$p_i = wa_i/(1-\lambda_i-\pi\lambda_i) \tag{10}$$

$$q_i = y_i\theta/(1-\lambda_i-g\lambda_i), \qquad i=1, 2, \ldots, n \tag{11}$$

As may be observed, the solutions for prices and quantities reveal a remarkable formal similarity. The wage component ($wa_i$) of each price $p_i$ is related to the price exactly in the same way as consumption of each commodity ($\theta y_i$) is related to the corresponding total quantity produced ($q_i$).

Very clearly, prices depend on technology and the distribution of income. When $\pi=0$, each price $p_i$ is proportional to $a_i\ (1-\lambda_i)^{-1}$, which is the vertically integrated labour coefficient, or direct and indirect labour required by the corresponding commodity. And when $\pi=g$, each price $p_i$ is proportional to $a_i(1-\lambda_i-g\lambda_i)^{-1}$, which represents direct, indirect and (as I have called it – see Pasinetti, 1977, 1981) hyper-indirect labour, required by the corresponding commodity. These are the features of a pure labour theory of value, both in its static and in its 'dynamic' version (see also Goodwin, 1974).

We can in fact represent all alternative income distributions in physical terms, by using any one of the n commodities. Take any commodity i, and consider the per capita net product in terms of that commodity. This clearly is $(1-\lambda_i)/a_i$, i.e. the reciprocal of $a_i/(1-\lambda_i)$, the latter representing the amount of direct and indirect labour in each unit of commodity i. By now putting:

$$p_i(1-\lambda_i)/a_i = 1 \tag{12}$$

we simply adopt the per capita net product in terms of commodity i as the *numéraire* of the price system. This also implies:

$$1 \geqslant w_i \geqslant 0 \tag{13}$$

where $w_i$ is the wage rate expressed in terms of the per capita net product of commodity i. Hence, in this way, the wage rate also coincides with the *proportion* of per capita net product, that goes to the workers. By substituting into (10) we obtain:

$$\pi = (1 - w_i)(1 - \lambda_i)/\lambda_i \tag{14}$$

which is the usual *linear* relation between $\pi$ and w (see Sraffa, 1960, p. 22).

We can use *any* commodity to obtain relation (14). In other words, any of the n commodities has the characteristics of Sraffa's 'standard commodity'. But of course, if the whole system is to be considered together, the maximum of the $\lambda_i$s (the maximum eigenvalue – call it $\lambda_m$) will put an upper limit – call it:

$$\Pi = (1 - \lambda_m)/\lambda_m \tag{15}$$

– to the rate of profit. As soon as $\pi > \Pi$, the price of that commodity that corresponds to $\lambda_m$ would become negative and the system of the n commodities which we consider could no longer, as a whole, be accepted as having economic meaning.

We may note that the physical quantity system gives rise to similar expressions. In particular, it is possible to set up a *linear* relation between g and $\theta$ (i.e. between accumulation and consumption) in terms of any commodity. Here, by the definition already given of vector y (i.e. that vector that expresses per capita demand for consumption, at $g = 0$, where $\theta = 1$), we have:

$$q_i = y_i/(1 - \lambda_i) \tag{16}$$

and therefore, substituting into (11),

$$g = (1 - \theta)(1 - \lambda_i)/\lambda_i \tag{17}$$

a linear relation between g and $\theta$, for which the same remarks made for (14) hold. The rate of growth for the system as a whole has an upper limit, call it G, set through the highest among the $\lambda_i$s (or maximum eigenvalue $\lambda_m$):

$$G = (1 - \lambda_m)/\lambda_m \tag{18}$$

which is the same as (15). For $g > G$, $\theta$ would become negative and this could not be accepted, as it would have no economic meaning.

It is interesting to note that, owing to absolute lack of interdependence among the sectors, the solutions for the two limiting cases represented by (15) and (18) would imply zero prices and zero quantities respectively, for all commodities except the one corresponding to the coefficient $\lambda_m$.

In other words, a uniform rate of profit (or else a uniform rate of growth) gives rise to solution with all positive prices (or else all positive physical quantities) as long as $\pi < \Pi$ (or else $g < G$), because wages (or else consumption) absorb the surplus left over after distributing profits (or else after providing for accumulation). But at the singular point $\pi = \Pi$ (or else $g = G$), all prices (or else all quantities) other than the one relating to the commodity with the highest self-coefficient, will have to be zero, to ensure compatibility among all relations.

There is of course an alternative way of expressing the same relations in physical terms, suggested by Goodwin, who prefers to look at them in terms of how *total* production gets distributed between wages, profits and replacements (and between consumption, net investments and replacements). By taking (10) and (11) and dividing through by $p_i$ and $q_i$ respectively, we obtain

$$\lambda_i + a_i w_i / p_i + \pi\lambda_i = 1$$

$$\lambda_i + \theta\lambda_i / q_i + g\lambda_i = 1$$

or, after calling

$$a_i w_i / p_i = \gamma_i$$

unit labour cost, and

$$\theta y_i / q_i = \delta_i$$

unit consumption, we may write:

$$\lambda_i + \gamma_i + \pi\lambda_i = 1 \tag{19}$$

$$\lambda_i + \delta_i + g\lambda_i = 1, \qquad i = 1, 2, \ldots, n \tag{20}$$

which are Goodwin's expressions.[3]

If rate of profits $\pi$ is given exogenously, (19) expresses for each single commodity, the proportions of its value which are accounted for by replacements, wages and profits, respectively. And similarly, if rate of growth g is exogenously given, (20) expresses, in physical terms, for each single commodity, the proportions of its total quantity produced that go to replacement, consumption and new investments, respectively. In the case considered here of course, all magnitudes are real, nonnegative numbers, and have an immediate economic meaning.

## 10.7 INTERDEPENDENCE THROUGH OVERALL EFFECTIVE DEMAND

There is one feature of Goodwin's formulations that might seem to have been lost in the analysis associated with simplified technology (9); this is the necessity that the equations here considered actually form a *system*. In Goodwin's general formulation the equations undoubtedly do form a *system*: for, although the diagonal eigen-technology makes each single eigen-industry dependent only upon itself, yet each eigen-industry is a linear combination of *all* industries in the whole economy. Technical interdependence disappears from the formulations, but remains in the background.

With simple technology (9) this is not so. Each industry is technologically (not only formally, but actually) dependent only upon itself. From a purely technological point of view, *any* industry, or group of industries, could be eliminated, and yet the remaining industries, by themselves and without the eliminated industry (or industries), would still form a (smaller but determinate) system with as many unknowns as there are equations.

It might in fact look as if equations (1) or (2), when (9) holds, do not form a system at all, but only a juxtaposition of a series of entirely independent equations.

However, this is not exactly the case. For, although the equations show no *technical* interdependence, the economic system is still linked together through the channel of overall demand.

The point is important and deserves further attention. A modern economic system is organised through extensive division of labour. This means that workers (and industries) specialise in producing a very small range of goods and services, sometimes even only a fraction of a good or of a service. This is the way to achieve high productivity. But then, each person contributing to any production will receive his/

her remuneration in terms of a certain amount of undifferentiated purchasing power over *all* commodities, and he/she will actually buy a 'basket' of commodities, composed of practically all goods and services. Thus, even when the production processes are not interdependent on the side of technology, they still remain interdependent on the side of *demand*. This means that, by itself, demand for all the produced goods and services links all the production processes together and therefore makes of them a system – a set of relations that has a sense only if it is considered as a whole.

Let me illustrate the point in a different way. From mere inspection of the technical coefficients, one might be tempted to say: 'Let us eliminate the industry with the highest self-coefficient ($\lambda_m$) and thus raise the upper limit to the rate of profit and to the rate of growth for the remaining industries.' But this would make no sense. If for example industry m produces a commodity that is demanded by all, even if in a small amount, for example a commodity that is absolutely necessary for the subsistence of all people, then that commodity will have to be produced. The whole system will depend on it (through the channel of demand), even if no other production process requires it as an input. This is of course an extreme case. But the channel of final demand links together the various processes in all cases, including those of nonnecessary goods.

In our formulation, there is something more specific – there is an overall constraint put on total effective demand by the requirement of full employment. To see it clearly, let us concentrate on time period t and on the physical quantity system, and multiply both sides of all equations by the total amount of labour N(t) – a scalar. By calling $Q(t) = qN(t)$, the equations system will appear as:

$$\left\{ \begin{bmatrix} I & 0 \\ 0 & 1 \end{bmatrix} - \begin{bmatrix} (1+\mathbf{g})A & \theta y \\ \mathbf{a} & 0 \end{bmatrix} \right\} \begin{bmatrix} Q(t) \\ N(t) \end{bmatrix} = \begin{bmatrix} 0 \\ 0 \end{bmatrix} \tag{21}$$

which is a system framed according to Leontief's closed model. Formally (21) is a homogeneous system of equations. Therefore, in order to assure non-null (i.e. economically meaningful) solutions, a necessary condition must hold. The determinant of the coefficient-matrix must be null, i.e.

$$\det \left\{ \begin{bmatrix} I & 0 \\ 0 & 1 \end{bmatrix} - \begin{bmatrix} (1+g)A & \theta y \\ a & 0 \end{bmatrix} \right\} = 0 \tag{22}$$

This necessary condition precisely represents the overall full employment condition. The technologically simple case (9) has the advantage of yielding a condition (22) which is particularly helpful in making us see immediately the relations that are involved. As may easily be checked, in the case (9), condition (22) becomes:

$$\sum_{i=1}^{n} (\theta y_i)[a_i/(1-\lambda_i-g\lambda_i)]=1 \tag{23}$$

This expression may be regarded as a sum of n addenda, each of which referring to each of the commodities produced. Each addendum has a very precise and straightforward economic meaning. What in (23) has been included in the first brackets is the per capita demand coefficient for consumption of commodity i, and what has been included in the square brackets is the vertically hyper-integrated labour coefficient for the same commodity, $i=1, 2, \ldots, n$. Expression (23) may in other words be regarded as a sum of binomials, each of which is the product of a demand coefficient and a labour coefficient. Its significance is that, through overall demand, it links together all production processes and thus the whole economic system!

I have had the opportunity elsewhere (see Pasinetti, 1965, 1981) of investigating the economic meaning, and of pointing out the important features, of necessary condition (23), which expresses in fact a macroeconomic condition on overall effective demand for keeping full employment over time. This condition obviously relates, in an immediate way, to Keynesian analysis. What is remarkable here is the simplicity with which these concepts are made to emerge, thanks to the particular properties of diagonal technology (9).

The message is clear – technology is not the only channel that makes the various sections of modern economic systems interdependent. There is another, symmetrical, and equally important channel: overall effective demand.

**Notes**

1. Financial help from a research grant of Ministero Pubblica Istruzione, Rome, is gratefully acknowledged.
2. Note that the solutions of (7), (8) may be expressed as:

$$\mathbf{p}=w\mathbf{v}[I-\pi H]^{-1}$$

$$\mathbf{q}=[I-gH]^{-1}\mathbf{z}\theta$$

3. See, for example, Goodwin, 1974, pp. 27–8. Actually, expressions (19) and (20) are even simpler than Goodwin's, because, following Sraffa, wages are here considered as paid *post factum*, while in Goodwin, following Marx, they are considered as paid in advance.

**References**

GOODWIN, R. M. (1974) 'The Use of Normalized General Coordinates in Economic Analysis', in Ashok Mitra (ed.) *Economic Theory and Planning: Essays in Honour of A. K. Das Gupta* (Calcutta: Oxford University Press) pp. 26–38.

GOODWIN, R. M. (1976) 'Use of Normalized General Coordinates in Linear Value and Distribution Theory', in K. Polenske and J. Skolka (eds), *Advances in Input–Output Economics* (Cambridge, Mass.: Ballinger Publ. Co.).

LEONTIEF, WASSILY W. (1951) *The Structure of American Economy, 1919–1939*, 2nd edn (New York: Oxford University Press).

PASINETTI, LUIGI L. (1965) 'A New Theoretical Approach to the Problems of Economic Growth', *Pontificiae Academiae Scientiarum Scripta Varia*, repr. in *The Econometric Approach to Development Planning* (Amsterdam: North-Holland).

PASINETTI, LUIGI L. (1973) 'The Notion of Vertical Integration in Economic Analysis', in *Metroeconomica*, vol. XXV, pp. 1–29; reprinted in L. L. Pasinetti (ed.), *Essays on the Theory of Joint Production* (London: Macmillan) 1980.

PASINETTI, LUIGI L. (1977) *Lectures on the Theory of Production* (London: Macmillan).

PASINETTI, LUIGI L. (1981) *Structural Change and Economic Growth – A Theoretical Essay on the Dynamics of the Wealth of Nations* (Cambridge: Cambridge University Press).

SRAFFA, PIERO (1960) *Production of Commodities by Means of Commodities – Prelude to a Critique of Economic Theory* (Cambridge: Cambridge University Press).

# 11 A Comparison Between Goodwin's Normalised General Coordinates and Pasinetti's Vertical Integration Methods

Terenzio Cozzi

## 11.1

There is always a conflict between macroeconomic aggregation and sectoral interdependence. The former makes for simplicity, the latter for realism. Is it possible not to sacrifice one most valuable aim to the other?

Two proposals have been put forth: Goodwin (1976, 1983) suggested the use of the normalised coordinates; Pasinetti (1965, 1977, 1981) that of the vertically integrated sectors. Both transform the original (observed) sectors to new ones defined in such a way as to become independent of each other. The transformations take full account of general interdependence. But, once they are performed, the new sectors are completely separated and can be analysed one at a time.

The aim of this paper is to compare the methods of Goodwin and Pasinetti. At first sight, they appear to be very different. But both encounter some difficulties in giving an exact solution to models in which the sectors' long-run growth rates are unequal. This does not mean that in the absence of exact solutions you can do nothing. For many problems the approximate ones are quite sufficient.

## 11.2

Let us consider the Goodwin's model as expounded in Goodwin

(1976) and reprinted in Goodwin (1983). In his notation, the original system is:

$$[I-(1+g)A]\mathbf{Q}_o=(1+g)\gamma\mathbf{C}_o \tag{1}$$

where $\mathbf{Q}_o$ is the output vector, A the square coefficient matrix, g the unique growth rate, $\mathbf{C}_o$ a given consumption vector, and $\gamma$ its scale factor. The value system is:

$$\mathbf{P}_o[I-(1+\pi)A]=w\mathbf{B}_o^l \tag{2}$$

where $\mathbf{P}_o$ is the price vector, $\pi$ the unique profit rate, w the money wage rate, and $\mathbf{B}_o^l$ the vector of direct labour inputs. Wages are assumed to be paid *post factum* to make easier the comparison with Pasinetti.

Under the Goodwin's assumptions on A, it is possible to transform the system to normalised general coordinates. Let $MAM^{-1}=\hat{\lambda}$, where $\hat{\lambda}$ is the eigenvalues diagonal matrix, M and $M^{-1}$ the matrices of value and output eigenvectors. Hence, by letting $\mathbf{P}M=\mathbf{P}_o$; $\mathbf{B}^lM=\mathbf{B}_o^l$; $M^{-1}\mathbf{Q}=\mathbf{Q}_o$; $M^{-1}\mathbf{C}=\mathbf{C}_o$, the system is transformed to:

$$[I-(1+g)\hat{\lambda}]\mathbf{Q}=(1+g)\gamma\mathbf{C} \tag{3}$$

$$\mathbf{P}[I-(1+\pi)\hat{\lambda}]=w\mathbf{B}^l \tag{4}$$

with sectors completely separated.

But, if we drop the assumption of a single g, the results are no longer so neat. In fact, the output system (1) should be written as:

$$[I-A(I+\hat{g})]\mathbf{Q}_o=(I+\hat{g})\gamma\mathbf{C}_o \tag{5}$$

where $\hat{g}$ is the growth rates diagonal matrix. Hence, we have to diagonalise $A(I+\hat{g})$. Assume that $NA(I+\hat{g})N^{-1}=\hat{\mu}$. But then, in general, $\hat{\mu}\neq\hat{\lambda}(I+\hat{g})$ with $\hat{\lambda}$ eigenvalues of A and independent of $\hat{g}$. In economic terms, this means that when the different sectors grow at different rates the composite commodities (i.e. the Goodwin's eigen-goods) depend on the whole set of growth rates.

Clearly, it is possible to use the Pasinetti assumption (Pasinetti, 1981, pp. 82–3) that time is divided into stretches of a given length within which, for each sector, the growth rate $g_i$ remains constant. Then, passing from one stretch of time to the next, $g_i$ changes, remaining then constant again for another stretch of time. This procedure overcomes most of the difficulties. But, at the points of time in which the $g_i$s change, it is necessary to rework the transformations, i.e. to define the new eigengoods.

For the value system, there is no other problems if it is assumed that the sectoral profit rates are equal to the sectoral growth rates. In this case, one is considering the theoretical construction that Pasinetti called the 'natural economic system' (Pasinetti, 1981, Ch. VII) from the analysis of which many interesting conclusions can be drawn. But, for any other hypothesis on the profit rates, including one of their equality among sectors, the transformations diagonalising the value and the output system are different. This means that the eigenprices are not the prices of the eigengoods.

## 11.3

Let us consider now the model developed by Pasinetti (1981). Assume, for the sake of comparison with Goodwin, that there is only circulating capital and, for the moment, that g is unique. The Pasinetti model can be written as:

$$\mathbf{X} = \mathbf{c}\mathrm{L} \tag{6}$$

$$\mathbf{X}_k = \mathrm{g}\mathbf{X}$$

$$\mathrm{L} = \mathbf{v}\mathbf{X} + \mathbf{v}_k\mathbf{X}_k$$

where $\mathbf{X}$ is the vector of production of the consumption goods, $\mathbf{X}_k$ that of the corresponding (circulating) capital goods, L is a scalar denoting employment, $\mathbf{c}$ the consumption vector per employee, $\mathbf{v}$ and $\mathbf{v}_k$ the vectors of direct and indirect labour content of the productions.

As assumed by Pasinetti, one unit of the final consumption in the i-th Pasinetti sector contains $(I-A)^{-1}\mathbf{u}_i$ units of the original goods of the system $\mathbf{Q}_o$.[1] One unit of the i-th investment good (circulating capital only) contains $H^i = A(I-A)^{-1}\mathbf{u}_i$ units of the original goods. Hence, in the original $\mathbf{Q}_o$ system, the Pasinetti model is equivalent to the following:

$$\mathbf{Q}_o = \mathbf{Q}_1 + \mathbf{Q}_2 \tag{7}$$
$$\mathbf{Q}_1 = (I - A)^{-1}Y$$
$$\mathbf{Q}_2 = gA(I - A)^{-1}Y$$
$$Y = \mathbf{c}_o L$$
$$L = \mathbf{v}\mathbf{Q}_1 + \mathbf{v}_k \mathbf{Q}_2$$

where $\mathbf{Q}_1$ and $\mathbf{Q}_2$ correspond to $\mathbf{X}$ and $\mathbf{X}_k$ of (6) and $(I - A)^{-1}\mathbf{c}_o = \mathbf{c}$. Since, according to Pasinetti,

$$\mathbf{v} = \mathbf{a}_{[n]}(I - A)^{-1} \tag{8}$$
$$\mathbf{v}_k = \mathbf{v}A$$

where $\mathbf{a}_{[n]}$ is the row vector corresponding to the $\mathbf{B}_0^{!}$ of Goodwin, it is easy to show that:

$$L = \mathbf{a}_{[n]}\mathbf{Q}_o \tag{9}$$

as it should be.

But, from the first three equations of (7), we see that

$$\mathbf{Q}_o = (I - A)^{-1}Y + gA(I - A)^{-1}Y \tag{10}$$

from which – taking into account that, under the usual assumptions on A, we have that $A(I - A)^{-1} = (I - A)^{-1}A$ as it can be seen by expanding in power series $(I - A)^{-1}$ – we can finally obtain:

$$\mathbf{Q}_o = A\mathbf{Q}_o + gAY + Y \tag{11}$$

which is rather different from the usual models like (1). The striking difference is not in the fact that for final consumption we have Y instead of $(1 + g)Y$. This can be accounted for quite easily. The main difference is that for investment we have gAY instead of $gA\mathbf{Q}_o$. This fact will produce an unpleasant consequence, as we shall see later on.

No problems arise with the value system. In fact, according to Pasinetti, we have:

$$\mathbf{P} = w\mathbf{v} + \pi\mathbf{P}_k \tag{12}$$
$$\mathbf{P}_k = \mathbf{P}A(I - A)^{-1}$$

the first equation expressing the price of the consumption goods (wages plus profits on the unit of capacity utilised), the second the price of the capital goods. Therefore:

$$\mathbf{P} = w\mathbf{v} + \pi\mathbf{P}A(I - A)^{-1} \tag{13}$$

and, taking account of (8),

$$\mathbf{P}[I - \pi A(I - A)^{-1}] = w\mathbf{a}_{[n]}(I - A)^{-1} \tag{14}$$

from which, after post-multiplication by $(I - A)$ and rearrangements, we get:

$$\mathbf{P}[I - (1 + \pi)A] = w\mathbf{a}_{[n]} \tag{15}$$

which is equivalent to (2) once considered that here $\mathbf{P} = \mathbf{P}_o$, by definition, and $\mathbf{a}_{[n]}$ is the Pasinetti notation for $\mathbf{B}^l$.

In conclusion, the value system (15) is equivalent to the traditional one; the output system (11) is not. One consequence of this fact is worth mentioning. Let us assume that all profits are invested and all wages are consumed. This implies that $\mathbf{P}_o Y = w\mathbf{a}_{[n]}\mathbf{Q}_o$. Now, if (11) is pre-multiplied by $\mathbf{P}_o$ and (15) is post-multiplied by $\mathbf{Q}_o$, after some rearrangements it is possible to obtain:

$$g\mathbf{P}_o AY = \pi\mathbf{P}_o A\mathbf{Q}_o \tag{16}$$

which shows that $g > \pi$, because $\mathbf{P}_o AY < \mathbf{P}_o A\mathbf{Q}_o$. The conclusion contrasts with all tradition. The economic reason for this striking result is that, for a given g, the level of investment required in (11) is less than that required in (1) while, for a given $\pi$, the profits in (15) are the same as in (2). If the same amount of profits is invested in both cases, the growth rate has to be greater in the system requiring less investment.

Undoubtedly, the result just obtained represents a shortcoming of the Pasinetti model so far considered. In contrast with this, it should be emphasised that the model has the advantage of being able to allow for the introduction of different sectoral growth and profit rates without any difficulty. In fact, it is sufficient to write $\hat{g}$ and $\hat{\pi}$ instead of g and $\pi$ and nothing else changes. Moreover, there is no problem in considering the existence of fixed capital which, of course, is a relevant advantage.

11.4

Pasinetti has utilised his method of vertical integration also in dealing directly with the traditional model (see Pasinetti, 1977). In what follows his approach will be utilised with very minor changes in notation.[2] The transformed model is once again that of (6) above. But the transformations are different, particularly the quantities of the original goods contained in a Pasinetti unit of capacity. In the previous model the i-th unit contained $H^i = A(I-A)^{-1}\mathbf{u}_i$ quantities of the original goods. In the present model, with g unique, it contains $H^i(g) = (G + gG^2 + g^2G^3 + \dots)\ (I-A)^{-1}\mathbf{u}_i$, where $G = (I-A)^{-1}A$. Hence, in (7) the third equation now reads:

$$\mathbf{Q}_2 = g(G + gG^2 + g^2G^3 + \dots)(I-A)^{-1}Y \tag{17}$$

so that:

$$\begin{aligned}\mathbf{Q}_o &= (I-A)^{-1}Y + g(G + gG^2 + g^2G^3 + \dots)(I-A)^{-1}Y \\ &= (I + gG + g^2G^2 + g^3G^3 + \dots)(I-A)^{-1}Y \\ &= (I-gG)^{-1}(I-A)^{-1}Y \\ &= [I-(1+g)A]^{-1}Y\end{aligned} \tag{18}$$

the last equality having been proved by Pasinetti (1977, p. 32). This final expression (18) shows that the model now considered corresponds to (1), apart from the already noticed unimportant change in the treatment of consumption growth.

Corresponding to the new definition of a unit of capacity, there is also a new definition of its labour content which can be proven to be:

$$\mathbf{v}_k = \mathbf{v}A[I-(1+g)A]^{-1} \tag{19}$$

The new $\mathbf{v}_k$ is greater than that considered in (8), this stemming from the fact that now it is considered the full amount of capacity necessary to produce growth at the rate g (i.e. $gA\mathbf{Q}_o$ and not $gAY$). The correctness of (19) can be checked by showing that $L = \mathbf{a}_{[n]}\mathbf{Q}_o$. In fact:

$$\begin{aligned}L &= \mathbf{a}_{[n]}(I-A)^{-1}Y + g\mathbf{a}_{[n]}(I-A)^{-1}A[I-(1+g)A]^{-1}Y \\ &\mathbf{a}_{[n]}[I + g(I-A)^{-1}A(I-gG)^{-1}](I-A)^{-1}Y\end{aligned} \tag{20}$$

$$= \mathbf{a}_{[n]}[I + gG(I + gG + g^2G^2 + \ldots)](I - A)^{-1}Y$$
$$= \mathbf{a}_{[n]}(I - gG)^{-1}(I - A)^{-1}Y = \mathbf{a}_{[n]}\mathbf{Q}_o$$

Let us now look at the price system. The new definition of a unit of capacity implies that (12) should now read:

$$\mathbf{P} = w\mathbf{v} + \pi\mathbf{P}_k \qquad (21)$$
$$\mathbf{P}_k = \mathbf{P}H(g)$$

where

$$H(g) = (G + gG^2 + g^2G^3 + \ldots)(I - A)^{-1}$$

By solving (21), after substitution for $\mathbf{v}$ from (8), we obtain:

$$\mathbf{P} = w\mathbf{a}_{[n]}(I - A)^{-1}[I - \pi H(g)]^{-1}$$

which is different from the usual solution one can derive from (15), unless $\pi = 0$.

Therefore, it is possible to conclude that the new model coincides with the traditional one for the output but not for the value system. There is not a complete separation between the two systems because g intervenes in the determination of prices. If g is a given constant, for a stretch of time, there is no other problem. But one has to rework the transformations at the points of time in which g is allowed to change. When different gs are introduced at the sectoral level, the transformations become functions of the matrix $\hat{g}$ so that we are in the same situation we had with the Goodwin's model. When the transformations are correct, the output and value systems are no longer completely separated and there is a difficulty in giving a consistent formulation for prices.

## 11.5

Neither Goodwin's nor Pasinetti's models are quite satisfactory. Both suffer from a shortcoming that seems to have the same logical origin: the impossibility of taking full account of interdependence and then finding a way to leave it out of consideration. But, perhaps, one can draw another conclusion. If it is impossible to find an exact solution to the problem of coupling the simplicity of macroeconomics with the realism of interdependence, it is possible to find some approximate solutions. The methods of both Goodwin and Pasinetti provide them. As the authors have shown, these solutions can be profitably utilised in many instances to obtain significant conclusions. The alternative of saying nothing of relevance on the behaviour of complex dynamic systems is, at least to me, clearly a worse option.

## Notes

1. The column vector $\mathbf{u}_i$ has 1 as the i-th component and zero elsewhere.
2. For instance, since here only circulating capital is considered, there is no difference between the matrices A and $A^-$, the latter being the matrix of technical coefficients net of the fixed capital depreciation. Moreover, owing to the already recalled property that $(I-A)^{-1}A = A(I-A)^{-1}$, also the Pasinetti matrices H and G are equal.

## References

GOODWIN, R. M. (1976) 'Use of Normalised General Co-ordinates in Linear Value and Distribution Theory', in K. Polenske and J. Skolka (eds), *Advances in Input–Output Analysis* (Ballinger).

GOODWIN, R. M. (1983) *Essays in Linear Economic Structures* (London: Macmillan) Chs 7 and 8.

PASINETTI, L. L. (1965) 'A New Theoretical Approach to the Problems of Economic Growth', in *The Econometric Approach to Development Planning* (Amsterdam: North Holland).

PASINETTI, L. L. (1977) 'The Notion of Vertical Integration in Economic Analysis', *Metroeconomica* (1973) vol. 25, repr. in L. L. Pasinetti (ed.), *Essays on the Theory of Joint Production* (London: Macmillan).

PASINETTI, L. L. (1981) *Structural Change and Economic Growth* (Cambridge: Cambridge University Press).

# 12 Generalised Diagonal Coordinates in Dynamical Analysis, and Capital and Distribution Theory

Lionello F. Punzo[1]

> Thus general equilibrium theory was fully stated by Walras but remained an empty box until the work of von Neumann and Leontief. (Goodwin, 1970, p. ix)

It is a favourite story of Richard Goodwin that he was recommended to read von Neumann's (1938) seminal paper by Schumpeter himself. He did not like the paper because he regarded joint production as a purely artificial device that deprived the model of all empirical interest. However, Goodwin did not reject linear economics, as it appears from his work starting with his beautiful (1947) paper on dynamical coupling of markets. Linear economics was in many ways an offspring of the crisis of Walrasian economics. Goodwin took linear models as theoretical compromises that allowed the phenomenon of interdependence typical of large-scale systems to be dealt with. To analyse economic interdependence, he developed in a number of papers a method in terms of generalised diagonal coordinates, making use of a linear transformation of the system matrix which goes under the name of diagonal canonical form.

In this work, he tackled some of the issues which inspired the much celebrated model of von Neumann. Both von Neumann and Goodwin saw that the system basic properties had their roots in the (spectral) properties of the matrix of system coefficients. From this perspective, Goodwin investigated the relations between dynamical and accounting properties of a given economy. Von Neumann, on the other hand, confined himself to establishing that a certain equilibrium state could be obtained under a sufficient number of mild assumptions. These could be justified on the grounds of the specific interpretation which the system matrix received in his model. We feel, however, that a comparison of Goodwin's and von Neumann's different mathematical approaches to the same set of issues arising in the theory of capital, growth and distribution could be particularly illuminating.

This paper is organised as follows. Goodwin's treatment of capital and distribution assumes the existence of a diagonal canonical form of the matrix of system coefficients. In sections 12.1 and 12.2 we review the conditions for the existence of such a canonical form for certain production and exchange economies and introduce the notion of systems with simple structure. The bridge between Goodwin's analysis in diagonal coordinates and von Neumann's equilibrium analysis is established by the notion that, under certain restrictions, a von Neumann solution is a triple ($\alpha$, x, y) of nonnegative vectors, where $\alpha$ is the reciprocal of an eigenvalue of the system coefficient matrix while x and y are the associated right and left eigenvectors. In section 12.3, the diagonalisation technique is extended to the case of systems with rectangular input and output matrices. The remainder of the chapter concerns the generalisation of the Goodwin theory, by allowing the output matrix to have any sign pattern. In this way, fixed capital and joint production are introduced.

## 12.1 THE ORIGINAL SETTING

The aim of this section is to illustrate the relation between the notion of a *system structure* (identified with the matrix of system coefficients) and the eigenvalues of such matrix. In the following section we shall introduce the definition of system with simple structure.

Let us recall an elementary notion of linear algebra. The diagonal canonical form of a matrix is a special similarity transformation of a given matrix, interpreted as the representation in a chosen system of coordinate axes of a linear operator. The diagonal canonical form synthesises the linear operator through the set of its eigenvalues. Thus, the diagonal canonical form of a matrix **W** is a matrix [$\Lambda$], similar to **W**, which is diagonal and displays along its main diagonal the eigenvalues of **W**.

Goodwin's use of the diagonal canonical form and of diagonal coordinates emerges as follows. Let A be the standard matrix (of order n) of input coefficients per unit levels of activity; let **B** stand for the corresponding output coefficient matrix; and let $\mathbf{a}_0$ be the vector of labour input coefficients. By assumption, A, B and $\mathbf{a}_0$ are derived from statistical observations in the sense that they refer to a technique actually in use.

Consider now the well known equation

$$\mathbf{p}\,B = (1+\pi)\,\mathbf{p}\,A + w\,\mathbf{a}_0 \tag{1}$$

which can always be written in the equivalent form

$$\mathbf{p}\,[B-(1+\pi)\,A] = w\,\mathbf{a}_0 \tag{2}$$

Let the nominal wage rate w be fixed at an arbitrary positive level. For any given value of the uniform rate of profit $\pi$, equation (1) defines a vector of *implicit prices* $\mathbf{p}$ associated with the profit rate $\pi$ and denoted by $\mathbf{p}(\pi)$, *provided* $\mathbf{p}(\pi)$ is unique. The theoretical justifications for such a definition (and the set of assumptions required to support it) are too well known to require explanation.

If H is a nonsingular matrix, (2) can be manipulated to yield

$$\mathbf{p}\,H^{-1}\,H\,[B-(1+\pi)\,A]\,H^{-1} = w\,\mathbf{a}_0\,H^{-1} \tag{3}$$

As $H\,(1+\pi)\,A\,H^{-1} = (1+\pi)\,H\,A\,H^{-1}$, introducing the change of variables $\mathbf{y} = \mathbf{p}\,H^{-1}$ and $\mathbf{a}_0\,H^{-1} = \boldsymbol{l}_0$, equation (3) becomes

$$\mathbf{y}[H\,B\,H^{-1} - (1+\pi)\,H\,A\,H^{-1}] = w\boldsymbol{l}_0 \tag{4}$$

We obtain two pairs of pairwise similar matrices: A and $[H\,A\,H^{-1}]$, B and $[H\,B\,H^{-1}]$, respectively. Similarity between A and $[H\,A\,H^{-1}]$ implies that they are alternative representations of the same structural coefficients, the former in *orthogonal* coordinates, the latter in the set of coordinate axes spanned by matrix H. Hence, they have the same set of eigenvalues. (The same holds true for the pair B and $H\,B\,H^{-1}$). The change of variables leading from (3) to (4) expresses input and output coefficients, the labour input vector and the vector of implicit prices in terms of the new coordinate axes. As vectors in H are generally *not* orthogonal to one another (unless H is a diagonal matrix), equation (4) is an equivalent formulation, albeit in *oblique* coordinates, of the price relations of the same model.

It is common to identify the description of *the system (inner) structure* with the pair of input and output matrices, in this case, A and B. However, as by assumption this structure is linear with constant coefficients, it is always possible to normalise it in such a way that only the (newly defined) input matrix, called system coefficient matrix, is informationally relevant.

Goodwin considers the particular case where $B \equiv [I]$. From an economic point of view, this amounts to excluding joint production of both the intrinsic type and of fixed capital goods at various stages of wear and tear. In this case, the system coefficient matrix coincides with the input matrix and all system properties can be ascertained by scrutinizing its eigenvalues (thus, by looking at its diagonal canonical form).

Matrix $[H\,A\,H^{-1}] = [\Lambda]$ is the diagonal canonical form of A *if and only if* H is the matrix of (left) eigenvectors of A. On the other hand, for such H: $H\,B\,H^{-1} = I$, so that both A and B are diagonalised by the matrix of eigenvectors of A. In this case, H provides a set of principal (diagonal) coordinate axes. As a result, the system of equations (3) is decoupled into n distinct scalar equations

$$y_j[1 - (1+\pi)\,\beta_j] = w\,\boldsymbol{l}_{o,j}, \qquad j = 1,2,\ldots,n \tag{5}$$

where $B_j$ is an eigenvalue of A, $\boldsymbol{l}_{o,j} = \mathbf{a}_o\,H^{-1,j}$, and $y_j = \mathbf{p}\,H^{-1,j}$, ($H^{-1j}$ being the j-th column vector of $H^{-1}$).

If we set $w = 0$, equation (5) becomes, if written in compact form,

$$\mathbf{y}[I - (1+\pi)\,\Lambda] = 0 \tag{6}$$

An arbitrarily given vector $\mathbf{p}$ is a solution of (1) for $w = 0$ if $\mathbf{y} = \mathbf{p}\,H^{-1}$ satisfies equation (6). In turn, this is true if and only if $\mathbf{p}$ is (one of the) eigenvectors of matrix A associated with one of its eigenvalues. All vectors $\mathbf{p}$ such that $\mathbf{y} = \mathbf{p}\,H^{-1}$ satisfies (6) are collected in H, which therefore provides a set of price eigenrays. For any scale factor arbitrarily given, we obtain a set of eigenprices. As $H\,H^{-1} = [I]$, equation (6) has exactly n linearly independent vectors of eigenprices.

A nonnegative vector of eigenprices lying on an eigenray associated with a nonnegative eigenvalue represents a vector of *implicit prices* corresponding to the value of the nominal wage rate $w = 0$. Eigenprices associated with the maximal eigenvalue of matrix A are also (equal to) implicit prices. A sufficient condition for the existence of such a vector is that, in equation (6), $\pi$ be such that $\sigma[(1+\pi)\,A] = 1$ or, equivalently, that $\pi = (1 - \sigma[A])/\sigma[A]$. (Here, $\sigma[.]$ stands for the dominant eigenvalue of matrix [.].) Such a value of the rate of profit will be denoted by $\Pi$ and the corresponding set of implicit prices by $\mathbf{p}(\Pi)$. If A is indecomposable, $\mathbf{p}(\Pi)$ is also unique (up to a scale factor).

When the wage rate is positive and is chosen as *numéraire* implicit prices are expressed in wage units. However, given the common nature of the solutions of decoupled equations (5) and (6), the following definition seems to be justified.

*Definition 1:* all prices $\mathbf{y}$ defined by the change of coordinates $\mathbf{y} = \mathbf{p}\,H^{-1}$, where H is the (left) eigenvector matrix of A and $\mathbf{p}$ is a solution of equation (3) are called *eigenprices and are parametrised by a value of the scalar* $\pi$. They are the projections, along the price eigenrays associated with matrix A, of the solutions of equation (3) corresponding to various nonnegative values of the profit rate.

## 12.2 DUALITY AND ACCOUNTING STRUCTURES

The solution $\mathbf{y}$ of (5) (and hence the solution of (3)) is unique only for those values of $(1+\pi)$ which are *not* reciprocals of eigenvalues of A. (In this case, matrix $[I-(1+\pi)\,H\,A\,H^{-1}] = [I-(1+\pi)\Lambda]$ is invertible.) Therefore, a distinction is to be made between the set of implicit prices $\mathbf{p}(\pi)$ corresponding to $\pi = \Pi$ and those associated with values of the profit rate lower than $\Pi$. In the former case, they generally form a set; in the latter the vector of wage prices $\mathbf{p}$ associated with a given value of $\pi$ is unique provided $[I-(1+\pi)\Lambda]$ is invertible. As a consequence, the conditions for the existence of implicit prices for any value $\pi{:}\pi < \Pi$ and for $\pi = \Pi$ are logically distinct. Eigenprices can always be defined *provided the system matrix be diagonalisable*, but they may not be directly interpretable.

When the output matrix is $B \equiv [I]$, the output equation dual to (3) can take the form

$$\mathbf{x} = (1+g)\,A\,\mathbf{x} + h\,\mathbf{D} \tag{7}$$

under the usual assumptions of a balanced growth equilibrium path. (Thus, $\mathbf{x}$ is the vector of activity levels, g a rate of balanced growth, $\mathbf{D}$ a vector of final demand and h a scale factor.) The 'state' of the jth eigensector is represented by the equation

$$z_j = (1+g)\,\beta_j\,z_j + h\,d_j, \qquad j = 1, 2, \ldots, n \tag{8}$$

Therefore, for the whole system, $\mathbf{z}=(z_1, z_2, \ldots, z_n)=X^{-1}\mathbf{x}$, $\boldsymbol{d}=X^{-1}\mathbf{D}$ and $\beta_j$, $j=1,2,\ldots,n$, are the n eigenvalues of A. X is the matrix of right eigenvectors associated with A. Hence, scalar $z_j=X^{-1,j}\mathbf{x}$ stands for the number of units of gross output of the jth eigencommodity produced. As $[H\,A\,H^{-1}]=[X^{-1}\,A\,X]=[\Lambda]$, then

$$H=X^{-1}$$

and, naturally,

$$H\,X=[I]$$

Equations of the form (8) describe the output sides of n *independent* eigensectors. Dividing throughout by the diagonal matrix $[Z]=[\delta_{ij}\,z_j]$, we obtain n accounting systems for output

$$[Z]^{-1}\mathbf{z}=(1+g)\,\Lambda\,[Z]^{-1}\mathbf{z}+h\,[Z]^{-1}\boldsymbol{d} \tag{9}$$

In fact, as $[Z]^{-1}\mathbf{z}=(1,\ldots,1)^T$, equation (9) yields the allocation of the output of the jth eigensector, represented by $\mathbf{z}_j$ units of the jth composite commodity, as the sum of the share used up for accumulation and replacement, the first term on the right, and the share of final demand.

Likewise, dividing throughout the set of equations (5) by the diagonal matrix $[Y]=[\delta_{ij}\,y_j]$,

$$\mathbf{y}\,[Y]^{-1}=(1+\pi)\,\Lambda\,\mathbf{y}\,[Y]^{-1}+w\,\boldsymbol{l}_o\,[Y]^{-1} \tag{10}$$

we obtain n accounting systems *in value*: one unit (in value) of gross output of the jth eigensector is the sum of the share of capital (accounting for both cost and profit rate) and the share of wages.

Therefore each eigensector is represented by an output ray and a price ray, vectors $X^{(j)}$ and $H_{(j)}$, where $X^{(j)}$ and $H_{(j)}$ are respectively the j-th column and row vectors of matrices X and H of eigenvectors of A. With each eigensector we associate a pair of scalars $(z_j, y_j)$, the former being the eigensector output and the latter its price (both expressed in eigenunits). Thus, for each eigensector, the two equations (8) and (10) define two (dual) accounting schemes or an *accounting structure*. These are linear for all eigensectors whose pairs $(z_j, y_j)$ are real (i.e. not complex) numbers.

Two conceptual difficulties arise in working with eigensectors instead of the sectors or 'industries' of the standard input–output analysis. First, each eigensector produces a bundle of commodities and therefore the productive activity taking place in it is purely fictitious. This implies that accounting in diagonal coordinates is meant only to give qualitative results. The second difficulty is more important. As is well known, eigenvalues (and eigenvectors) of a general real matrix are generally complex numbers (vectors with complex entries, respectively), subject only to the qualification that each complex number has its own conjugate. We can pair conjugate eigenvalues and obtain the so-called real diagonal canonical form: this is made up of blocks of submatrices along the main diagonal of dimension two for each pair of complex eigenvalues and dimension one for all real eigenvalues (Hirsch and Smale, 1974). In a similar way, eigenvectors associated with conjugate eigenvalues can be paired and rendered in real coordinates. All the preceding discussion should be understood as referring to the real canonical form and a pair of real eigenvector matrices H, X.

None the less, eigensectors corresponding to pairs of complex conjugate eigensolutions are not independent of one another. In such cases (value or output), accounting does not yield a pair of independent linear relations and the classical beauty of the accounting structures defined above would be lost. To save the diagonalisation as an analytical tool, we have to require that at least one solution (i.e. one eigensector) be real. Furthermore, for such an eigensector to have immediate economic significance, we have to require that its associated scalars $z_j$ and $y_j$ both be nonnegative for some acceptable values of g and $\pi$. Systems with at least one eigensector satisfying all the above requirements are amenable to direct economic interpretation. This justifies the following paraphrase of a well-known definition (see Gantmacher, 1960):

*Definition 2:* a system with square, real input and output matrices A and I has simple structure if and only if the following conditions are all simultaneously satisfied:

(i) A has a diagonal canonical form;
(ii) the dominant eigenvalue of A is real and positive;
(iii) its dominant eigenvalue is larger in modulus than any other eigenvalue;
(iv) with the dominant eigenvalue is associated a pair of left and

right nonnegative, nontrivial eigenvectors, each of them being unique up to a scale factor.

Matrix A must be of simple structure (in the algebraic sense) to obtain (i), and the necessary and sufficient condition for this is that all of its eigenvalues have geometric multiplicities equal to one (Gantmacher, 1960; Hirsch and Smale, 1974). That A be nonnegative is sufficient to ensure (iv). Indecomposability of $A \geqslant [0]$ is sufficient to ensure property (ii). Finally, primitivity of A is sufficient for (iii). Thus, this is a set of sufficient conditions for a system to have a simple structure. However, in the present case, the input matrix and the system coefficient matrix (or matrix in normal form, cf. below) coincide because the output matrix is the identity matrix. In the general case, the above set of conditions apply to the system matrix in normal form.

*Proposition:* if a system has simple structure, the eigensector associated with the dominant eigenvalue can be represented by a pair of nonnegative left and right eigenrays which are unique up to scale factors, and the associated scalars $z_j$ and $y_j$ (solutions of equation (5) and (8)) are positive for all g, $\pi < \Pi$ as they are obtained from

$$z_j = \mathbf{p}(\pi)\, X^{(j)}$$

and

$$y_j = H_{(j)}\, \mathbf{x}$$

(where $H_{(j)}$ and $X^{(j)}$ are the nonnegative (left and right) eigenvectors associated with the dominant eigenvalue of A).

Notice that, in this case, the corresponding equations in (5) and (8) have positive resolvents:

$$[1-(1+\pi)\,\sigma[A]]^{-1} > 0 \text{ and } [1-(1+g)\,\sigma[A]]^{-1} > 0$$

If any one of the properties stated in Definition 2 does not hold, the system is said to have *a complex structure*. We can dispose of cases where either (i) and/or (iii) fail to be met on the grounds of the empirical relevance of the system matrix. By appealing to a classic perturbation argument, it can be argued that such systems are 'rare' and can be treated as mathematical flukes.[2] Cases where (ii) and/or (iv) are not met lend themselves to economic interpretation: in either occurrence, the system does not admit a full capacity equilibrium path. The prototype of a model holding both (ii) and (iv) is the model of an exchange (and production) economy. Fixed capital models typically fail to meet at least one of these two requirements. Hereafter, we shall concentrate on such models.

Let us first look back at equation (3) and at the dual equations (7) in their full generality, by removing the assumption $B \equiv [I]$. We assume that there exists a price solution $\mathbf{p}$ of equation (3) and an output solution $\mathbf{x}$ of equation (7), associated with a pair of given values of $\pi$ and of g.

The jth eigensector is now defined by a pair of (left and right coordinated) eigenvectors $H_{(j)}$ and $X^{(j)}$ of matrices H and X such that $[B-(1+\pi)A]$ and $[B-(1+g)A]$ are diagonalised. On the other hand, a *state* of the eigensector is represented by the projections, already defined,

$$y_j = H_{(j)}\, \mathbf{x}$$

and

$$z_j = \mathbf{p}(\pi)\, X^{(j)}$$

for eigenoutput and eigenprice, respectively.

*Definition 3:* in a meaningful accounting structure in diagonal coordinates, there is at least one eigensector whose price and output rays are both real and at least one of them is positive.

This definition applies to systems with and without simple structure.

## 12.3 AN EIGENSYSTEM FOR A RECTANGULAR INPUT MATRIX

The properties of an accounting structure which have been identified as 'desirable' in Definition 3 are equivalent to certain well-known dynamical properties.

The model discussed so far reflects an actual economy, whose data are represented by matrices A and I and by vectors $\mathbf{a}_0$ and **D**. When A is indecomposable, requirement (iv) is satisfied. Multiplicity of eigensectors associated with one and the same eigenvalue can only arise if A is a rectangular matrix.

If A is a nonnegative, rectangular matrix of dimension (m x n), we may in principle formulate the pair of equations

$$\alpha \mathrm{A} \mathbf{x} = \mathbf{x} \tag{11}$$

$$\beta \mathbf{y} \mathrm{A} = \mathbf{y} \tag{12}$$

and add the restrictions

$$\mathbf{x} \neq 0 \tag{13}$$

$$\mathbf{y} \neq 0 \tag{14}$$

The unknowns are now the (n + 1) vector ($\mathbf{x}$, $\alpha$) and the (m + 1) vector ($\mathbf{y}$, $\beta$). If both $\alpha$ and $\beta$ are nonzero and equal to a common value, by setting $\lambda = \alpha^{-1} = \beta^{-1}$, equations (11) and (12) can be rewritten as

$$\mathrm{A} \mathbf{x} = \lambda \mathrm{E} \mathbf{x} \tag{15}$$

$$\mathbf{y} \mathrm{A} = \lambda \mathrm{E} \mathbf{y} \tag{16}$$

where E is a rectangular matrix with 1 and 0 entries as appropriate. If system (15)–(16) bordered by (13) and (14), has a solution, it is a generalisation of the eigenvalue–eigenvector problem to the case where A is rectangular. However, when $n > m$, the *columns* of matrix $[\mathrm{A} - \lambda \mathrm{E}]$ are linearly dependent for all scalars $\lambda$ and therefore the radius of A is unbounded (thus the maximal eigenvalue of A, $\sigma[\mathrm{A}] = \infty$) and any vector $\mathbf{x} \neq 0$ is an eigenvector of A. On the other hand, there will generally be no value for the scalar $\lambda$ for which the *rows* of $[\mathrm{A} - \lambda \mathrm{E}]$ become linearly dependent. Hence, equation (16) has only the trivial solution $\mathbf{y} = 0$, violating (14). A totally symmetric situation arises when $m > n$, with roles interchanged between the two equations (Punzo, 1980; Punzo and Velupillai, 1984).

Therefore, when A is rectangular, we cannot in general solve meaningfully *both* equations (15) and (16). For this reason, in the study of the properties of a closed model of production with choice of techniques (i.e. with $m < n$), von Neumann has resorted to inequalities. He has shown that a solution ($\alpha$, $\beta$, **x**, **y**) exists where: (i) $\alpha$ is the maximin and (ii) $\beta$ the minimax of a bilinear form; (iii) vectors **x** and **y** belong to *whole sets* of economically meaningful solutions associated with $\alpha$ and $\beta$, respectively; (iv) finally, $\alpha \geqslant \beta$ and equality holds *if* matrix [A + E] is positive. Von Neumann *interpreted* the solution to his model as a Balanced Growth Path (BGP) at the expansion factor $\alpha$.

There is clearly a relation between von Neumann result and our generalised eigenvalue problem. A translation of the minimax theorem into the language of spectral analysis shows the requirement which must be satisfied for a meaningful use of equations.

## A theorem of von Neumann

Given a system matrix A of dimension (m by n), where $m \leqslant n$, there is *at least* one square submatrix A* of *order* k, $k \leqslant m$, such that

$$A^* \mathbf{x} = \alpha^{-1} \mathbf{x} \tag{17}$$

for some (k by 1)-dimensional nonnegative, nonzero vector **x** associated with a positive scalar $\alpha$. Dually, there is a (1 by k)-dimensional nonnegative, nonzero vector **y** such that

$$\mathbf{y} A^* = \beta^{-1} \mathbf{y} \tag{18}$$

In the language of spectral analysis, $\alpha$ ($= \beta$) is the reciprocal of the *minimal* of the dominant eigenvalues of the kth order submatrices that can be formed from A. This matrix being nonnegative, scalars $\alpha$, $\beta$ are nonnegative. Vectors **x** and **y** are the associated right and left eigenvectors of submatrix A*. If all submatrices of order m of A are indecomposable, then A* has order n and both **x** and **y** are positive (Punzo, 1989). Finally, scalar $\alpha^{-1} = \beta^{-1}$ is the unique eigenvalue of A* to which are associated positive solutions **x** and **y**.

If we obtain a square submatrix A*, we can proceed to diagonalise it and to derive the two, dual or parallel, accounting systems (8) and (10). Thus,

> *Proposition:* if a system has a Balanced Growth Path supported by a square submatrix A*, it has a meaningful accounting structure in

diagonal coordinates (i.e. a structure complying with the requirements stated in Definition 3).

## 12.4 DATA AND ABSTRACT ECONOMIES

The analytical requirement emerging in the accounting framework and stated in Definition 3 is therefore equivalent to the existence of a special balanced growth equilibrium path. On the other hand, this entails the existence of a full capacity monotonic expansion path, as a dynamical path ensuring the full employment of all capital goods. This path is a solution of homogeneous equations of the type (7) or (8) for $h=0$.

For systems with simple structure, the unifying mathematical approach is offered by the set of theorems of the Perron–Frobenius class, discovered for the economists by R. M. Goodwin as early as 1950. For complex systems, or systems in general, we have to rely upon generalisations of the same set of theorems. To be able to treat the problem in its full generality, we have resort to von Neumann's approach.

Von Neumann discussed the following general mathematical problem. Let A, **B** be nonnegative rectangular input and output matrices of dimension (k by z). They are connected by the set of inequalities

$$\alpha \, A \, \mathbf{x} \leqslant B \, \mathbf{x} \tag{19}$$

coupled with

$$\beta \, \mathbf{p} \, A \geqslant p \, \mathbf{B} \tag{20}$$

If we add to (19)–(20) the restriction that unknowns **x** and **p** be nonnegative and nonzero, and $\alpha$, $\beta$ positive scalars, we obtain a *von Neumann system*, with A and B as *data matrices*. (The generalisation discussed above (pp. 181–4) corresponds to a special von Neumann system with $B=E$.)

Von Neumann's data matrices are derived from an axiomatics of production relations and describe laws of technological transformation. This 'origin' does not exclude the possibility of deriving them from 'empirical' observations (as we do when we follow Goodwin and Sraffa).

In the sequel, a set of data will be referred to as the *data economy*. A distinction characteristic of the von Neumann approach is between data and the set of structures which are realised in certain system states. We have said that such a structure 'supports' a given system state. (In von Neumann this is a particular quasi-stationary equilibrium.)

*Definition 4:* A *von Neumann equilibrium* is described by the (possibly empty) subsets of inequalities (19) and (20) such that

$$\alpha\, A^*\, \mathbf{x}^* = B^*\, \mathbf{x}^* \tag{21}$$

and

$$\beta\, \mathbf{p}^*\, A^* = \mathbf{p}^*\, B^* \tag{22}$$

$$\alpha > 0,\ \beta > 0;\ \mathbf{p} \geqslant 0;\ \mathbf{x} \geqslant 0, \tag{23}$$

$$\mathbf{p}\,\mathbf{u} = 0;\ \mathbf{v}\,\mathbf{x} = 0 \tag{24}$$

where $A^*$, $B^*$ are *rectangular* submatrices of A, B; $\mathbf{p} = (\mathbf{p}^*, 0)$ and $\mathbf{x} = (\mathbf{x}^*, 0)^T$.

In the mathematical literature, the set of equations (21) and (22) are known as matrix pencils. In physics they arise in optics where either matrix is assumed to be symmetric. Given the economic interpretation of the two matrices, however, a crucial role is played by the assumption that both A and B are nonnegative (but in general they are not symmetric) and by the additional requirements (23) and (24).

The pair of equations (21) and (22), obtained as the subset of inequalities (19) and (20), describe von Neumann's Balanced Growth Equilibrium path, as a path where all output levels grow at the same pace, so that the structure of the economy remains unchanged, and competitive equilibrium prices are stationary.[3]

As pointed out, submatrices $A^*$, $B^*$ of A, B are generally rectangular of consistent dimension. They sum up all the data economically relevant for a system in the rather special state represented by a von Neumann equilibrium. Such a state entails a *particular realisation* of the data economy. A von Neumann economy involves a realisable structure which may or may not coincide with the data economy (in other words, with the realised structure). For this reason a realisation may also be called an *abstract economy*. The definition is meant to stress the distinction between the set of data that is assumed to be experimentally known, and a kernel of the data that becomes economically relevant only if the system happens to be in a certain theoretically postulated state.

Let an *economy* be defined by the set of processes fetching a positive activity level and the set of goods fetching a positive price in a certain system state. Von Neumann has shown that any model (19)–(20), subject to mild assumptions on data matrices, *contains at least* one nonempty von Neumann economy (i.e. an economy on a von Neumann path). This is the set of columns and rows of the pair of coordinated submatrices $A^*$, $B^*$ of A and B, respectively (von Neumann, 1938; Kemeny, Morgenstern and Thompson, 1956; Morishima, 1971; Morgenstern and Thompson, 1976).

The *dimension* of an economy is the product of the cardinality of the processes to be used and of the goods that are also commodities. It is embodied in the common dimension of the two starred submatrices, say (m by n), where $m \leqslant k$, $n \leqslant z$. For geometrical reasons, and an important theorem, a von Neumann economy (i.e. its supporting structure) can be called *degenerate* if $m > n$. (In other words, when there are less processes activated than commodities produced. See, for instance, Morishima, 1969.)

It is clear from our discussion above (pp. 174–7) that if $B \equiv E$, this sort of degeneracy cannot arise. It can only arise when we allow for joint production. In other words, when B contains some nonzero off-diagonal entries.

Assume that the economy has a nondegenerate structure (i.e. $A^*$, $B^*$ are square). As $\alpha$ and $\mathbf{x}$ solve a homogeneous equation associated with two *square* submatrices of A, B, they can be thought of as representing a generalised eigenvalue and the associated right eigenvector of the two submatrices. The same can be said of the dual solution ($\beta$, $\mathbf{p}$). In this case, the two vectors $\mathbf{x}$ and $\mathbf{p}$ are called central solutions or eigensolutions. Thus, any nondegenerate von Neumann economy corresponds to an eigensolution and the economy is an eigensystem (see Morgenstern and Thompson, 1971).

The motion of a von Neumann economy corresponding to a *central solution* of system (19) is a path along an eigenray of matrix $A^*$ with respect to matrix $B^*$. It describes a razor-edge dynamics which is a close relative of Harrod's knife-edge path (Goodwin and Punzo, 1987).

## 12.5 A UNIFIED APPROACH

There is however a fundamental and not purely formal difference between von Neumann's and Goodwin's approaches. While in the former the data economy is represented by a pair of generally rectangular matrices, in Goodwin data matrices are themselves square. For this reason, von Neumann analysis relies on inequalities and allows for degeneracy, while the structure of Goodwin data implies the assumption of a nondegenerate economy and the data themselves can, in principle at least, be related via equations. Rationalising Goodwin's assumption from the point of view of von Neumann, this procedure presupposes the existence of a *realisation* of a suitably defined von Neumann system. Such a realisation (taken to be the *data economy*) is an observed or actual economic system. Diagonalisation is meant to render explicit the *abstract economy* implicit in the actual economy. In this light, the requirements for a meaningful diagonalisation (and thus a meaningful accounting structure) imply the requirement of the coincidence of the abstract (or realisable) and the actual economies.

Hereafter, we shall investigate the conditions for the existence of a realised nondegenerate economy. This is required to analyse an economy through its spectral properties. We generalise von Neumann's approach in several ways, by allowing input and output coefficient matrices to have any sign patterns, and we analyse cases of equations admitting central solutions.

In fact, a number of economically interesting cases can be described either by the equation

$$\mathrm{B}\,\mathbf{x} = \alpha\,\mathrm{A}\,\mathbf{x}$$

or by

$$\lambda\,\mathrm{B}\,\mathbf{x} = \mathrm{A}\,\mathbf{x}$$

where A, B are *real* square, but sign unrestricted (input and output) matrices of order n.

We can manipulate the equations above to obtain

$$[\mathrm{A}^{-1}\mathrm{B}]\,\mathbf{x} = \alpha\,\mathbf{x}, \qquad \text{if } \det \mathrm{A} \neq 0 \tag{25}$$

$$\lambda\,\mathbf{x} = [\mathrm{B}^{-1}\mathrm{A}]\,\mathbf{x}, \qquad \text{if } \det \mathrm{B} \neq 0 \tag{26}$$

In (25), any scalar $\alpha$ to which there corresponds a vector $\mathbf{x} \neq 0$, is an eigenvalue of B with respect to A or an eigenvalue of matrix $[A^{-1}B]$, while $\mathbf{x}$ is one of the associated eigenvectors. Such a set of scalars $\alpha$ spans the spectrum of B versus A or the spectrum of $[A^{-1}B]$: formally, sp(B/A) or sp($A^{-1}B$). An analogous definition applies to $\lambda$ and $\mathbf{x}$ in (26). If both det $A \neq 0$ *and* det $B \neq 0$, scalar $\alpha$ is in sp(B/A) if and only if $\alpha^{-1} = \lambda$ is in sp(A/B).

However, the spectrum of a real matrix is generally spanned by complex numbers whose associated eigenvectors have complex entries. In our applications to von Neumann's equilibrium theory and to Goodwin's accounting structures, the crucial issue is to establish the existence of at least one positive eigenvalue with an associated nonnegative eigenvector $\mathbf{x}$.

The *sufficient* condition for obtaining such result is that the *system matrix in normal form* $[B^{-1}A]$ and/or $[A^{-1}B]$ be nonnegative. If $[B^{-1}A]$ or equivalently $[A^{-1}B] \geqq [0]$, the Perron–Frobenius theorem applies to the system in normal form. Thus, in this treatment, matrices A and/or B are allowed to contain some negative entries, although in most economic applications one of the two matrices is nonnegative by construction.

In fact, the following crucial relation holds in general (Mangasarian, 1971; Punzo and Velupillai, 1984). Given two real sign unrestricted matrices Z and X of order n,

(i) $[Z^{-1}X] = W$, where W is a real matrix, provided det $Z \neq 0$; while rk $(W) \leqslant n$;

on the other hand,

(ii) $[Z^{-1}X] = W \geqq [0]$ if and only if $\Delta(X) \subseteq \Delta(Z)$.

Assume $[Z^{-1}X] \geqq [0]$. Hence, the maximal eigenvalue of W (the *spanning matrix*) is nonnegative and has an associated eigenvector which is also nonnegative. As $[Z^{-1}X] = [X^{-1}Z]^{-1}$, the dominant eigenvalue of $[Z^{-1}X]$ is equal to the minimal (in modulus) eigenvalue of $[X^{-1}Z]$.

This quick review of elementary facts shows that we may start from models whose matrix in normal form, either $[B^{-1}A]$ or $[A^{-1}B]$, is nonnegative. We begin with the case where $[B^{-1}A] \geqq [0]$ and consider output equations first. We also review a number of standard cases to show that their treatment can be unified once it is recognised that they rely upon the satisfaction of the above cone inclusion condition.

**Model (A.1)**

The simplest case is represented by the aggregate model of income determination, with the equation

$$\lambda \, Y = c \, Y \tag{27}$$

where the input matrix A reduces to the scalar (positive) matrix $0 < c \leqslant 1$, the cone spanned by input matrix $A \equiv [c]$ is the half line: $k \, c \, Y$, where scalar $k \geqq 0$, and the output cone is spanned by positive matrix $B \equiv Y$. Thus, for all values of $c \leqslant 1$, the input cone is included in the output cone. Hence, there is a dominant eigenvalue of the input matrix [c] which is: $\sigma \, [c] = c^{-1}$.

**Model (B.1)**

The second example is offered by the standard multisectoral model of production (with circulating capital goods only) and exchange. This model has been already analysed: the homogeneous equation for output is

$$\lambda \, \mathbf{x} = A \, \mathbf{x} \tag{28}$$

where $A \equiv A \geqq [0]$
and $B \equiv I \geqq [0]$

In terms of our inclusion proposition, $\Delta \, (A) \subseteq R^{n}{}_{+} \equiv \Delta(I)$, as $A \geqq [0]$, implies $I \, A \geqq [0]$. Thus, A has a dominant eigenvalue which is positive if $\det A \neq 0$, or if A is indecomposable.

**Model (C.1)**

As a generalisation of the preceding case, consider the equation

$$\lambda [I - A] \, \mathbf{x} = g \, A \, \mathbf{x}, \text{ with} \tag{29}$$

$B \equiv [I - A]$

$A \equiv g \, A \geqq [0]$

where g is a given and *positive* value of the (balanced) growth rate.

In this case the output matrix $B \equiv [I - A]$ is a Z-matrix: $[I - A]_{ij} \leqslant 0$ (Berman and Plemmons, 1979). Thus, if A is productive and therefore $\sigma[A] < 1$, $\Delta(I) \equiv R^n_+ \subseteq \Delta[I - A]$. This is sufficient to ensure $[I - A]^{-1} A \geqq [0]$, because $\Delta(A) \subseteq \Delta[I - A]$. Then, equation (29) becomes

$$\lambda \mathbf{x} = g [I - A]^{-1} A \mathbf{x}$$

Growth rate g is feasible if and only if $g^{-1}$ is in $sp([I - A]^{-1}A)$. If this matrix is indecomposable, the condition is strengthened because g must be equal to the reciprocal of its dominant eigenvalue.

**Model (D.1)**

As a further generalisation, take the equation

$$\lambda[\mu I - A] \mathbf{x} = A \mathbf{x}, \qquad \mu > 0 \tag{30}$$

with

$$B(\mu) \equiv [\mu I - A]$$

$$A \geqq [0]$$

where **B** is parametrised by a scalar $\mu$. In normal form equation (30) becomes

$$\lambda \mathbf{x} = [\mu I - A]^{-1} A \mathbf{x}, \qquad (\mu \in sp(A))$$

(Equation (29) corresponds to the special case where $\mu = 1$.) Assume $\Delta(A) \subseteq \Delta[\mu I - A]$, for some given $\mu > 0$. Then, the dominant eigenvalue of $[\mu I - A]^{-1} A$ is nonnegative and has an associated nonnegative eigenvector **x**.

When the output matrix is a Z-matrix, the system holds a global property: if the inclusion relation between input and output cones holds for $\mu = 1$, it holds for all $\mu > 1$ up to a positive maximal value, and vice versa.

**Model (E.1)**

We consider now a model with capital stocks, commonly identified with the dynamic version of Leontief closed model. In this case, the n by n matrix K is the stock matrix while A is the flow matrix of replacement goods. We have the balance equation

$$\lambda[I - A + K]\,\mathbf{x} = K\,\mathbf{x} \tag{31}$$

which describes an elementary path: $\mathbf{x}_t = \lambda^t\,\mathbf{x}_o$.

Here,

$$A \equiv K \geqq [0]$$

while the output matrix

$$B \equiv [I - A + K]$$

has no specified pattern. The equation above can be transformed into

$$\lambda\,\mathbf{x} = [I - A + K]^{-1}\,K\,\mathbf{x}$$

or, if $\lambda \neq 1$,

$$\mu[I - A]\,\mathbf{x} = K\,\mathbf{x}, \qquad \mu = \lambda(1 - \lambda)^{-1}$$

with $B \equiv [I - A]$

which is a Z-matrix.

Thus, as $\Delta(K) \subseteq \Delta(I)$, a *sufficient condition* for $[I - A]^{-1}K$, to be nonnegative is that $\Delta(R^n{}_+) \subseteq \Delta[I - A]$, which in turn requires that the flow matrix be productive.

(Obviously, models C.1 and D.1 are special cases of this model.)

**Model (F.1)**

Finally, in the model of joint production, B is the gross output matrix and A the input matrix with the properties

$$B \geqq [0]$$

$$A \geqq [0]$$

The input and output coefficients may refer to finished goods as well as to partly worn-out machines. In the case of a model specialised to deal with fixed capital goods, the input and output matrices may have a special pattern. In fact, if capital goods once installed are not transferable over their lifetimes, each matrix can be decomposed into a direct sum

$$B \equiv I \oplus M_1$$

$$A \equiv A \oplus M_0$$

where matrices $M_1$ and $M_0$ record output and input coefficients of installed (old) capital goods at various stages of their lifetimes, and I, A refer to finished goods only (including brand new capital goods).

Equation

$$B\,\mathbf{x} = \alpha\, A\,\mathbf{x}$$

can be transformed into the equivalent system

$$\mathbf{x} = \alpha\,[B^{-1} A]\,\mathbf{x}$$

provided det $B \neq 0$, with input matrix $\hat{A} \equiv [B^{-1} A]$ and output matrix $B \equiv I$. In this case, if $[B^{-1} A] \geqq [0]$, there is a nonnegative scalar $\alpha$ which is the reciprocal of the dominant eigenvalue of the system matrix in normal form.

Otherwise, we can obtain the equivalent system

$$[B - A]\,\mathbf{x} = (\alpha - 1)\,A\,\mathbf{x}$$

with $A \geqq [0]$ and a general real sign unrestricted matrix $\hat{B} \equiv [B - A]$ as output matrix. In fact, the difference between $[B - A]$ and the output matrix $[I - A]$ associated with model C.1 above is that while the latter is always a Z-matrix the former may or may not have this required sign pattern. Hence, the condition for the nonnegativity of the system matrix in normal form cannot be 'mediated' by the nonnegative orthant. Thus, we shall directly assume $[B - A]^{-1} A \geqq [0]$, or equivalently that $\Delta(A) \subseteq \Delta[B - A] \bigcap R^n{}_+ \neq \Phi$. This amounts to assuming that $[B - A]$ is productive: in this case, the maximal eigenvalue of $[B - A]^{-1}$ A is $\sigma = (\alpha - 1) > 0$. (Notice that this is a particular version of assumption: $\Delta(A) \subseteq \Delta[\mu\, B - A]$, for some $\mu > 0$. If this condition is satisfied, we say that $[B - A]$ is productive *above* the value of scalar $\mu$.)

The following implication holds

$$\Delta(A) \subseteq \Delta(B) \rightarrow \Delta(A) \subseteq \Delta[\mu B - A], \qquad \text{some } \mu > 0$$

but the opposite is not necessarily true. Thus, we may have that

$$\Delta(A) \subseteq \Delta[\mu B - A], \qquad \text{some } \mu > 0$$

while Δ (A) is not included in Δ (B).

## 12.6 THE PRICE SIDE

In the preceding section we examined fairly standard examples of productive systems whose technologies belong to the class of backward narrowing (BN) technologies (see Hicks, 1965). The leading representative of this class is the production model with neither joint production of intrinsic type nor fixed capital goods (Hicks, 1965). For all such models, the relation holds

$$\{\Delta(A) \subseteq \Delta(R^n{}_+)\} \rightarrow \{\Delta(A) \subseteq \Delta(B)\}$$

The relation above can be taken to be typical of all BN technologies with input and output matrices both nonnegative. On the other hand, the general relation when the input matrix A is nonnegative and the output matrix B is sign unrestricted is

$$\{\Delta(A) \subseteq \Delta[I - A]\} \rightarrow \{\Delta(A) \subseteq \Delta[\mu I - A]\} \rightarrow \{\Delta(A) \subseteq \Delta[\mu B - A]\}$$

We may now turn succinctly to the price dual relations of models with techniques of the backward narrowing class. It can be seen at once that by construction, model (A.1) has no price dual; models (B.1)–(C.1)–(D.1) are special cases of (F.1). In fact, they correspond to the case where the flow input matrix A = [0]. Therefore, we can treat the equation

$$\lambda\, p\,[I - A + K] = \mathbf{p}\, K$$

or

$$\mu\, \mathbf{p}[I - A] = \mathbf{p}\, K$$

as the general case. Easy manipulation yields

$$\mu \mathbf{p} = \mathbf{p} \, K \, [I - A]^{-1}$$

A sufficient condition for **p** to be nonnegative is that $\mu$ be the maximal eigenvalue of $K\,[I-A]^{-1}$. Now, matrix $K\,[I-A]^{-1}$ is similar to matrix $[I-A]^{-1}\,K$, which is nonnegative if the technology is of the backward narrowing type. Therefore, the two matrices have the same nonnegative dominant eigenvalue. Let **y** be the left eigenvector of $[I-A]^{-1}\,K$ associated with the dominant eigenvalue. Then, the corresponding eigenvector of $K\,[I-A]^{-1}$ is $\mathbf{p} = \mathbf{y}\,[I-A]^{-1}$.

In this particular case, as $[I-A]^{-1}$ is a Z-matrix, eigenvectors **y** and **p** associated with the dominant eigenvalue are both nonnegative. In general this is not true.

In fact for the general equation (F.1), the following relation holds between left and right eigenvectors associated with the dominant eigenvalue. In normal form the equation is

$$\lambda \mathbf{x} = [B^{-1} A]\,\mathbf{x}$$

(provided $\alpha \neq 0$!). As there exists a nonnegative solution **x** associated with the maximal eigenvalue $\sigma\,[B^{-1}A]$, there is also a nonnegative left eigenvector **y** for $\lambda = \sigma$, i.e. a vector **y** such that

$$\sigma \mathbf{y} = \mathbf{y}\,[B^{-1} A]$$

Hence, $\mathbf{p} = \mathbf{y}\,B^{-1}$ is an eigenvector of $[A\,B^{-1}]$ associated with its dominant eigenvalue. The latter is nonnegative notwithstanding $[A\,B^{-1}]$ generally contains some negative entries. By definition, **p** is such that

$$\sigma \mathbf{p} = \mathbf{p}\,[A\,B^{-1}], \text{ or } \sigma\,\mathbf{p}\,B = \mathbf{p}\,A$$

Thus, eigenprices associated with the dominant eigenvalue of a matrix similar to a nonnegative matrix can only be partly negative. (They cannot be complex.)[4]

## 12.7 COMPLEXITY

We have provided the appropriate generalisations for the class of backward narrowing production systems. The standard Perron–Frobenius theorem applies to a member of this class. Systems with simple structure are also special cases in the same class.

However, *when the output matrix is not diagonal*, equation

$$\lambda \, B \, \mathbf{x} = A \, \mathbf{x}$$

can give rise to a case which is entirely dual to the Perron–Frobenius case. Let us assume det. $A \neq 0$ *and* $[A^{-1} B] \geqq [0]$.

Assuming that $[A^{-1} B] \geqq [0]$ is equivalent to assuming that $\Delta(B) \subseteq \Delta(A)$. Then the above system becomes

$$\lambda [A^{-1} B] \, \mathbf{x} = \mathbf{x}$$

In this case, we can still apply standard results, though we have to deal with the dominant eigenvalue of B versus A which would be the minimal (in modulus) eigenvalue of A versus B. The minimal eigenvalue of $[A^{-1} B]$ is surely economically relevant: it is nonnegative with a nonnegative right eigenvector associated to it. This is the forward narrowing (FN) case.

However, when B is not diagonal, two entirely new cases can present themselves. The first is when the cones spanned by the input and output coefficient matrices only have a nonempty intersection. (They simply overlap.) Otherwise, their intersection may be empty. In either case, neither matrix $[B^{-1} A]$ nor $[A \, B^{-1}]$ can be nonnegative. We are at a loss because there are no sufficient conditions ensuring the existence of a pair of real eigensolutions. We have to abandon the algebraic approach and resort to von Neumann's maximin theorem. A nonempty intersection between input and output cones is in fact the *necessary*, though not sufficient, condition for the (output and/or the value) equations to have real solutions. It is the condition upon which Goodwin's diagonalisation rests.

The requirements established above (pp. 177–81) for a pair of parallel accounting schemes in diagonal coordinates to be meaningful, are very mild: they amount to requiring the system technology to allow for a full capacity expansion path. They are naturally satisfied if the technology is either of the forward or of the backward narrowing types. However, if we treat our models as mathematically general systems, these requirements may not be met. The abstract economy that is associated with the accounting structure in diagonal coordinates may, therefore, not be defined. This 'strange occurrence' is, nevertheless, perfectly compatible with the hypothesis that the data economy exhibits nonnegative price and output solutions at some given levels of the rate of profit or of growth. Thus, the abstract economy emerging from an accounting structure may have no immediate interpretation as a realisable economy, even though the actual or data economy does have an obvious one.

Here, Goodwin's diagonalisation raises methodological issues very close to those involved in Sraffa's treatment of an economic system and of the Standard System.

**Notes**

1. Financial support from the Italian Ministry of Education is gratefully acknowledged.
2. Semisimplicity is a generic property of linear operators. See Hirsch and Smale, 1974.
3. Morgenstern and Thompson, 1971; Morgenstern and Thompson, 1976. Note that **u** and **v** are appropriate vectors of (nonnegative) slack variables: hence, (24) establishes the rule of free goods and the rule of profitability.
4. An analogous exercise can be performed with matrices [B − A] and A.

**References**

BERMAN, A. and R. J. PLEMMONS (1979) *Nonnegative Matrices in the Mathematical Sciences* (New York: Academic Press).

GANTMACHER, F. R. (1960) *The Theory of Matrices*, vol. II (New York: Chelsea).

GOODWIN, R. M. (1947) 'Dynamical Coupling with Especial Reference to Markets Having Production Lags', *Econometrica*, reprinted in Goodwin (1982).

GOODWIN, R. M. (1949) 'The Multiplier as Matrix', *Economic Journal*, reprinted in Goodwin (1983).

GOODWIN, R. M. (1950) 'Does the Matrix Multiplier Oscillate?', *Economic Journal*, reprinted in Goodwin (1983).

GOODWIN, R. M. (1953) 'Static and Dynamic Linear General Equilibrium Models', in The Netherlands Economic Institute (eds), *Input and Output Relations* (Leiden: H. E. Stenfert Kroese N. V.); reprinted in Goodwin (1983).

GOODWIN, R. M. (1970) *Elementary Economics from the Higher Standpoint* (Cambridge: Cambridge University Press).

GOODWIN, R. M. (1974) 'La teoria economica lineare nell'analisi dinamica della produzione, del valore e della distribuzione', in *Annali della Fondazione Luigi Einaudi*, Torino, vol. III.

GOODWIN, R. M. (1976) 'Use of Normalised General Coordinates in Linear Value and Distribution Theory', in Polenske and Skolka (eds),

*Advances in Input–Output Analysis*, Proceedings of the 6th International Conference held in Vienna.
GOODWIN, R. M. (1977) 'Capital Theory in Orthogonal General Coordinates', Wicksell Symposium, Frostavallen, Sweden; printed in Goodwin (1983).
GOODWIN, R. M. (1980) 'The World Trade Multiplier', *Journal of Post Keynesian Economics*; reprinted in Goodwin (1983).
GOODWIN, R. M. (1982) *Essays in Economic Dynamics* (London: Macmillan).
GOODWIN, R. M. (1983) *Essays in Linear Economic Structures* (London: Macmillan).
GOODWIN, R. M. (1986) 'Swinging Along the Autostrada', in W. Semmler (ed.), *Competition, Instability and Nonlinear Cycles* (Berlin, New York: Springer Verlag).
GOODWIN, R. M. and L. F. PUNZO (1987) *The Dynamics of a Capitalist Economy. A Multisectoral Approach* (Cambridge: Polity Press).
HICKS, J. (1965) *Capital and Growth* (Oxford: Oxford University Press).
HIRSCH, M. W. and S. SMALE (1974) *Differential Equations, Dynamical Systems, and Linear Algebra* (New York: Academic Press).
KEMENY, J. G., O. MORGENSTERN and G. L. THOMPSON (1956) 'A Generalization of von Neumann Model of an Expanding Economy', *Econometrica.*
MANGASARIAN, O. (1971) 'The Generalized Perron–Frobenius Theorem', *Journal of Mathematical Analysis and Applications.*
MORGENSTERN, O. and G. L. THOMPSON (1971) 'Von Neumann Systems are Eigensystems', in G. Brückmann and W. Weber (eds), *Contributions to the von Neumann Growth Model*, Zeitschrift für Nationalökonomie, Supplementum 1 (New York: Springer Verlag).
MORGENSTERN, O. and G. L. THOMPSON (1976) *Mathematical Theory of Expanding and Contracting Economies* (Lexington, Mass.: Heath Lexington Books).
MORISHIMA, M. (1969) *Theory of Economic Growth* (Oxford: Clarendon Press).
MORISHIMA, M. (1971) 'Consumption–Investment Frontier, Wage–Profit Frontier and the Von Neumann Equilibrium', in G. Brückmann and W. Weber (eds), *Contributions to the von Neumann Growth Model*, Zeitschrift für Nationalökonomie, Supplementum 1 (New York: Springer Verlag).
PUNZO, L. F. (1980) 'Economic Applications of a Generalized Perron–Frobenius Problem', *Economic Notes.*
PUNZO, L. F. (1989) 'Von Neumann and K. Menger's Mathematical Colloquium', in S. Chakravarthy, M. Dore and R. M. Goodwin (eds), *John von Neumann and Modern Economics* (Oxford: Oxford University Press), forthcoming.
PUNZO, L. F. and K. VELUPILLAI (1984) 'Multisectoral Models and Joint Production', in F. van der Ploeg (ed.), *Mathematical Methods in Economics* (New York: J. Wiley and Sons).
VON NEUMANN, J. (1938) 'Über ein ökonomisches Gleichungssystem und eine Verallgemeinerung des Brouwerischen Fixpunktsatzes', *Ergebnisse Math. Kolloquiums*; English translation as 'A Model of General Economic Equilibrium', *Review of Economic Studies* (1945–6).

# PART IV
# Exotica

# 13 The Specification of Error Terms

Jan Tinbergen

It is customary to introduce into a relationship we are going to test with the aid of regression analysis, added to the systematic terms, an error term. The systematic terms are those containing one or more independent variables; in a relation used to explain national income as a dependent variable we may use as an important independent variable exports. This will especially apply to small open countries. The error term is introduced as a catchall for less important independent variables and for measuring errors of both the dependent variable and the independent variables. The error term is usually assumed to be a random variable with an average value of zero and a normal distribution.

Essentially the introduction of an error term is a second-best setup and in a way a *testimonium paupertatis*. It will be considered preferable to replace it, at least partially, by a specified additional independent variable (multiplied by a regression coefficient). In the example of the explanation of a small country's national income by its exports it is possible that part of the error term can be replaced by the crop yield of some agricultural product. Crop yields interfere with any country's economy, either because the country produces agricultural commodities or because it imports or exports them.

In this essay some more examples of possible specifications of error terms will be discussed, and one recently come across by the author shown in some detail. In a volume to honour Richard Goodwin this subject can only play a subordinate role. Goodwin did highly interesting and creative work which has been evaluated clearly, for instance, by Professor K. Velupillai (1982), who gave some impressive examples of Goodwin's creativity. His econometric work must have brought him in permanent contact, however, with the modest problem I propose to deal with. All of us experience the pleasant surprise of 'discoveries', however, of particularly good fits and we also know that doing scientific work partly consists of such discovery excursions.

It is my hope that this satisfaction will be experienced by the readers of this modest discovery I propose to report on, after some other examples which will be described more sketchily.

To begin with, let us dig somewhat more deeply into the example already given: the impact of crop-yield figures on national income. Time series of crop yields for numerous agricultural and horticultural products show fluctuations which are close to random series. But they are not the result of a lottery. Agricultural economists know, on the basis of various types of research, that yields can be explained to a very large degree by temperature and rainfall, often in particular weeks or months of the year, depending on the geographical latitude and other geographical data concerning the area studied. So a large part of seemingly random crop-yield figures can be explained by specific variables that can be measured. These variables may, if one wishes, be considered as the deeper causes of fluctuations in national income. If the country is large and produces a great variety of agricultural and horticultural products the data on temperature and rainfall may have to be specified in great detail.

A similar but very specific example may be taken from fishery in the Netherlands. Before the dyke was built which was constructed in order to reclaim parts of the Dutch Zuiderzee one of the important products of that sea was anchovy. The annual reports of the Dutch Ministry of Agriculture and Fisheries provide figures on the anchovy catch for the period 1855–1930. These figures show very large random fluctuations and the amplitude is characterised by a maximum catch 200 times the minimum. As can be expected, the prices are negatively correlated with catches and because of the large amplitude of supply factor ‘catch’ this independent determinant of prices is much larger than the impact of demand factor ‘income of consumers’ and the impact of competing consumer goods. Moreover, the best explanation of price fluctuations is obtained by transforming catch figures into four-year moving averages. The explanation is that anchovy is not consumed shortly after it has been caught, but is preserved and considered to taste best after some four years.

In this case too the fluctuations, although practically random, can be explained by a climate variable, as research of the Dutch Fishery Research Station has shown. The main independent variable appeared to be the temperature of seawater close to the station (in the part of the Waddenzee called Marsdiep), where the anchovy young live for the first few months.

The relationships discussed so far have been the subject of research for many institutions. Begun by the American Department of Agriculture and several American universities, the subject was quickly taken up by European institutions, both political and scientific – and in some cases both – such as the German Institut für Konjunkturforschung. Mathematical–statistical methods had been developed in connection with other subjects than economic ones, and some of these methods were later adapted to the special needs of economic applications.

As stated above, this essay will deal with an issue the author recently came across. It deals with an attempt to allocate a number of workers with varying levels of schooling over an equal number of jobs characterised by a required level of schooling (Tinbergen, 1984). The expression 'required level' should not be interpreted to mean that individuals with a different level would not be able to choose such a job, but only that he or she might then feel less satisfied, because the job would be either to easy or too difficult. The problem considered was to test a theory on the allocation of 1000 workers over 1000 jobs arranged in a six-row six-column matrix. The number of workers in each cell of that matrix will be indicated by $\varphi_{hh'}$, where $h$ is the level required and $h'$ the actual level of schooling. Rows contain individuals with jobs $h=1$, 2, etc., and the row total $\varphi_h$ represents the demand for workers on job $h$; columns contain individuals with the same $h'$, and the column total is written $\varphi_{.h'}$. Evidently $\Sigma_h\varphi_{h'} = \Sigma_{h'}\varphi_{\cdot h'} = \Sigma_h\Sigma_{h'}\varphi_{hh'} = 1000$. Two sets of data were available from Rumberger (1981a) based on a much larger sample, of which the unit used here constitutes one promille.

The theory tested is the theory of minimum tension; by tension the expression $(h-h')^2$ is meant, implying that both workers and employers dislike differences between $h$ and $h'$, irrespective of its algebraic sign and proportionally to the square of $(h-h')$.

In the article quoted it is shown that a minimum of 'total tension' $\Sigma_h\Sigma_{h'}\varphi_{hh'}(h-h')^2$ is obtained by an allocation according to the so-called Northwest-corner rule formulated by Hitchcock (1941). This rule allocates to cell 1,1 (the northwest-corner)

$$\varphi_{11} = \min\,(\varphi_{1.}, \varphi_{.1}) \tag{1}$$

and as step 2 leaves empty cell 2, 1 if $\varphi_{1.} > \varphi_{.1}$ and cell 1, 2 if $\varphi_{1.} < \varphi_{.1}$, whereas in the former case $\varphi_{12} = \min\,(\varphi_{1.} - \varphi_{.1}, \varphi_{.2})$ and in the latter case $\varphi_{21} = \min\,(\varphi_{.1} - \varphi_{1.}, \varphi_{2.})$. These two steps may have clarified the rule.

In the article quoted it is shown that this solution which we indicate by

$$\varphi_{hh'} = \beta t \tag{2}$$

provides us, as stated, with the minimum of total tension. It is interesting then to study equation (2) in the conventional way by estimating the regression equation corresponding with (2), by adding an error term. In the spirit of the introductory paragraph we propose to specify the error term in advance and to choose two specifications, to be called *n* and *p*. Here *n* stands for a (two-dimensioned) normal or Gaussian distribution and *p* for a probability distribution built on the assumption that the probability for an observation to supply an additional unit (i.e. promille) in each cell is based on the independence of demand and supply. This leads to

$$P_{hh'} = \gamma \varphi_{h.} \varphi_{.h'} 1000 \tag{3}$$

where $\gamma$ is the weight of *p* in the regression (2) formed with OLS. In other words we estimate as alternative checks of (2)

$$\varphi_{hh'} = \beta' t + \alpha n \tag{4}$$

$$\varphi_{hh'} = \beta'' t + \gamma p \tag{5}$$

The data used are Rumberger's (1981a) for $\varphi_{hh'}$, from which the *t* and *p* can be derived in the way described. Rumberger offers two educational groupings and we will indicate these by lower indices 1 and 2, omitting the *h* and *h'* indexes to the $\varphi$ figures. The normal distribution *n* is the same for both educational groupings. Since we have to work with discrete figures, we approach the one-dimensional distributions of the row sums and the column sums by the terms of the binomium $(1/2+1/2)^5$ which are 1, 5, 10, 10, 5, 1, all divided by 32. The frequencies in each cell of the $\varphi$ matrix are obtained by multiplying the row total by the column total corresponding with the cell considered; multiplied by $32^2$ they are:

| | | | | | | |
|---|---|---|---|---|---|---|
| 1 | 5 | 10 | 10 | 5 | 1 | 1 |
| 5 | 25 | 50 | 50 | 25 | 5 | 5 |
| 10 | 50 | 100 | 100 | 50 | 10 | 10 |
| 10 | 50 | 100 | 100 | 50 | 10 | 10 |
| 5 | 25 | 50 | 50 | 25 | 5 | 5 |
| 1 | 5 | 10 | 10 | 5 | 1 | 1 |
| 1 | 5 | 10 | 10 | 5 | 1 | 32 |

Expressed in 10 000th and adjusting the four central frequencies so as to let all frequencies add up to 10 000 we obtain for the normal distribution the matrix where the following transformation is applied:

| | | | | | | |
|---|---|---|---|---|---|---|
| original frequencies: | 1 | 5 | 10 | 25 | 50 | 100 |
| transformed frequencies: | 10 | 49 | 98 | 244 | 488 | 976 |

Upon inspection it will be found that this transformation yields figures adding up to 10000.

With the aid of the data described the following estimates of equations (4) and (5) for the two educational groupings are found. Figures in parentheses indicate standard deviations of regression coefficients.

$$\hat{\varphi}_1 = \underset{(0.0583)}{0.4087}\, t_1 + \underset{(0.1338)}{0.6948}\, n \qquad \bar{R}^2 = 0.8128 \tag{4.1}$$

$$\hat{\varphi}_2 = \underset{(0.0475)}{0.6410}\, t_2 + \underset{(0.1109)}{0.3678}\, n \qquad \bar{R}^2 = 0.8936 \tag{4.2}$$

$$\hat{\varphi}_1 = \underset{(0.0441)}{0.2276}\, t_1 + \underset{(0.0721)}{0.7995}\, p_1 \qquad \bar{R}^2 = 0.9258 \tag{5.1}$$

$$\hat{\varphi}_2 = \underset{(0.0637)}{0.4146}\, t_2 + \underset{0.0923)}{0.5513}\, p_2 \qquad \bar{R}^2 = 0.9502 \tag{5.2}$$

For our evaluation of these results the following values of the simple correlation coefficients will be useful:

$$r_{\varphi_1 t_1} = 0.8315 \qquad r_{\varphi_2 t_2} = 0.9222$$
$$r_{\varphi_1 n} = 0.5865 \qquad r_{\varphi_2 n} = 0.6264$$
$$r_{\varphi_1 p_1} = 0.9372 \qquad r_{\varphi_2 p_2} = 0.9236$$
$$r_{t_1 n} = 0.5582 \qquad r_{t_2 n} = 0.5104$$
$$r_{t_1 p_1} = 0.7184 \qquad r_{t_2 p_2} = 0.8073$$
$$r_{p_1 n} = 0.8125 \qquad r_{p_2 n} = 0.6430$$

The following conclusions may be drawn from the evidence shown.

(i) The high values of $\bar{R}^2$ in all four cases show that both the random errors *n* and *p* are able to explain a large part of the variance left unexplained by *t* (31 per cent in grouping 1, namely $1-0.8315^2$, and 15 per cent in grouping 2).

(ii) The error term *p* performs better than the conventional error term *n*, as shown by the $\bar{R}^2$. So the specification implied in *p*, namely that supply and demand are independent variables appears to be better able to explain the error term left by the minimum-tension theory than the conventional Gaussian error term does.

(iii) Educational grouping 2 figures can be better explained than grouping 1.

(iv) The assumption made in Tinbergen (1984), from which our example was taken, namely that the sum of the coefficients in each equation equals 1 is not far from our regressions which do not make that assumption.[1]

## Notes

1. The equations mentioned in Tinbergen (1984) were estimated with the restriction that the two coefficients add up to unity and hence are different from (5.1) and (5.2). With these restrictions they are not OLS estimates with two independent variables. The formulae used to calculate $R^2$ and $\bar{R}^2$ were those for OLS estimates and as a consequence $R^2$ and $\bar{R}^2$ are overestimated. They must be replaced by those shown in this article; so must the (underestimated) formulae for the standard deviations of their regression coefficients.

## References

HITCHCOCK, F. L. (1941) 'The Distribution of a Product from Several Sources to Numerous Localities', *Journal of Mathematics and Physics*, vol. 20, pp. 224–30.

RUMBERGER, R. W. (1981a) 'The Changing Skill Requirements of Jobs in the U.S. Economy', *Industrial and Labor Relations Review*, vol. 34, pp. 578–90.

RUMBERGER, R. W. (1981b) 'The Rising Incidence of Overeducation in the U.S. Labor Market', *Economics of Education Review*, vol. 1, pp. 293–314. The material collected and computed by Dr Rumberger was kindly made available to me in 1982, during a meeting at the University of Amsterdam.

TINBERGEN, J. (1984) 'Allocation of Workers over Jobs', *De Economist*, vol. 132, pp. 23–29. (See, however, note 1 to the present article.)

VELUPILLAI, K. (1982) 'Linear and Nonlinear Dynamics in Economics: The Contributions of Richard Goodwin', *Economic Notes*, vol. 11, pp. 73–91.

# 14 Rationality in Disequilibrium

Siro Lombardini

## 14.1 THE TRADITIONAL STATIC DEFINITION OF RATIONALITY

Rational behaviour has been traditionally defined as *maximising (optimising) behaviour*. Such a definition is grounded on the assumption of certainty (individuals have complete and certain informations) and by reference to an equilibrium structure of the system. From the individual rational behaviour so defined we can infer a criterion for rationality of the whole system: the Pareto criterion. Pareto optima are, in fact, consistent sets of individuals' rational choices.

The simple knowledge of the equilibrium structure of the system does not, however, allow us to explain why and how the system moves. Even in the pseudo-dynamic generalisation of the Walrasian equilibrium, which can be obtained by assuming that individual choices span over a certain number of periods and can be implemented in forward markets, what the equilibrium analysis offers us is a rational structure (increased by the time dimension), not a *law of movement*, the explanation of a *process*.

It is true that the Walrasian equilibrium concerns an economy that can grow. Firms may indeed find it convenient to invest because of their *expectations* of increasing demand (due essentially to increase in population and employment; technical progress being ruled out). The interest rate is then pushed to such a level as to induce consumers to save the amount which is required to finance investments. Yet the factor that causes movement of the economy (population growth) is to be found outside the system. What the equilibrium model does explain is not how such a factor operates (and why it operates) but what are the effects that *individuals' expectations* exert on the rational structure at a given moment of time.

Some equilibrium models have been produced to explain *processes*; more precisely to define *equilibrium paths*. It is sufficient to recall von

Neumann's model. Yet the optimality conditions for the economy stated by these models, are not derived by the optimising behaviour of autonomous individuals acting independently from one another. Some of these models (the aggregate Harrod–Domar for instance) have been utilised to describe mechanisms by which the system is brought to an equilibrium path (golden age path).[1] Such mechanisms are conceived as adjustment processes aiming at producing a rational structure, hence not at inducing one among the various possible processes. One can of course state the conditions under which equilibrium structures are compatible with processes envisaging equilibrium paths of growth (Lombardini and Nicola, 1975). But the *dynamic equilibrium model* does not allow us to explain how such conditions are produced. Such a model cannot indeed explain how individuals can move from one equilibrium path to another; even if when some of the structural conditions are changed the new equilibrium path becomes more convenient for the economy as a whole. In order to leave an equilibrium path, a disequilibrium situation must be produced; unused capacity must be available to make it possible for supply to match a suddenly increased demand.

We can summarise our remarks by saying that rational behaviour has been essentially defined in a static context, which can indeed justify the assumption of complete and certain information.

## 14.2 THE THEORY OF EQUILIBRIUM: AN APORETIC APPROACH TO RATIONALITY

Optimising behaviour analysis yields sets of relations – between individuals' decision variables and market parameters (and exogenous variables) – that represent *virtual movements* of the system. The virtual movements enable us to define the state of equilibrium. It is with reference to such a state that choices resulting from optimising behaviour are rational choices.

As Boland has stated (Boland, 1986), even if prices are not equilibrium prices, there may be individuals that have succeeded in attaining their goals. They find themselves on the 'short' side of both the markets in which they act as purchasers and those in which they operate as suppliers. Disequilibrium is revealed by the fact that other individuals did not succeed in implementing their rational choices. In opposition to Boland we cannot consider the first set of individuals in equilibrium. The reason can be easily explained. The second set of individuals will not be satisfied with the results of their activities. This means that, even if no change in parameters or exogenous variables occurs, they will change their decisions inducing changes in the system that will be reflected on the results of the choices of the first set of individuals. Thus the latter are not justified in assuming the prices as given (until changes occur in parameters and exogenous variables). For the system to be in equilibrium expectations must be appropriate. In fact this is not usually required in the analysis of one-period equilibrium (or more generally in one-point equilibrium).[2] But then a situation that can be qualified as equilibrium at the end of one period, may end up as a disequilibrium situation if it is considered in the context of the same period with the information acquired in the successive period.

In fact equilibrium theory does not enable us to find a meaningful solution for the problem of rational behaviour in spite of the fact that equilibrium theory has been conceived in order to describe rational structures. In order to visualise the state of equilibrium we must assume that individual choices are rational. For individual choices to be rational equilibrium has to be assumed. Walras has tried to escape this vicious circle by converting – through the *escamotage* of the auctioneer – the virtual movements into a procedure by which the equilibrium state may be reached without inducing changes in those conditions that must be assumed as given in framing the optimisation problems of the various individuals. When we consider several markets interrelated one with another, the Walras procedure is deemed impossible even on a logical plan. Few markets (the stock exchange for instance) behave in a way that resembles the Walras procedure. Unfortunately such markets are rather exceptional. For other markets the equilibrium models do not provide a theory to explain the price formation. Paradoxically, a theory originally conceived in order to explain how prices are determined is unable to interpret the process by which prices can be established.[3]

The vicious circle which we have just mentioned reminds us of the contradiction between the hypothesis of *substantive rationality* on which equilibrium analysis is based and the assumption of *adaptive behaviour* that enables us to associate a dynamic model to the equilibrium model in order to study its stability property. In equilibrium analysis individuals are considered to be rational men able to compare all alternatives. In the analysis of the process by which the equilibrium state can be attained individuals are supposed to act according to the logic of the conditioned reflexes. From superman to animal!

A similar contradiction is to be found in the Hahn process in which the stability of equilibrium has been analysed. Hahn assumes that markets are so well organised that if in a market there is excess demand only purchasers will be unable to implement their plans; all purchasers perceiving the state of excess demand in the same way. Then in Fisher's words

> Since prices adjust in the direction of aggregate excess demand, he [the individual] finds that, outside of equilibrium, the things he wishes to buy and cannot buy are getting more expensive, while the things he wishes to sell and cannot sell are getting cheaper unless they are already free. Accordingly, he finds himself getting worse and worse off in the sense that his *target* utility . . . is going down. Accordingly, the sum of such target utilities (which it is trivial to assume bounded below) will serve as a Lyapounov function and quasi-stability can be proved.
>
> (Fisher, 1983, p. 32)

We do not want to discuss the hypothesis of well-organised markets which is more questionable than it appears to be; nor do we want to deal with the hypothesis of uniformity of individuals' reactions. In fact similar hypotheses are the Achilles' heel of all aggregation procedures.[4] What we want to emphasise is that even in Hahn's scheme the process by which prices are changed is not explained in terms of individuals' rational choice. Therefore the contradiction between the superman who makes his rational choice and the animal that reacts (through his expectations, in Hahn's scheme) to disequilibrium remains.

The new classical macroeconomics has only apparently escaped the vicious circle in which the analysis of rational behaviour is entrapped. In fact it assumes that some kinds of mechanism like the Walrasian auctioneer can operate to bring all markets in equilibrium. If that can occur – no proof has been yet produced by the new classical macroeconomists – then the hypothesis of rational expectations is sufficient to ensure that individual behaviour is rational. Such an approach begs the question of how prices are formed.

What the classical macroeconomic equilibrium model can tell us is how information about changes in parameters or exogenous variables will induce changes in individuals' behaviour such that the system may be brought from the old to the new equilibrium. Comparative statics becomes the conceptual framework for the analysis of system dynamics. The dynamics of the system is thus conceived as mere adaptation of the system to changes in external factors, contrarily to the opinion of quite a few economists – like Smith and Schumpeter – that the main factors explaining economic development are internal factors; accumulation interacting with technical innovations. We do not want to consider here the assumptions required for such a procedure to be logically acceptable.[5] We want to lay stress on the role played by one specific assumption – already mentioned – which is rarely explicitly analysed, i.e. that of uniformity of individual behaviour. Even if the set of information is the same for all individuals there is no reason to think that all individuals infer the same expectations. Even though all expect prices of some commodities to increase, there might be divergent views concerning the speed of adjustment. If all individuals know that prices have been declining for some time, some may believe that the trend might soon be inverted, while others may expect the past trend to continue for some time.

Last but not least let us make some remarks on the understatement of the role of money in the traditional models of general equilibrium. It is essentially because of the role of money that the set of information offered by markets is not adequate. Then it is difficult to accept the idea that individuals can have rational expectations about the virtual price changes. It is because of this difficulty that some economists were led to analyse how individuals react to disequilibria by adjusting the quantities purchased and sold under the assumption that prices remain unchanged. Such an assumption seems reasonable in the short term.[6] Unfortunately in the short run it becomes difficult to think that individuals can complete the adjustment of their quantities to make it possible for the system to reach an equilibrium. The equilibrium is, of course, a non-Walrasian equilibrium which no longer represents a rational structure for the system. It is not this feature of the new approach that we want to emphasise but rather the fact that the process of adjustment that has to be assumed for the system to be brought to a state of equilibrium is no less difficult to conceive in operational terms than the process of price adjustment in Walrasian analysis.

Any process for the price formation that may be conceived entails either some market power of individuals or firms, or a specific power of some special agent (the Walrasian auctioneer) being able to induce other agents to change their decisions. If one wants to adhere to methodological individualism, the fact that auctioneers are necessary to run markets entails that there must be a market for auctioneers and an auctioneer to run the market for auctioneers: an *infinite regress*. If one allows individuals to have market power in order that a process for price formation can be conceived, then one of the ideological justifications for methodological individualism fails.

In fact the normal state of the economy – especially of a monetary economy – is a disequilibrium state. This means that prices will not remain unchanged. People will therefore expect price changes. As we mentioned, individuals' expectations cannot be uniform. If so the system of individuals would operate as the Walrasian auctioneer, and the new classical macroeconomics would look well founded.

A disequilibrium state may enjoy a certain stability if the actions that disappointed people should take to improve their conditions entail a cost; their outcome being uncertain and the expected improvement rather scanty. We could even convert such a state of disequilibrium into an equilibrium state by re-phrasing the individuals' problems into an uncertainty context (of limited information) and by considering the cost that actions required to change given structures (of individual wealth for instance) entail. Yet, as we noticed at the beginning of our paper, the state of equilibrium has a clear meaning (and can provide meaningful theorems in the Samuelson sense (Samuelson, 1947, pp. 3–5)) if we assume that all individuals possess certain and complete information. *If they are all alike* then it is easy to infer, from the property of the relations obtained from the solution of the individual problems, the properties of relations concerning the whole economy. A sad outcome for those people that have married methodological individualism to Benthamite liberalist ideology.[7] If the peculiarities of individuals are taken into account (in particular their creative capacities) then the state of equilibrium, as it has been interpreted by the Walrasian theory, is inconceivable.

## 14.3 RATIONAL STRUCTURES AND ECONOMIC PROCESS

Individual choices are always made in a dynamic context under uncertainty. Let us ignore for the time being the specific implications of uncertainty. The dynamics of the system are the result of internal mechanisms (accumulation and to some extent technical innovations) and of external factors (population growth, for instance).

If the system has been growing at a constant and uniform rate, then expectations can be both rational and certain. In fact the problem of expectations is ruled out. The nature of some factors of growth (technical progress) and some features of the economy (scarce natural resources that have to be utilised in combination with labour) do not allow for a uniform and constant rate of growth. So the problem of expectations arises. In a dynamic context there are additional reasons for the individuals' expectations to diverge. In fact this occurs not only because people have different opinions about the speed of adjustments (and possibly about the adjustment mechanism) but also because they have different opinions about the way the growth factors operate. All individuals may agree that a certain technical innovation is forthcoming and yet they may differ on the date of such a future event. We may all be convinced that in a near future all families will have a personal computer: but opinions may diverge on the question of how soon this will happen.

The divergencies in expectations are not only inevitable: they are also necessary for the development of the economy. Uniformity of expectations is incompatible with some entrepreneurs being innovators. Speculation is possible because people have different expectations.

Expectations must then be considered as an essential ingredient of any dynamic process. Can they be rational?

If by rationality we mean congruence between the individual's beliefs, needs, and decisions (actions) we could accept the assumption of rationality, ignoring in a first approximation the arguments by which a psychologist could explain why incoherence may occur between the individual's beliefs, his needs and his actions. Yet, before such an assumption can be made, economists must face the related problem of how expectations are formed (of why certain beliefs emerge).

Rational-expectation theorists assume that all individuals know the relevant facts and the economic mechanism and that from such knowledge they will infer the same future events. To be rational, expectations must be essentially the same.

As is well known to all students of epistemology, facts do not exist independently from theory, or, as some say, facts are 'theory laden'. We are thus caught into a vicious circle: people need a theory to single out facts; they need facts to infer (or test?) the theory. The learning process is not indeed uniform. Even on the relevance of known facts there may be divergencies between individuals. Let us ignore this difficulty. Even if we assume that information is the same for all individuals, there is no reason to believe that individuals will derive from it the same expectations. Differences may occur not only because they may have different opinions on the economic mechanism and, in particular, on the interrelations between the economic and the political systems, but also because they may differ in assessing the speed of certain adjustments and in evaluating possible future events that cannot be inferred from previous experiences.

If by rational choice we mean a process leading various individuals having the same tastes and the same (complete) information and being endowed with the same resources, to take the same decisions, which we label as *rational*, what we really do is to deprive the notion of *choice* of its proper meaning. In fact we adopt a mechanistic approach to the problem of human behaviour. Thus we ought to leave the task of explaining the individual behaviour to psychologists who do not label in advance the result of their research as *rational behaviour* and, therefore, are free to analyse all factors accounting for what the economists label as individual choices. Some economists – like von Mises – have avoided this logical trap by adopting a praxeological approach: the economists' rational behaviour is not a description of actual behaviour but a normative model. Such an approach does not avoid the logical difficulties mentioned above, on which we shall further comment; yet it helps to clarify the economists' role in explaining individuals' behaviour. There is indeed an economists' role in so far as the individual behaviour is not mechanistically determined, even when tastes are assumed as given and all information is available. This amounts to saying that past experience does not suffice to determine future activity; that uncertainty is the inevitable result of man's propensity to *explore* the future: that goals (and tastes) cannot be assumed as independent from the actual experiences.

Let us ignore some of the implications of these remarks (as we do with implications of the means–goals distinction usually drawn by economists) and return to the reasons why equilibrium models are inadequate to define rational behaviour. Our argument can be strengthened by considering one more reason as to why equilibrium models are inadequate to explain economic development. If the essential features of economic development are all taken into account, some disequilibrium states are more *efficient* than the equilibrium states that at the time can be associated with the same set of initial conditions. In fact for some factors of development to operate (for innovations to be implemented, for instance) some disequilibria must occur: unused capacities must exist in certain industries.[8]

It is true that when the system is in disequilibrium a different structure may be obtained which makes some individuals better off, with no other individual being worse off. But this is true with reference to the resources available at the beginning of the period and to the preferences of the same period. Yet the disequilibrium will allow changes in the available resources and, possibly, in individuals' preferences. After development has taken place, should people be able to come back in time with the experience acquired, they will assess the disequilibrium state as preferable to the corresponding equilibrium state.

Such a consideration raises some difficult problems concerning the rationality of the system: (a) how to compare states to which different sets of preferences are associated; (b) to what extent and under what conditions should views of those being able to promote economic development be at a premium as compared with the views of common people. We do not intend to deal with these problems. It is for this reason that we said that there can be situations in which the disequilibrium state is *more efficient* (rather than *more rational*) than the associated equilibrium. Efficiency is usually defined with regard to the rate of growth of income.

The arguments in favour of the disequilibrium approach should not lead us to think that equilibrium analysis no longer has citizenship in economic theory. In fact equilibrium analysis can still play three roles in economics:

(i) it can offer operational models that can be used to solve planning problems at various levels (firm, complex organisation, nation);
(ii) it can help in understanding some essential features of an economic structure. It makes a difference to ascertain that an economy – as can be interpreted by a disequilibrium model – admits, as logical possibilities, paths of steady growth (the models allowing us to state the conditions for such logical possibilities) with respect to alternative structures that require, for instance, ceilings or floors to prevent the system from exploding;
(iii) it helps in stating problems of economic policy. If the structure is such that normal states are disequilibrium states and if steady growth paths are logically possible, then we ought to look for

parameters or exogenous variables or relations of the model that a government can change in order to stabilise the economy; to bring the economy on a steady growth path or to keep it close to such a path. There is no doubt that in the long run, changes capable of restoring some equilibrium relations must occur, as Pasinetti has proved in his analysis of economic dynamics (Pasinetti, 1981).

In fact to define rationality for the whole system we must consider both the structural features accounting for the distribution of resources in a given period and those features that determine the capacity of the economy for growth and development. To lay stress on the conditions entailing disequilibrium, that are required for an efficient growth (difficult to assess because of the problem we have just mentioned) does not mean to ignore that the structural features of the economy determining the distribution of resources in a given period may cause some inefficiencies. Changes in the allocation of resources, as can be envisaged by equilibrium models, can then have positive effects on the development of the system. The Pareto criterion must be combined to some Schumpeterian criteria for efficient development. The combination is not easy because no Schumpeterian criterion can be defined without referring to some features of the social system, as well as to those of the economic system, while the Pareto criterion implies that all effects of the social system on the economy can be synthetised by the notion of individual *tastes*.

## 14.4 A CYBERNETIC APPROACH TO THE PROBLEM OF RATIONALITY IN DISEQUILIBRIUM

Both the traditional substantive rationality approach and the adaptive behaviouristic approach must be discarded when dealing with the problems of rationality in disequilibrium states that have to be considered – at least in the short run – as normal states. That means that individual behaviour must be explained in terms of rational (efficient?) choices. There are four mechanisms that enable us to define the individual decision problem:

(i) an optimisation model. To be rational an individual must operate in order to reach the goals he is pursuing in the most efficient way. In an uncertain context there may be some difficulties even in defining the individual's goals. In fact for a firm one alternative may be preferable to another that is more profitable if the former is likely to make easier the adjustment of its structure to unforeseeable changes – or, we can say, if it entails a higher degree of *flexibility*. The goals are not decided once and for all. As we shall see below they will be adjusted in the light of experience gained during the adjustment process.

(ii) a model for the formation of expectations. The individual has to utilise all available information to estimate some of the variables entering into the optimisation model. Such an operation is performed according to a model that the individual, more or less consciously, has built in his mind;

(iii) a mechanism of learning. In the process, the individual acquires experiences and information that enable him to revise:

 (1) the optimisation model (the goals can be revised: the flexibility requirement, for instance may increase or decrease);
 (2) the set of facts that are deemed to be relevant and the mechanism by which they are utilised for the formation of expectations and for the acquisition of experience (process of learning);
 (3) the model for the formation of expectations;
 (4) the mechanism of learning;

(iv) a model for error correction. When expectations are disappointed (for instance stocks increase faster than expected) the individual has to make some corrections in his expectations or in the models by which the problem is framed. The model for error correction establishes some links between the other models.

It is usually assumed that the decision process produces continuous relations. Discontinuities are usually associated with decisions of economic policies. In fact – as Goodwin has shown in one of his fundamental contributions (Goodwin, 1951) – discontinuities may also result as a consequence of market decisions. Even at an individual level, there may be reasons for discontinuities. When some inequalities reverse, such as those between the rate of assets rentability and the rate of interest, the individual may find it convenient to change abruptly his behaviour; for example, to stop purchasing assets and to increase his money funds.

So far we have assumed that individuals are autonomous and act independently of one another. Even in this case, if individuals are not the same under those aspects that are relevant for the process of aggregation – and even in the context of the theory of equilibrium – the aggregation of the relations explaining their behaviour raises difficult problems, which have already been hinted at. The difficulties increase tremendously if interactions between individuals are taken into account.

A first set of difficulties arises with regards to the same choice criteria. As E. F. McClennen has proved, the expected-utility principle as a basic criterion of rational behaviour, looks less plausible than is usually thought to be (McClennen, 1978). A second set of difficulties concerns the learning mechanism. As A. K. Bierring has remarked

> Sometimes we 'know' our opponent and sometimes we don't. Exactly what is involved in 'knowing' our opponent is a large issue ... In short 'knowing' an opponent means that every particular interaction with him should be viewed as one in a *series* of interactions; and that series itself has an important unity overlooked by traditional game theory.
>
> (Bierring, 1978, p. 45)

A third specific set of difficulties concerns the strategy that the various individuals have to adopt concerning the interrelations between their decisions. The analysis of situations like those reminiscent of the prisoners' dilemma, to which the von Neumann criteria are not applicable, leads T. R. Burns and D. Meeker to state that

> knowledge of the action structure is not sufficient. Also necessary are procedures capable of coordinating decision-making. This may pose obvious difficulties in the case of social action. For instance, coordination generally requires certain opportunities for implicit or explicit communication among the actors involved. Even if the conditions for a 'cooperative game' – possibly for communication and making 'binding agreements' obtain – the social relationships between the actors may be such as to preclude or inhibit utilization of available opportunities.
>
> (Burns and Meeker, 1978, p. 107)

Even in the von Neumann and Morgenstern theory of games context, if we want to make the result of the model manageable, we have to make some assumptions about the social relations among actors, as R. Luce and H. Raiffa have shown (Luce and Raiffa, 1957).

## 14.5 EMPIRICAL RESEARCH VERSUS THEORETICAL ANALYSIS

Quite a few economists will agree on the arguments we have so far advanced. Yet they will stick to the equilibrium paradigm that produces less heterogeneous results and lets the profession of economists recognise a common matrix. In fact in the last 20 years economic theory has been developing along two different lines that are becoming more and more disconnected: that of abstract models that do not intend to interpret actual processes, and that of empirical research. In spite of the advent of the theories of rational expectations and of the new classical macroeconomics, the latter has not been able to remove the aporias of the theoretical models on which it relies more or less consciously.

There are further remarks more pertinent to the issue in hand. The orientations of epistemology that prevailed in the thirties and the Keynesian revolution have led many economists to turn to the second of the two options just mentioned. This has been done without paying sufficient attention to the peculiarities of empirical research in economics.

(i) Facts are theory laden as we have already been reminded. Yet in macrophysics we can observe facts that can be singled out by using the common parlance and then look for empirical, theoretical explanations. The eclipses of the sun and of the moon could (and can) be foreseen on the basis of Kepler's laws before Newton could offer a theoretical explanation. The facts that the empirical economist utilises – and that are usually observed (evaluated) for some specific reasons that are different from those that concern scientific research – are singled out according to some previous theory and may be incapable of either confirming or falsifying a different theory. This peculiarity of research in the field of economics is linked to the fact that the economic system – that is a theoretical construction – must be conceived as an *open system* not only because some of the inputs come from outside, but also because it interacts with the social system.

(ii) Even if facts could be observed for the sake of scientific research, they would hardly represent empirical correlates of theoretical concepts. The meaning of most theoretical concepts (like that of unemployment) varies with the theoretical context in which they are defined. Empirical data are what they are.

(iii) Empirical research is in general carried out in macroeconomic terms. Changes in the structure of the aggregate variables may invalidate the theoretical model underlying the research. Some composition of public expenditure may justify the theoretical models that emphasise the inflationary effects. A different composition of public expenditure may strengthen other, positive, effects.

When the relevant structural features of the economy are maintained, it is not difficult to build various empirical models – grounded on some of the different and possibly opposing theories of the set available – that enable us to make correct forecasts. It is sufficient to choose properly the form of the relations, the distribution of lags and the trends in order to have the model confirmed by facts.

These remarks are sufficient to throw doubts on the problem of empirical criteria for validation of the theories as it is usually posed even by the supporters of the most sophisticated falsificationist criteria.[9]

## 14.6 A NEW APPROACH: THE COMPUTATIONAL ECONOMICS

If individual decision problems in disequilibrium are properly stated, having of course accepted adequate simplifications to make the analysis workable, the model obtained is in general too complex to be analysed with respect to structural properties by means of mathematical algorithms.

It is instead possible to use the model for simulations to produce *theoretical-empirical data* that can be utilised to establish *hypothetical-empirical laws*. Given the assumptions, these laws are not indubitably the operational meaningful theorems that can be derived from an axiomatic theory, but they may be more operational. They are not drawn by the observations of facts as the empirical laws claim (but are they?). Yet they may help in understanding the working of the system, in producing suggestions to rebuild the theoretical model, in stating the problems of economic policy by investigating – in more realistic contexts – the effects of governments' actions, in stimulating collection of new empirical data. Such a theoretical empirical approach has been already developed in other fields such as physics and chemistry. We can adopt the same terminology and qualify the new approach we are proposing for economics: *computational economics*.

**Notes**

1. The neo-Keynesian mechanism assumes that the effect of the change in wages – occurring when the labour market is in disequilibrium – on income distribution and that of the change in income distribution on the level of consumption can occur almost simultaneously and in such a short period as to bring forth an adjustment of the warranted rate of growth to the natural rate.

   The neo-classical mechanism entails an assumption even more unrealistic: that, because of the change in wages, entrepreneurs will change the production techniques, in such a way as to produce a change in the (aggregate) capital input and, therefore, in the warranted rate of growth large enough to set the warranted rate of growth in line with the natural rate.

   In both arguments it is assumed that after the disequilibrium has occurred in the labour market, entrepreneurs are able to adjust their expectations to the new conditions brought forth by the changes in the level of consumption or in the techniques of production and are ready to believe that the new conditions will prevail in all relevant future. It is difficult to find grounds for such an assumption.
2. It is for this reason that equilibrium at one period may be incompatible with the equilibrium in the successive periods as it has been outlined by Arrow and Hahn (1971).
3. In fact, all attempts to explain price formation on the basis of individuals' behaviour had to drop the assumption of perfect competition. See Negishi (1962) and Diamond (1984).
4. As has been proved by Wold (1953), some of the fundamental theorems of the theory of consumers' behaviour can remain valid for the aggregate demand function only if the consumers are similar. Such an assumption is required also to avoid the complications that – in a dynamic context – aggregation of individual behaviour equations entails. See Lippi (1985).
5. Let us confine ourselves to recollecting some of the assumptions that are far from being given: the uniqueness of equilibrium, its stability, the capacity of the system to come close to equilibrium in a sufficiently short time.
6. See for instance Leijonhufvud (1968)
7. The liberalist ideology has been justified with reference to individuals having the same rights and being potentially equal in their capacity to take part in economic and social life. In fact there is another interpre-

tation of liberalism, closer to a Darwinistic concept of the social system, which can be found in the works of Schumpeter and Hayek on the assumption that individuals are unequal.

8. Such disequilibria can be induced by abrupt changes in prices occurring as a consequence of a sudden change in the quantity of money. Money is the key variable in disequilibrium processes.
9. I have dealt with this problem in my paper 'Dalla teoria dell 'eqilibrio alla economia computazionale' (Lombardini, 1988).

**References**

ARROW, K. J. and F. H. HAHN (1971) *General Competitive Analysis* (San Francisco: Holden Day).

BIERRING, A. K. (1978) 'The "Tracing Procedure" and a Theory of Rational Interaction', in Hooker, *et al.* (1978), pp. 1–54.

BOLAND, L. A. (1986) *Methodology for a New Microeconomics, The Critical Foundations* (Boston, Mass.: Allen & Unwin).

BURNS, T. R. AND D. MEEKER (1978) 'Conflict and Structure in Multiple-objective Decision-making System', in Hooker, *et al.* (1978), pp. 67–114.

DIAMOND, P. A. (1984) *A Search–Equilibrium Approach to the Microfoundations of Macroeconomics, The Wicksell Lectures 1982* (Cambridge, Mass.: MIT Press).

FISHER, F. (1983) *Disequilibrium Foundations of Equilibrium Economics* (Cambridge: Cambridge University Press).

GOODWIN, R. M. (1951) 'The Nonlinear Accelerator and the Persistence of Business Cycles', *Econometrica*, vol. 19, no. 1, pp. 1–17.

HOOKER, C. A., J. J. LEACH and E. F. McCLENNEN (eds) (1978) *Foundations and Applications of Decision Theory, Volume I: Theoretical Foundations* (Boston, Mass.: E. Reidel Publishing Company).

LEIJONHUFVUD, A. (1968) *On Keynesian Economics and the Economics of Keynes* (New York: Oxford University Press).

LIPPI, M. (1985) 'Sulla dinamica delle relazioni tra variabili aggregate', *Politica economia*, (August), pp. 141–65.

LOMBARDINI, S. (1988) 'Dalla teoria dell'equilibrio alla economia computazionale', in *Rundiconti del Seminario Matematico di Brescia Saggi in onore di F. Manara*, a cura di S. Lombardini, G. Melzi, P. C. Nicola (Milano: Vita e Pensiero).

LOMBARDINI, S. and P. C. NICOLA (1975) 'Income Distribution and Economic Development in Ricardian and Walrasian Models', in *Proceedings of the Second Polish–Italian Conference, On Applications of System Theory to Economics* (Rome).

LUCE, R. and H. RAIFFA (1957) *Games and Decisions* (New York: John Wiley & Sons).

McCLENNEN, E. F. (1978) 'The Minimax Theory and Expected-utility Reasoning', in Hooker, *et al.* (1978), pp. 337–67.

NEGISHI, T. (1962) 'The Stability of a Competitive Economy', *Econometrica*, (Oct.).

PASINETTI, L. L. (1981) *Structural Change and Economic Growth, A*

*Theoretical Essay on the Dynamics of the Wealth of Nations* (Cambridge: Cambridge University Press).
SAMUELSON, P. A. (1947) *Foundations of Economic Analysis* (Cambridge, Mass.: Harvard University Press).
WOLD, H. (in association with LARS JUREEN) (1953) *Demand Analysis: A Study in Econometrics* (New York, John Wiley & Sons, Inc.).

# 15 Probabilistic Causality and Economic Models: Suppes, Keynes and Granger

Alessandro Vercelli

> As our knowledge is partial, there is constantly, in our use of the term cause, some reference implied or expressed to a limited body of knowledge.
>
> (Keynes, 1921, p. 306)

## 15.1 INTRODUCTION

Concepts of causality have played an important role in economics since the early fifties. They have been involved in many theoretical and methodological debates as well as in the appraisal of alternative theories and models.

At the roots of modern conceptions of causality in economics we find authors like Keynes, who often used causal concepts in developing his economic arguments, and Tinbergen, who gave a version of 'process analysis' that lent itself particularly well to causal analysis. A crucial step for working out a conception of causality rigorous and general enough for economic analysis was taken in the late forties and early fifties, when causality was redefined in the language of matrix algebra which was to find a widespread application in economics. A seminal contribution in this direction came from Goodwin (1947) who was able to clarify the relation between 'unilateral coupling' (as he preferred to call what would later be called a 'causal relation') and the formal properties of matrices necessary to express it.[1] This contribution inspired the papers written in the early fifties by Simon (1952, 1953, 1954), who built on the suggestions of Goodwin.[2] He adopted an explicitly causal language, referring openly to the philosophical literature on causality. Simon's conception of causality rapidly became the most influential one in economics, and remained so until very recently. Its dominance was challenged only much later by the conception worked out by Granger (1963, 1969, 1980) and developed by Sims (1972, 1977). This conception has been found congenial by many new classical economists trying to undo the Keynesian revolution, while that of Simon has often been favoured by Keynesian economists.[3] Concepts of causality are thus crucially involved in the current lively debate on the foundations of macroeconomics.

In order to clarify certain aspects of this debate I shall use the rigorous conception of probabilistic causality recently worked out by the well-known epistemologist Suppes (1970, 1984) with the aim of explicating[4] the causality concepts of Keynes and Granger.

I will argue in particular that:

(i) Keynes' conception of causality is probabilistic and in many respects anticipates that of Suppes;
(ii) Granger's conception of causality is *prima facie* philosophically legitimate (which was denied by Zellner (1979) among others), since it may be interpreted in its turn as a version of Suppes' probabilistic causality, but its application to economic models is philosophically questionable;
(iii) there are no grounds for believing that in economic analysis Granger causality should in general be preferred to that of Simon.

## 15.2 SUPPES' PROBABILISTIC CAUSALITY

Probabilistic causality has occupied a central place in the philosophic debate on causality since the publication in 1970 of a monograph by Suppes which rapidly became a classic of epistemological literature. Thus probabilistic causality has a very short history, though we could mention a few earlier seminal contributions which remained completely neglected (Reichenbach, 1956; Good, 1961, 1962; and, as we shall see, Keynes, 1921). At first sight this might appear quite surprising, because both ingredients of the concept have been on the stage of philosophical debate for a very long time (more than two millenia for causality and more than two centuries for probability). This may be ascribed to the fact that causality and determinism were considered mutually inseparable until very recently, when the quantum physics revolution (which began in the thirties) had had time to percolate through into common wisdom, and probabilistic language (after Kolmogorov's axiomatisation in 1933) began to acquire the sophistication needed to fit the subtleties of causal language.

It is rather early to attempt a full appraisal of the usefulness of probabilistic causality in single disciplines, such as economics. Preliminary work is needed to develop and adapt it to the specific requirements of economic analysis. Suppes' conception is particularly fruitful for this purpose because his point of view is taxonomic rather than prescriptive.

The starting point of his analysis is not, as was typical in earlier literature, a stipulative definition of causality proposed as the paradigm for a correct use of the concept. All attempts in this direction had proved rather unsuccessful because the range of application of each of these concepts was shown to be very narrow compared to the wide variety of meanings that may be found in scientific languages.

Suppes thus prefers to start from a 'weak' definition of causality which may be considered the 'least common denominator' of a wide variety of causal concepts. This is seen as a necessary premise for articulating the definition so that the ensuing causal analysis may evolve in diverse directions to fit the different characteristics of many subjects and languages. This approach agrees very well with a discipline like economics, where the causal intuitions are particularly varied and heterogeneous.

The starting point is the concept of '*prima facie* cause', which may be roughly defined in the following way: 'An event B is a *prima facie* cause of an event A if and only if (i) B occurs earlier than A, (ii) the conditional probability of A occurring when B occurs is greater than the unconditional probability of A occurring' (Suppes 1984, p. 48). In other words, the occurrence of event B increases the probability of the occurrence of event A. *Prima facie* causality is thus a necessary, though not sufficient, condition for identifying a peculiar causal relation. Such a weak concept is unable to discriminate between 'genuine' causes and 'spurious' causes because even spurious causes appear to increase the probability that the effect will occur.

In order to discuss this and the following problems, we must now introduce a slightly more precise definition of *prima facie* causality. Let us assume that $A_t$ and $B_t$ are events defined as 'subsets of all the possible outcomes', i.e. in the sense, introduced by Kolmogorov (1933), of the mathematical theory of probability. In addition, let us assume that the events are referred to a well-defined instant in time. We may thus introduce the following definition:

*Definition 1*: $B_t$ is a *prima facie* (potential) cause of $A_{t'}$ as regards the background information $Z_t$ iff

(i) $P(B_t \cap Z_t) > 0$ and $t < t'$

(ii) $P(A_{t'}/B_t \cap Z_t) > P(A_{t'}/Z_t)$

This definition is identical to that put forward by Suppes (1970) except for two specifications, implicit in Suppes, which are particularly relevant for what follows.

First of all we have stated explicitly that *prima facie* causality does not necessarily presuppose the actual occurrence of events. This allows a consistent utilisation of Suppes causality within an explicit theoretical context, because the concept becomes applicable not only to single events but also to types of events, and not only to directly observable magnitudes but also to dispositions. As is generally agreed, types of events and dispositions are essential ingredients in any theoretical argument.[5]

We also stated explicitly from the very outset that in Suppes' approach any causal statement or inference is always relative to a *corpus* of information organised by theoretical hypotheses which we may define as 'background information'. This should be kept firmly in mind in order to understand the nexus linking the conceptions of causality of Suppes, Keynes and Granger.

We are now in a position to analyse the distinction between genuine and spurious causes. Let us begin by examining a couple of examples. One of the favourite examples of a spurious cause, at least since Laplace, has been that of the barometer. The sudden shift of the barometer pointer is a *prima facie* cause of the storm which breaks out shortly afterwards, because the first event induces an upward revision of the probability of the second event. But the barometer shift is not a genuine cause of the storm, for as everyone knows both events are effects of a third cause: the drop in atmospheric pressure. In other words, as soon as we take account of the common cause, the effect becomes stochastically independent of the spurious cause. In Reichenbach's terminology, the common cause *screens off* the *prima facie* influence of the spurious cause (Reichenbach, 1956). This suggests the following definition:

*Definition 2*: $B_t$ is a *spurious* cause of $A_{t'}$ iff
(i) $B_t$ is a *prima facie* cause of $A_{t'}$
(ii) there is a $t'' < t$ and an event $C_{t''}$ such that

$$P(B_t \cap C_{t''}) > 0$$

$$P(A_{t'}/B_t \cap C_{t''}) = P(A_{t'}/C_{t''})$$

$$P(A_{t'}/B_t \cap C_{t''}) \geqq P(A_{t'}/B_t)$$

The barometer example might, because of its theoretical obviousness, obscure the crucial role played by the conceptual framework in any argument aimed at discriminating between spurious and genuine causes. An example drawn from economics may better illustrate this point. Both Keynes and classical economists would readily have admitted that an increase in real wages above the full employment level could be seen as a *prima facie* cause of a reduction in employment. However, Keynes would have considered such a cause to be spurious, since both events would have been interpreted as joint effects of a reduction in effective demand. On the other hand a classical economist, who rejected the principle of effective demand and accepted Say's Law, would have considered such a cause to be genuine.

Suppes' approach refers back to the prestigious Humean tradition aiming to extend its range of validity to the analysis of probabilistic phenomena. In addition he goes 'beyond Hume' in two other points which have great epistemological importance.

First of all, as we have already emphasised, any causal statement has meaning only in relation to a given theoretical framework. Suppes is here influenced by the contributions of post-positivist philosophers (such as Kuhn, Lakatos, Feyerabend), which he integrates into his own version of critical empiricism.

The second point gives a stimulating perspective on the *vaexata questio* of 'causal production', which many authors consider an essential characteristic of any satisfactory causal concept, but which Hume and his followers considered as a bit of metaphysical baggage to be carefully avoided. Suppes finds a way to analyse the problem without violating the Humean anti-metaphysical principles. There is no point in denying the existence of 'causal mechanisms' that describe and explain how the causal influence is produced or transmitted from cause to effect, provided that we are aware that these mechanisms may vary in different phenomena and may be interpreted in multifarious ways by different theories. In the history of thought we find diverse paradigms of the typical, or 'ultimate', causal mechanism. In Descartes' philosophy the paradigmatic causal mechanism was based on the impact of physical bodies, whereas for Kant it was based on the reciprocal influence of attractive and repulsive forces. Analogously, in economics we may easily detect a traditional contrast between authors who base the intelligibility of phenomena on individual reactions to external stimuli, and authors who base it on an equilibrium configuration of interdependent relations.

Suppes' own point of view, consistently with his epistemological pluralism and relativism, rejects the existence of an 'ultimate' causal mechanism. Different causal mechanisms may coexist in different empirical and/or theoretical contexts. Moreover, even within the same empirical and theoretical contexts, the paradigmatic causal mechanism accepted by one generation of scholars tends to be further analysed and explained by a subsequent generation of scholars in terms of simpler and more basic mechanisms. Suppes is led by these arguments to consider causal mechanisms as 'black boxes' which may be analysed without contravening the Humean anti-metaphysical principles.[6]

On these premises Suppes was able to work out a very flexible concept of causality which may be applied in different empirical and theoretical contexts. We cannot survey here the interesting articulations, specifications and developments of the concept explored by Suppes and his followers. We shall only briefly recall two aspects which are particularly useful for the following analysis.

First of all, Suppes defines deterministic causality as a particular instance of probabilistic causality:

*Definition 3*: $A_t$ is a sufficient cause of $B_{t'}$ iff

(i) $A_t$ is a *prima facie* cause of $B_{t'}$

(ii) $P(B_{t'}/A_t) = 1$

Suppes causality may thus be applied also to deterministic causality.

In addition, Suppes causality also applies whenever probability is not measurable on a cardinal scale. This is particularly important in disciplines like economics where these unhappy circumstances often prevail, as Keynes and many other economists have recognised. As Hicks recently maintained, in economics probabilities are in most cases only ordinable, and then often not even in a complete way (Hicks, 1979, p. 115). Suppes' theory may be easily adapted to these cases by translating his quantitative theory into a qualitative one, following the suggestions put forward by Keynes (1921) and developed by Koopman (1940). According to Keynes and Suppes the qualitative conception of probability is essentially comparative and is founded on the following primitive relation:

*Definition 4*: B given A is at least as probable as D given C:

$$(B/A) \geqq (D/C)$$

As Keynes wittily observed: 'no proposition is in itself either probable or improbable, just as no place can be intrinsically distant' (Keynes, 1921, p. 7).

## 15.3 SUPPES' THEORY OF PROBABILISTIC CAUSALITY: OPEN PROBLEMS AND GLIMPSES BEYOND

As Suppes himself recognised, his theory of causality raises more problems than it is able to solve. That, however, may well be considered as the hallmark of a progressive research programme. Suppes himself points out and discusses many of these open questions with a very constructive and anti-dogmatic attitude. Let us examine a couple of them which are particularly relevant for application in the field of economics.

First of all, Suppes' definition of cause applies only to events. Suppes admits that this assumption is potentially restrictive because 'many causes are not conceived as events' (Suppes, 1970, p. 71). This limitation is common to many theories of causality, but is particularly awkward for that of Suppes which is meant to explicate the current use of the term rather than to stipulate 'the right one'.

Moreover, the concept of 'event' chosen by Suppes appears, at first sight, very different from the usual one. In ordinary language, by 'event' we mean a change of state rather than a state described in terms of set theory. However, nothing prevents a definition of a change of state in set-theoretic terms, so that in this sense ordinary events are Suppes events, although the opposite is not always true. Moreover in ordinary language events are *actual* events, while Suppes events are *possible* events which may or may not be actualised. As we see Suppes' acceptation includes the ordinary acceptation but is much broader, and ultimately overlaps with philosophers' definition of 'state of affairs' or 'proposition'.[7] Summing up, any object defined in set-theoretic terms may be considered as a Suppes event.[8] This is true in particular for economic variables, which are often defined in set-theoretic terms and are indeed easily definable in that way. We may conclude that Suppes' probabilistic causality may be widely applied in economics.

The second difficulty is more serious. Suppes' probabilistic causality in the existing version applies only to instantaneous events. This is a grave limitation for a discipline like economics which often deals with events having a significant temporal extension ('chunk events' in Suppes' language). This is true in particular of the stock variables (such as wealth, capital, inventories, etc.); as for flow variables (such as income, saving, investment, etc.), they are almost never measured in an instant of time. Moreover this problem is particularly serious whenever aggregation is likely to introduce a temporal extension into the variables involved, and thus especially in macroeconomics.

We may, however, entertain a reasonable hope that Suppes causality can be extended to chunk events. The theory of probabilistic causality recently worked out by Salmon,[9] which is in many respects complementary to that of Suppes, concentrates precisely on the causal analysis of chunk events (called 'processes'). An integration of both theories seems not impossible, and it would be invaluable for working out a theory of probabilistic causality suitable for economic analysis.

The second set of problems is no less serious. The assumption introduced by Suppes, in the spirit of Hume, that the cause must precede the effect, excludes contemporaneous causation, although we may find many instances of it in ordinary language as well as in various scientific languages. This assumption is thus inconsistent with the explicative rather than stipulative point of view adopted by Suppes' theory. This difficulty cannot be overcome within the current version of Suppes causality, because if we drop the requisite of strict temporal inequality it is possible to prove that any cause is spurious (Suppes, 1970, p. 22). Suppes justifies this assumption for the physical world by appealing to the principle of 'retarded action'; and, for social sciences, to a time-consuming process of communication which necessarily mediates individual decisions. Both arguments can be accepted only from a well-defined theoretical and methodological point of view. In social sciences, for example, methodological individualism and behaviourism are presupposed. A serious attempt to extend Suppes' theory in such a way as to include contemporaneous causation would seem to me more consistent with the spirit of his contribution. I wish here to suggest the outline of an extension which could achieve this result.

The basic idea, following a time-honoured tradition in economic theory, is to distinguish between the 'historical' (or 'ontological') time t and the 'epistemic' time θ (often called by economists 'logical').[10] By historical time I mean the time characterising natural and social history, which is completely independent of any kind of human activity; by epistemic time I mean any irreversible order of succession, independent of the historical sequence, attributed by the epistemic subject to the elements of a process. A good example of epistemic time is given by the irreversible order of computation implied by a recursive function (this kind of order of succession gives the formal foundation for both Goodwin's unilateral coupling and the causal relation in Simon and Wold).

I am now in a position to reformulate Suppes' first definition in the following way:

*Definition 5*: $B_{t\theta}$ is a (potential) *prima facie* cause of $A_{t'\theta'}$ relative to the background information $Z_t$ iff

(i) $P(B_t \cap Z_t) > 0$

(ii) $t < t'$ and/or $\theta < \theta'$

(iii) $P(A_{t'\theta'}/B_{t\theta} \cap Z_t) > P(A_{t'\theta'}/Z_t)$

This definition overcomes the difficulties Suppes encountered in defining a concept of contemporaneous causation consistent with his theory. We may define a relation of contemporaneous causation whenever (5) is specified in the following way: $t = t'$ and $\theta < \theta'$. In other words, the order of succession between cause and effect is in this case merely epistemic and does not imply a temporal succession in the historical sense. The relation between investment and income in Keynes' static multiplier may be considered as an example of contemporaneous causation. In this case we have an epistemic succession based on the exogeneity of investment relative to the income–expenditure circuit, but we do not have a succession in historical time.

Suppes causality is a special case of (5) whenever $t<t'$. I will call this kind of causality 'sequential', following the terminological suggestion of Hicks (1979). We may distinguish two different kinds of sequential causality: e-sequential whenever $t<t'$ and $\theta<\theta'$, i.e. when the order of succession is both historical and epistemic, and h-sequential whenever $t<t'$ and $\theta=\theta'$, i.e. when the order of succession is historical but not epistemic. An example of e-sequential causality may be given by a lagged recursive function (for example, Keynes' dynamic multiplier where the autonomous investment, being exogenous, cannot be an effect), while an example of h-sequential causality would be a lagged reversible function (for example, the Keynesian equality between aggregate expenditure and lagged aggregate income; here both variables are considered as endogenous: the only reason to individuate a causal order lies in the historical temporal lag).

## 15.4 KEYNES AND SUPPES

In his economic contributions Keynes often employs a causal language, but in these writings he never clarifies the precise meaning of the causal concepts utilised. However, the issue is discussed in some detail in *A Treatise on Probability* (1921), where he worked out the foundations of his epistemological point of view. We find there a very interesting outline of a theory of probabilistic causality which in many respects anticipates the more mature and sophisticated theory of Suppes. The interpreters of Keynesian thought have neglected this link,[11] partly because they could not be acquainted with a fully-fledged theory of probabilistic causality, which is very recent. Keynesian causality has thus been interpreted as a version of deterministic causality close to that of Simon and Wold. The trouble is that Keynes explicitly judges deterministic causality to be not very useful, especially for 'Moral Sciences':[12]

> One is led, almost inevitably, to use 'cause' more widely than 'sufficient cause' or than 'necessary cause', because, the necessary causation of particulars by particulars being rarely apparent to us, the strict sense of the term has little utility.
>
> (Keynes, 1921, p. 306)

Keynes feels the need of a much more comprehensive concept of causality than the traditional one. What is required is a concept of '*probable cause*, where there is no implication of necessity and where the antecedents will sometimes lead to particular consequents and sometimes will not' (Keynes, 1921, p. 306). He is fully aware of the novelty and difficulties of this task, because 'a partial or possible cause involves ideas which are still obscure' (Keynes, 1921, p. 182). The main problems arise from the conviction, then universally shared, that physical determinism could not be questioned.[13] Keynes manages to get round the obstacle, in a way, by introducing a crucial distinction between the *causa essendi*, i.e. the ontological cause which in the physical world must be conceived as deterministic, and the *causa cognoscendi*, i.e. the epistemic cause which may be conceived as probabilistic. He puts the main emphasis on the second, because

> we wish to know whether knowledge of one fact throws light *of any kind* upon the likelihood of another. The theory of causality is only important because it is thought that by means of its assumptions light *can* be thrown by the experience of one phenomenon upon the expectation of another.
>
> (Keynes, 1921, p. 308)

Ontological causality (*causa essendi*) is interpreted as a limiting case of epistemic causality, whenever we have accurate enough knowledge of a certain set of phenomena to be able to individuate a necessary or sufficient cause. This is possible only if we are able to determine the nomic conditions K, both formal and theoretical, and the existential conditions (both general $L_t$ and hypothetical $H_t$) which make the causal influence of one event on another sufficient or necessary.

The nexus between ontological and epistemic causality is clarified by Keynes through a succession of formal definitions of causality, which constitutes a sort of descent from the paradise of certainty to the hell of uncertainty. The starting point is given by a definition of *causa essendi*;

> *Definition 6*: An event A described by proposition a is a sufficient cause in conditions kl of an event B described by proposition b, iff
>
> (i) event A is referred to moments which are all prior to those at which event B occurred;
>
> (ii) $b/akl = 1$ and $b/kl \neq 1$

This definition may be easily translated into Suppes' language setting $a = A_t$, $b = B_{t'}$, $kl = K \cap L_t = Z_t$. This is possible because, as we have seen, Suppes' events are strictly analogous to Keynes' propositions. Definition (6) is translated in the following way:

*Definition 7*: $A_t$ is a sufficient cause of $B_{t'}$ relative to $Z_t = K \cap L_t$, iff

(i) $P(A_t \cap Z_t) > 0$ and $t < t'$

(ii) $P(B_{t'}/A_t \cap Z_t) = 1$ and $P(B_{t'}/Z_t) \neq 1$

Notice that $A_t$ is a (potential) *prima facie* cause of $B_{t'}$ because (ii) implies that $P(B_{t'}/A_t \cap Z_t) > P(B_t/Z_t)$. Keynes' formulation (7) is thus strictly equivalent to Suppes' definition (3).

Keynes then progressively weakens definition (7) by relaxing the conditions under which a concept of ontological causality may be defined. An intermediate step is, for example, the definition of a 'possible sufficient cause', when the background information $Z_t$ includes a set $H_t$ of existential hypotheses. The last step in this chain of definitions is that of the *causa cognoscendi*:

*Definition 8*: $A_t$ is a *causa cognoscendi* of $B_{t'}$ relative to $Z_t$ iff

(i) $P(A_t \cap Z_t) > 0$

(ii) $P(B_{t'}/A_t \cap Z_t) \neq P(B_{t'}/Z_t)$

We may easily verify that a *causa cognoscendi*, which does not imply a necessary or sufficient nexus between cause and effect, corresponds to a (potential) *prima facie* cause as stated by Suppes in definition (1), apart from the two following differences:

(i) the temporal lag is not required. Keynes does not exclude the possibility of an epistemic cause contemporaneous with its effect. It is no wonder that contemporaneous causation may be found in his economic contributions;

(ii) the positive statistical relevance of the cause for the effect is not required. In other words a cause might also reduce the probability of the occurrence of the effect (in which case the cause is 'negative' or inhibitory).[14]

Keynes stops here in the *Treatise* because the theory of epistemic causality ends up by overlapping with his theory of probability. Still, I believe it is not improper to consider Keynes as a forerunner of the theory of probabilistic causality, especially of the Suppes version.

## 15.5 GRANGER'S PROBABILISTIC CAUSALITY

The causality concept worked out by Granger in the sixties (1963, 1969), following a suggestion by Wiener (1958), has been and still is at the centre of a lively debate over its range of validity and its implications for economic theory. A few economists and econometricians have even questioned its epistemological legitimacy on the grounds that it was inconsistent with an alleged philosophical tradition (see in particular Zellner, 1979). Even so, Granger causality rapidly became the prevailing conception of causality in economics and econometrics, probably because it was found particularly congenial to the monetarist tendencies which became very popular in the seventies.

Its fortune may be dated back to the publication of an influential article by Sims (1972), who used Granger causality to argue that the money stock exerts a strong causal influence on nominal income and not vice versa. Granger causality rapidly became very popular with the new classical economists (Lucas, Sargent, Barro, etc.), partly because it was found to fit in well with the rational-expectations hypothesis.[15] This notion also became an important source of inspiration for the new econometrics founded on time-series analysis, 'without pretending to have too much *a priori* economic theory' (Sargent and Sims, 1977). An appraisal of its epistemological legitimacy and its range of validity is thus very important. The observations developed above turn out to be very useful for this task.

Granger develops his conception of causality through a succession of definitions which, not unlike that of Keynes, follows a downward path towards the hell of uncertainty. It is justified in this case by the need to reach a definition of causality which is 'operative', i.e. amenable to empirical verification.

Let us assume that $Y_n$ and $X_{n+1}$ are two stochastic variables, and $\Omega_n$ is a complete set of information available at time n, and F is the function describing the distribution conditional to X.

The starting point is the following definition:

*Definition 9*: $Y_n$ is cause of $X_{n+1}$ iff

$$F(X_{n+1}/\Omega_n) \neq F(X_{n+1}/\Omega_n - Y_n)$$

In other words 'for causation to occur, the variable $Y_n$ needs to have some unique information about what value $X_{n+1}$ will take in the immediate future' (Granger, 1980, p. 330). In order to make this definition operative, Granger has to substitute for the complete information set $\Omega_n$ the incomplete information sets $J_n$, the information set actually available at time n, and $J'_n$, the information set $J_n$ plus the past and present values of $Y_n$. We obtain the following definition:

*Definition 10*: $Y_n$ is a *prima facie* cause of $X_{n+1}$ relative to the information set $J'_n$ iff

$$F(X_{n+1}/J'_n) \neq F(X_{n+1}/J_n)$$

The use of incomplete information sets makes it necessary to introduce two qualifications which bring Granger's definition closer to that of Suppes:

(i) the causal statement must be interpreted in relation to a certain complex of background information;
(ii) $Y_n$ thus becomes only a *prima facie* cause since we cannot exclude the possibility that new information might turn it spurious.

The definition is not yet operative because an empirical test should up to now refer to population attributes of $X_{n+1}$, which we cannot know. Granger is thus compelled to be content with the first moment of the distribution, introducing the following definition:

*Definition 11*: $Y_n$ is a *prima facie* cause in mean of $X_{n+1}$ relative to the information set $J'_n$ iff

$$E(X_{n+1}/J'_n) \neq E(X_{n+1}/J_n)$$

In addition Granger limits himself to point forecasts of $X_{n+1}$ using a least-squares criterion. We may eventually express an operative definition of Granger causality, assuming that $\sigma^2(X/J_n)$ is the variance of the one-step forecast error of $X_{n+1}$ given $J_n$.

*Definition 12*: $Y_n$ is a *prima facie* cause in mean of $X_{n+1}$ relative to the information set $J'_n$ iff

$$\sigma^2(X_{n+1}/J'_n) < \sigma^2(X_{n+1}/J_n)$$

In other words, the knowledge of $Y_n$ increases one's ability to forecast $X_{n+1}$ in a least-squares sense, because it reduces the variance of the forecast errors. Since much current economic and econometric practice is prediction oriented, we may well understand why this definition, although very restrictive, has appealed to many. However, the definition actually tested is further restricted to linear predictors (Granger, 1969, p. 429, and 1980, p. 338), owing to the limitations of the available modelling and forecasting techniques:

*Definition 13*: $Y_n$ is a linear *prima facie* cause in mean of $X_{n+1}$ relative to the information set $J'_n$ iff (12) is applied to a class of linear predictors.

From now on the term 'Granger causality' will stand for the concept stipulated in this last definition.

Before discussing the concept's range of validity, we must recall that its operational implementation is subject to further limitations. The principal ones are made explicit by Granger himself through the following axioms:

*Axiom A*: 'The past and present may cause the future, but the future cannot cause the past' (Granger, 1980, p. 330).

This axiom excludes not only backward causation, whose relevance is questionable, but also 'contemporaneous causation' which – as we have seen – is considered important by many economists.

*Axiom B*: 'the information sets contain no redundant information' (Granger, 1980, p. 330).

This axiom is much more restrictive than it may appear at first. Redundant information could generate the erroneous conviction that a certain *prima facie* cause is spurious. This difficulty is particularly serious with economics, whose time series often follow very similar patterns.

*Axiom C*: 'all causal relationships remain constant in direction through time' (Granger, 1980, p. 335).

This axiom has been considered very stringent by a few critics (see, for example, Zellner, 1982, p. 314). However, Granger is right in pointing out that this assumption, though not literally true, is usual in causal inference and, indeed in scientific inference. Much more disturbingly restrictive is the related hypothesis, routinely accepted in testing procedures of Granger causality, that the series are jointly covariance stationary. This assumption, according to Granger, is not strictly necessary for the definition of causality but is required for practical implementation. He admits that economic time series are often non-stationary, but he believes that they can be made stationary by transformations such as those suggested by Box and Cox and by Box and Jenkins. Unfortunately it may be shown that these transformations do not preserve the causal properties of the original time series (see Conway, Swamy and Yanagida, 1983, pp. 17–23).

In addition, we have to emphasise that, as Granger himself stressed (1980), his definition of causality does not apply to single events, to deterministic processes, or to data not measureable on a cardinal scale.

## 15.6 GRANGER AND SUPPES

As we have seen, the range of applicability of Granger causality is much narrower than that of Suppes causality. We may further clarify the issue by translating into Suppes' language Granger's definition 10, which is the most general definition that postulates incomplete information as in Suppes. Let us assume that $A_{t'} = X_{n+1}$, $B_t = Y_n$, $Z_t = J_n$, $B_t \cap Z_t = J'_n$, and that both $A_{t'}$ and $B_t$ occurred. Granger's definition 10 may thus be expressed in the following way:

*Definition 14*: $B_t$ is a *prima facie* Granger cause of $A_{t'}$ relative to background information $Z_t$ iff

(i) $A_{t'}$ and $B_t$ occur and $t < t'$

(ii) $F(A_{t'}/B_t \cap Z_t) \neq F(A_{t'}/Z_t)$

As we may easily verify by comparing (14) with (1), Granger causality appears as a particular case of Suppes causality.[16] This suffices to confer upon Granger causality a *prima facie* philosophical legitimacy, which Zellner wrongly denies. Moreover, it seems possible that the conception of causality adopted by Keynes and that adopted by the new classical economists, though the latter are uncompromising anti-Keynesians, both belong to the same philosophic family.

However, the formal analogy conceals a profound difference. In both Keynes and Suppes background information encompasses a theoretical framework, while in Granger it includes only the past and present values of the relevant stochastic variables. The other peculiarities of Granger causality, such as the exclusive reference to single events which have actually occurred, and hence not to types of events or to dispositional magnitudes, all follow this inductivist point of view. The supporters of Granger causality see this as vindicating its superiority over competing notions of causality. In their opinion, Granger causality is the only conception of causality which is actually operative, in the sense that the results of empirical tests are 'non-conditional', i.e. independent of *a priori* theoretical assumptions. This alleged superiority is argued in particular *vis-à-vis* Goodwin–Simon–Wold causality, which was and still is the main existing alternative for economic analysis. It is shown that from the formal point of view these two conceptions are strictly analogous, and that the only significant difference is that Goodwin, Simon and Wold always explicitly refer their causal statements to a theoretical framework. Moreover, it is admitted that the range of applicability is broader in this second case. If we could prove that the unconditionality claim is wrong, the superiority claim would in general be denied, if not reversed.

Many empirical tests of Granger causality have been devised, with different advantages and disadvantages. However, they all have in common a two-stage procedure of implementation. In the first stage a few statistical tests are applied to empirical data, and in the second stage the results of these tests are interpreted. In the first stage the theoretical hypotheses are not clearly defined. It could be objected that any procedure of selection and manipulation of data already presupposes a theoretical point of view, even if only implicitly.[17] Whatever one may think of this objection, in the second stage serious difficulties emerge which I consider insuperable. The crucial problem is to discriminate between genuine and spurious causes. This cannot be done without an *explicit* intervention of theoretical hypotheses.

Granger, Sims and other supporters of Granger causality believe that they can get round this obstacle. They discuss a list of circumstances under which a *prima facie* cause is likely to be spurious, in order to prove that all these circumstances are extremely unlikely in the case of Granger causality. Unfortunately this strategy fails.

For example, in order to exclude the possibility of finding a third variable that would make a *prima facie* cause spurious, it is suggested that certain empirical tests be applied to all the variables that might have this effect. This procedure is clearly unacceptable, unless we make a sufficient number of *a priori* theoretical assumptions regarding the behaviour of the economic system. Otherwise the list of third variables which could induce spuriousness would be virtually infinite.

More generally, we may observe that one cannot demonstrate the exhaustiveness of any list of circumstances which might induce spuriousness. An *a priori* discussion on the likelihood of certain spuriousness-inducing circumstances cannot substantially increase the confidence in the 'genuineness' of a certain *prima facie* cause, unless one explicitly declares his theoretical background. Thus even Granger causality refers implicitly to a certain theoretical conceptual framework. The only real difference in this respect is that the theoretical hypotheses are made explicit by Goodwin, Simon and Wold, while they remain implicit in the arguments of Granger and Sims. The charge of presupposition against Simon and Wold may thus be turned against Granger and Sims. What we really cannot do is to assert the truth of a causal statement, claiming that it is 'unconditional' with regard to a given theoretical framework.

Granger and Sims seem occasionally unaware of the well-known limits of inductive methods, which have been clarified by the prestigious philosophical tradition going from Hume to Popper and beyond. They apparently accept one or more of the following mistaken axioms:

(a) measurement is possible without theory;
(b) correlation implies causation;
(c) *post hoc ergo propter hoc.*

Each of these theses is at times provocatively entertained by the supporters of Granger causality,[18] perhaps in order to flaunt the novelty of their conception, as if the new techniques of time series were by themselves able to overcome the traditional methodological principles. In so doing they slip into the pitfalls of 'operationism' and 'inductivism', long since noted and rejected by the philosophy of science.

However, there is a second line of defence for Granger causality which is less pretentious and more convincing. Granger causality is considered particularly relevant for certain specific scientific aims. We recall in particular the following claims (see, for example, Sargent, 1977; Sims, 1972, 1976):

(i) Granger causality is a necessary and sufficient condition for exogeneity, which is a necessary condition for efficient estimation;
(ii) Granger causality is a necessary and sufficient condition for optimal forecasts;
(iii) Granger causality is a necessary, though not sufficient, condition for economic policy (forecast and control).

Unfortunately even these claims are exaggerated. Granger causality is a necessary but not sufficient condition for predicting the outcomes of processes which are not influenced by policy, or are in any case structurally stable. But it is neither a necessary nor a sufficient condition for correct estimation, nor for prediction and control of processes which are influenced by policy interventions, or which are in any way structurally unstable (Engle, Hendry and Richard, 1983).

We may thus conclude that Granger causality is not useless for a few well-defined and circumscribed scientific aims. But the claim of its general superiority over alternative conceptions of causality, in particular that of Goodwin, Simon and Wold, is totally groundless.

## 15.7 CONCLUSIONS

The conception of probabilistic causality in the version given by Suppes has been very useful for clarifying two conceptions of causality which are particularly important for economic analysis: that of Keynes and that of Granger. We have ascertained that Keynes causality is probabilistic and in many ways anticipates the more recent and mature theory of Suppes.

Granger's conception, which today is very popular particularly among anti-Keynesian economists and econometricians, can in turn be interpreted as a particular version of Suppes causality. However, we have seen that, behind the formal analogies, profound philosophical divergences between Keynes and Granger are detectable.

While Keynes, together with the supporters of the main alternative (Goodwin–Simon–Wold), insists that it is necessary to relate any causal statement to a well-defined theoretical background, the supporters of Granger causality claim that their concept is superior precisely because of its alleged independence of theoretical hypotheses. This presupposition proves completely groundless, and so does that of Granger causality's general superiority over alternative conceptions, although this does not exclude its utility for well-defined and circumscribed scientific purposes. In particular we have seen that it is a necessary, though not sufficient, condition for efficient predictions of the outcomes of processes which are not influenced by policy interventions, or which are in any case structurally stable.

The preceding considerations are not without implications for the lively debate between new classical economists and Keynesian economists. All the claims of superiority based on the results of Granger causality tests have to be considered as open to question, because they depend on *a priori* theoretical hypotheses which are not explicitly discussed in these studies.

**Notes**

1. The importance of this contribution for the modern development of causal analysis in economics is pointed out by Velupillai (1982, p. 79).
2. This is explicitly recognised by Simon himself (1953, fn. 5). We should recall that a similar conception of causality was independently worked out during the same years by Wold (1949, 1954).
3. See, for example, Pasinetti, 1974.
4. On the concept of explication see, for example, Carnap, 1950, Chapter 1.
5. See, for example, Suppe, 1977.
6. Bunge (1982) and other authors criticised Suppes' theory of causality because in their opinion it completely neglects causal production. In my opinion this criticism is not well founded.
7. See on the same line Spohn, 1983. The same opinion has been recently expressed by Suppes himself (1981, p. 25).
8. The conviction that the traditional meaning of 'event', defined as a change of state, is too restrictive for many uses of the term, has recently become widespread among philosophers and methodologists. On this subject see, for example, Kim, 1973.
9. Since the early sixties Salmon, following Reichenbach, has been developing a very interesting theory of probabilistic causality. An excellent

synthesis has been recently given by Salmon himself in an important monograph (1984).

10. This distinction appears, though with somewhat different meanings, in authors such as J. Robinson, Hicks, Shackle, Georgescu-Roegen.
11. An important exception is the excellent essay by Carabelli (1988), where Keynesian causality is correctly interpreted as probabilistic causality. However, the author does not try to formalise this conception, or to compare it with alternative definitions.
12. Keynes classifies economics among moral sciences, whose method is contrasted to that of the natural sciences. See, for example, Keynes, CW, vol. XIV, p. 300.
13. As is rightly observed by Weatherford (1982) this depends very much on the fact that Keynes was writing in that happy epoch that preceded the quantum-mechanics revolution (p. 106).
14. This possibility is admitted by Suppes himself, though it is not made explicit in the definitions here recalled.
15. Lucas and Sargent explain why 'Granger causality is of natural interest for scholars of rational expectations' in the Introduction to Lucas and Sargent, 1981, pp xxii–xxiv.
16. A thesis in many respects analogous is maintained by Spohn (1983). Moreover, he rightly emphasises a few notational problems of Granger's definitions. However, Spohn's analysis does not perceive the crucial point: the profoundly different role that background information plays in the causal theory of the two authors.
17. See, for example, Blaug, 1980, p. 14.
18. An example is given by the following passage of Sims: 'The method of identifying causal direction employed here does rest on a sophisticated version of the *post hoc ergo propter hoc* principle' (Sims, 1972, p. 543).

**References**

BLAUG, M. (1980) *The Methodology of Economics* (Cambridge: Cambridge University Press).

BUNGE, M, (1982) 'The Revival of Causality', in G. Fløistad (ed.), *Contemporary Philosophy*, vol. 2, pp. 133–55.

CARABELLI, A. (1988) *On Keynesian Method*, (London: Macmillan).

CARNAP, R. (1950) *Logical Foundations of Probability* (London: Routledge and Kegan).

CONWAY R. K., P. A. V. B. SWAMY and J. F. YANAGIDA (1983) 'The Impossibility of Causality Testing', *Federal Reserve Board, Special Studies Papers*, No. 178.

ENGLE, R. F., D. F. HENDRY and J.-F. RICHARD (1983) 'Exogeneity', Econometrica, vol. 51, no. 2.

GALAVOTTI, M. C. and G. GAMBETTA (eds) (1983) *Causalità e modelli probabilistici* (Bologna: CLUEB).

GEWEKE, J. (1984) 'Inference and Causality in Economic Time Series Models' in Griliches and Intriligator (eds), *Handbook of Econometrics*, vol. II, pp. 1101–44.

GOOD, I. J. (1961) 'A Causal Calculus I', *British Journal for the Philosophy of Science*, vol 11, pp. 305–18.

GOOD, I. J. (1962) 'A Causal Calculus II', *British Journal for the Philosophy of Science*, vol. 12, pp. 43–51.

GOODWIN, R. M. (1947) 'Dynamical Coupling with Especial Reference to Markets Having Production Lags', *Econometrica*, vol. 5, pp. 181–204.

GRANGER, C. W. J. (1963) 'Economic Processes Involving Feedback', *Information and Control*, vol. 6, pp. 28–48.

GRANGER, C. W. J. (1969) 'Investigating Causal Relations by Econometric Models and Cross-spectral Methods', *Econometrica*, vol. 37, pp. 424–38.

GRANGER, C. W. J. (1980) 'Testing For Causality: A Personal Viewpoint', *Journal of Economic Dynamics and Control*, vol. 2, pp. 303–28.

HICKS, J. (1979) *Causality in Economics* (Oxford: Blackwell).

KEYNES, J. M. *The Collected Writings of J. M. Keynes* ('CW'), ed. by D. E. Moggridge and E. Johnson, in thirty volumes (London: Macmillan).

KEYNES, J. M. (1921) *A Treatise on Probability* (New York: Macmillan); repr. as vol. VIII of Keynes' CW.

KIM, J. (1973) 'Causation, Nomic Subsumption and the Concept of Event', *Journal of Philosophy*, vol. LXX, no. 8.

KOLMOGOROV, A. N. (1933) *Grundbegriffe der Wahrscheinlichkettsrechnung* (Berlin: Springer), trans. *Foundations of the Theory of Probability* (New York: Chelsea), 1956.

KOOPMAN, B. O. (1940) 'The Bases of Probability', *Bulletin of American Mathematical Society*, vol. 46.

LUCAS, R. E. and T. J. SARGENT (eds) (1981) *Rational Expectations and Econometric Practice* (London: Allen and Unwin).

PASINETTI, L. L. (1974) *Growth and Income Distribution. Essays in Economic Theory* (Cambridge: Cambridge University Press).

REICHENBACH, H. (1956) *The Direction of Time* (Berkeley: University of California Press).

SALMON, W. C. (1984) *Scientific Explanation and the Causal Structure of the World* (Princeton, NJ: Princeton University Press).

SARGENT, T. J. and C. A. SIMS (1977) 'Business Cycle Modelling Without Pretending to Have Too Much *a priori* Economic Theory', in C. A. Sims (ed.), *New Methods in Business Cycle Research* (Minneapolis: Federal Reserve Bank of Minneapolis).

SIMON, H. A. (1952) 'On the Definition of the Causal Relation', *The Journal of Philosophy*, vol. 49, pp. 517–28.

SIMON, H. A. (1953) 'Causal Ordering and Identifiability', in Hood and Koopmans (eds), *Studies in Econometric Methods* (New York: J. Wiley) pp. 49–74.

SIMON, H. A. (1954) 'Spurious Correlation: A Causal Interpretation, *Journal of the American Statistical Association*, pp. 467–79.

SIMS, C. A. (1972) 'Money, Income and Causality', *American Economic Review*, vol. 62, pp. 540–52.

SIMS, C. A. (1977) 'Exogeneity and Causal Ordering in Macroeconomic Models', in C. A. Sims (ed.), *New Methods in Business Cycle Research* (Minneapolis: Federal Reserve Bank of Minneapolis).

SIMS, C. A. (1980) 'Macroeconomics and Reality', *Econometrica*, vol. 48, pp. 1–48.
SPOHN, W. (1983) 'Probabilistic Causality: From Hume via Suppes to Granger', in Galavotti and Gambetta (1983).
SUPPE, F. (ed.) (1977) *The Structure of Scientific Theories* (Urbana, Ill.: University of Illinois Press).
SUPPES, P. (1970) A *Probabilistic Theory of Causality* (Amsterdam: North-Holland).
SUPPES, P. (1981) *La logica del probabile*, trad. it., (Bologna: CLUEB) 1984.
SUPPES, P. (1984) *Probabilistic Metaphysics* (Oxford: Blackwell).
VELUPILLAI, K. (1982) 'Linear and Nonlinear Dynamics in Economics: The Contributions of Richard Goodwin', *Economic Notes*, no. 3.
WEATHERFORD, R. (1982) *Philosophical Foundations of Probability Theory* (Routledge and Kegan Paul).
WIENER, N. (1958) 'The Theory of Prediction', in E. F. Beckenbach (ed.), *Modern Mathematics for Engineers*, Series 1, Ch. 8 (New York: McGraw-Hill).
WOLD, H. O. (1949) 'Statistical Estimation of Economic Relationships', *Econometrica*, vol. 17, suppl. (July), pp. 1–21.
WOLD, H. O. (1954) 'Causality and Econometrics', *Econometrica*, vol. 22, pp. 162–77.
ZELLNER, A. (1979) 'Causality and Econometrics', in Brunner and Meltzer (eds), *Rochester Conference Series on Public Policy*, 10 (Amsterdam: North Holland).
ZELLNER, A. (1982) 'Comment to J. Geweke, Measurement of Linear Dependence and Feedback Between Multiple Time Series', *Journal of the American Statistical Association*, vol. 77, pp. 313–14.

# Index of Names

# Index of Subjects